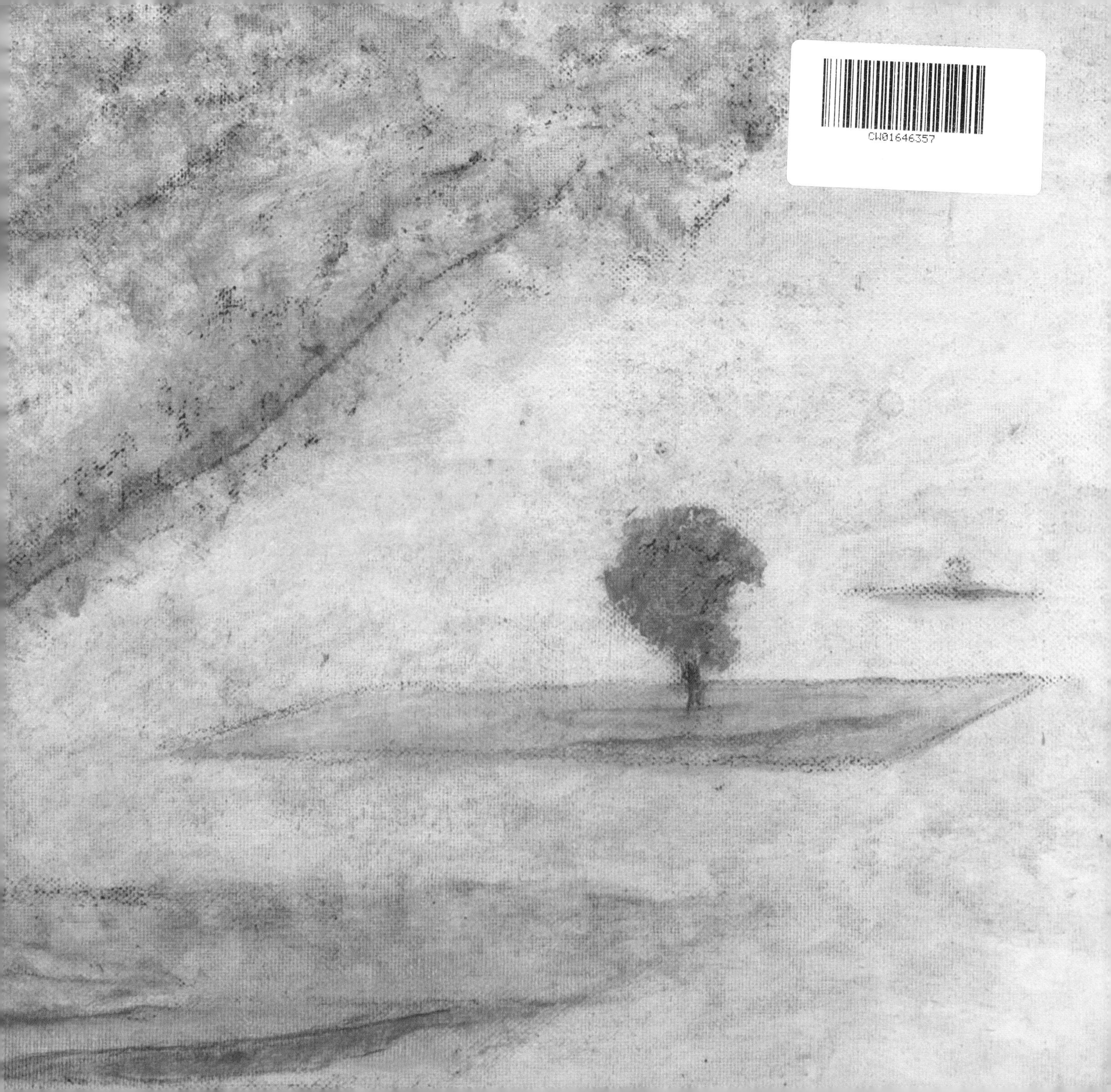

RAPHAEL MAKLOUF

Life, Art & The Making of The Mint

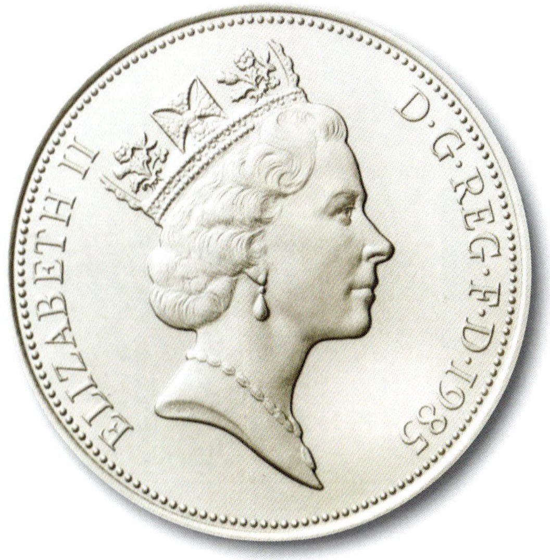

JENNY PERY

HALSTAR

First published in Great Britain in 2018

All sculpture and painting is by Raphael Maklouf unless otherwise stated

British Library Cataloguing-in-Publication Data
A CIP record for this title is available from the British Library

ISBN 978 1 906690 65 6

HALSTAR
Halsgrove House, Ryelands Business Park,
Bagley Road, Wellington, Somerset TA21 9PZ
Tel: 01823 653777   Fax: 01823 216796
email: sales@halsgrove.com

Part of the Halsgrove group of companies
Information on all Halsgrove titles is
available at: www.halsgrove.com

Printed and bound by Parksons Graphics, India

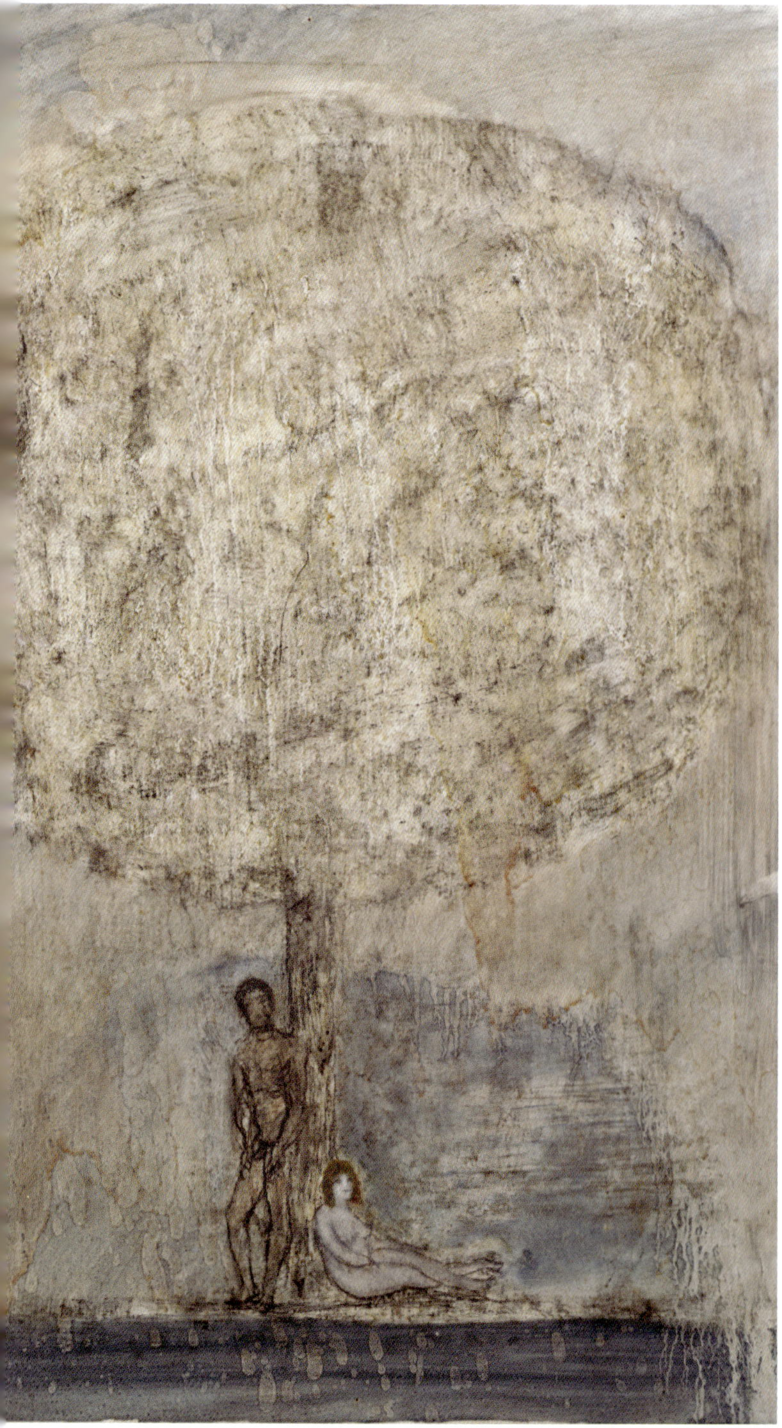

Photo by Paul Webster

Contents

For Marillyn, who changed my life

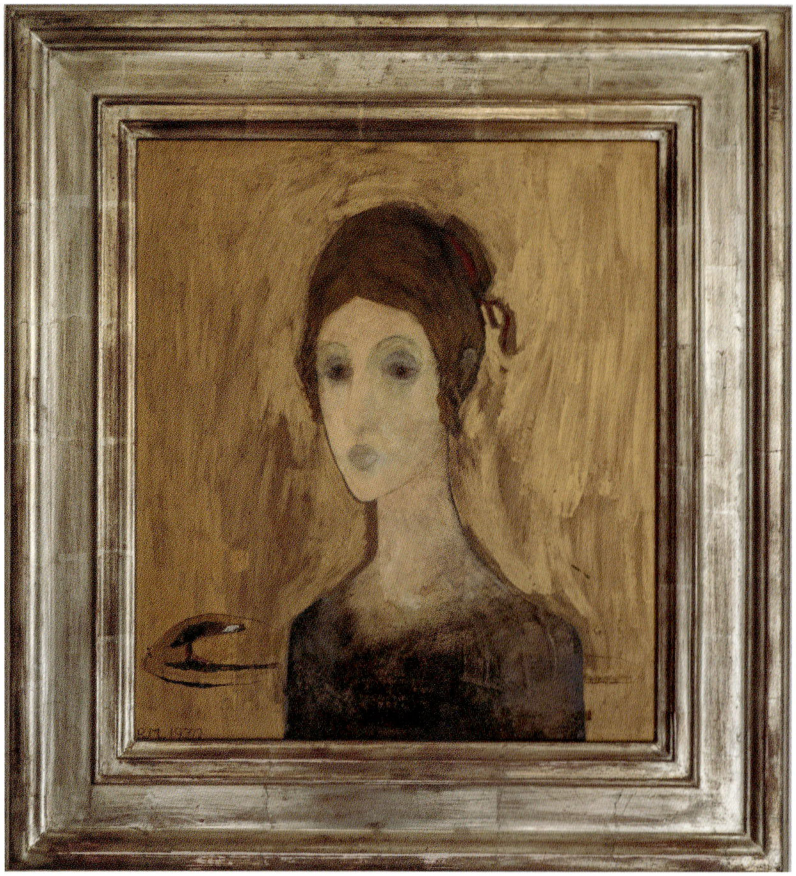

Golden Portrait of Marillyn by Raphael (1970)
Photo by Kirsten Scully

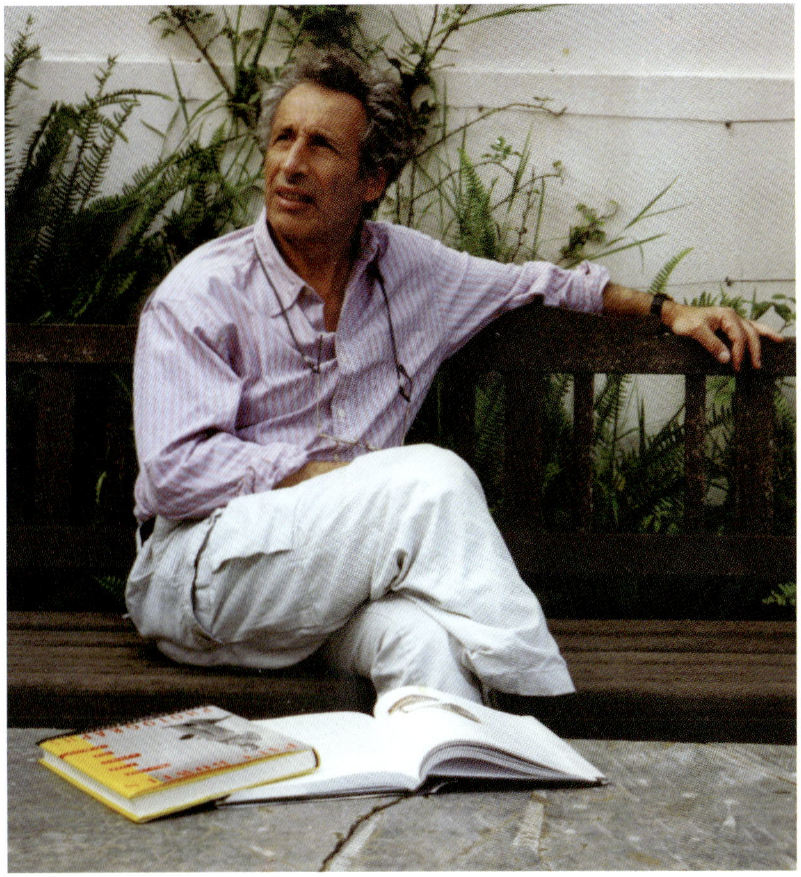

Raphael

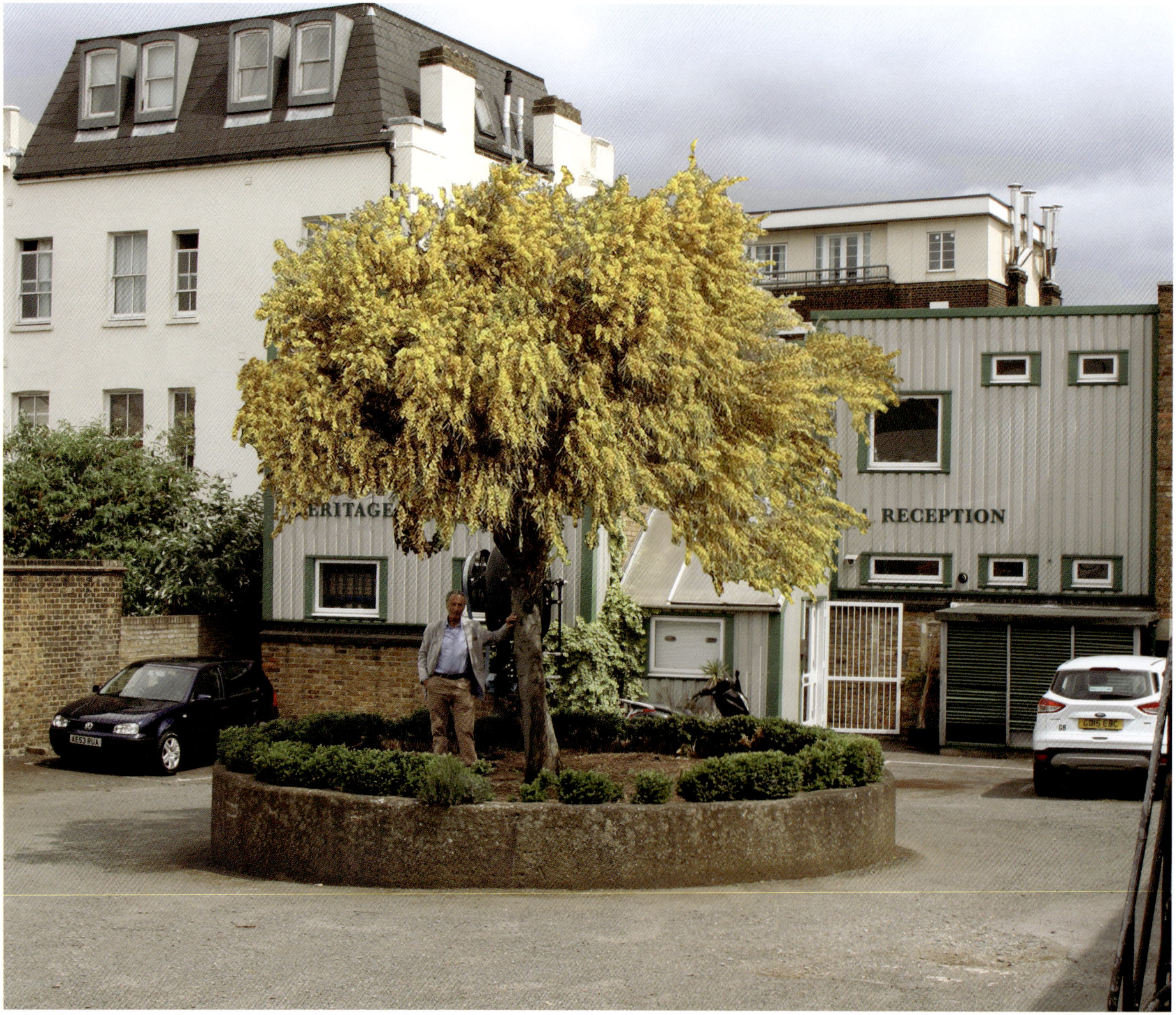

The mimosa tree at Tower Mint

Chapter 1

The Tree of Life

IF IT IS THE business of the wise man to be happy, as Dr Johnson suggests, then Raphael Maklouf is that wise man. Artist, sculptor and minter, Raphael's natural optimism has carried him happily through the ups and downs of his extraordinary life. He has had a lot of luck and he knows how fortunate he has been. But he has also made his own luck, seizing chances as they have arisen. In Shakespeare's words, 'there is a tide in the affairs of men which, taken at the flood, leads on to fortune.' On almost every occasion Raphael has caught the flood tide.

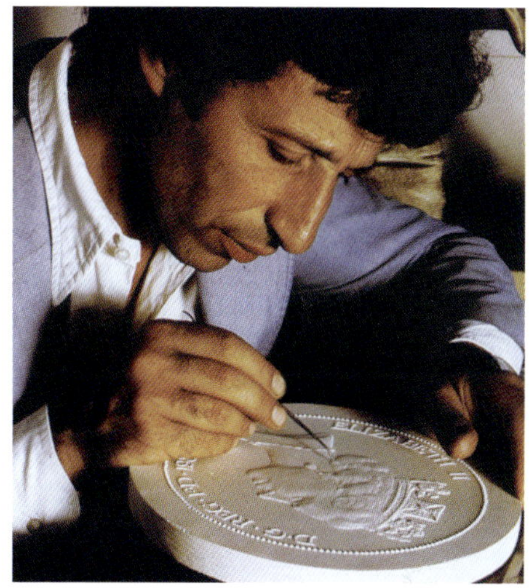

Raphael working on the plaster of the Queen's effigy

It is Raphael's sunny personality that has created the relaxed atmosphere in Tower Mint, the company that he has built from scratch. Now in its fortieth year, the Mint is thriving and diversifying into new areas. Raphael had already established himself as a portrait sculptor and a teacher of sculpture when a series of unexpected opportunities led him into the world of minting. With no previous business experience he has built the Mint into the successful company it is today. And it has remained true to his values, with its entrepreneurial approach, loyalty to the workforce and concern for their welfare, the family feeling of everyone pulling together.

The company, initially named Sovereign Medallions, supplied medals to places of historic interest. On 13th September 1967 it was registered for striking coins and renamed Tower Mint. Now Tower Mint is a multi-stranded manufacturer of commemorative medallions of all descriptions as well as the legal tender for several countries. It is also the sole UK manufacturer of chocolate coins, its Heritage Chocolates being a business within a business. The Mint's current employees now number thirty. Raphael is Chairman of the Board, which also includes his elder son David. Other members of the team include the Office Staff, the Press Operators and the Polishers, Platers and Packers. Having nursed Tower Mint to maturity from a standing start, Raphael is very proud of it but says bemusedly as he looks around 'I still find it difficult to believe that this all started with me!'.

Tower Mint's premises in a light industrial estate are based in Camberwell, close to Raphael's old alma mater, Camberwell School of Arts and Crafts. He knows the area

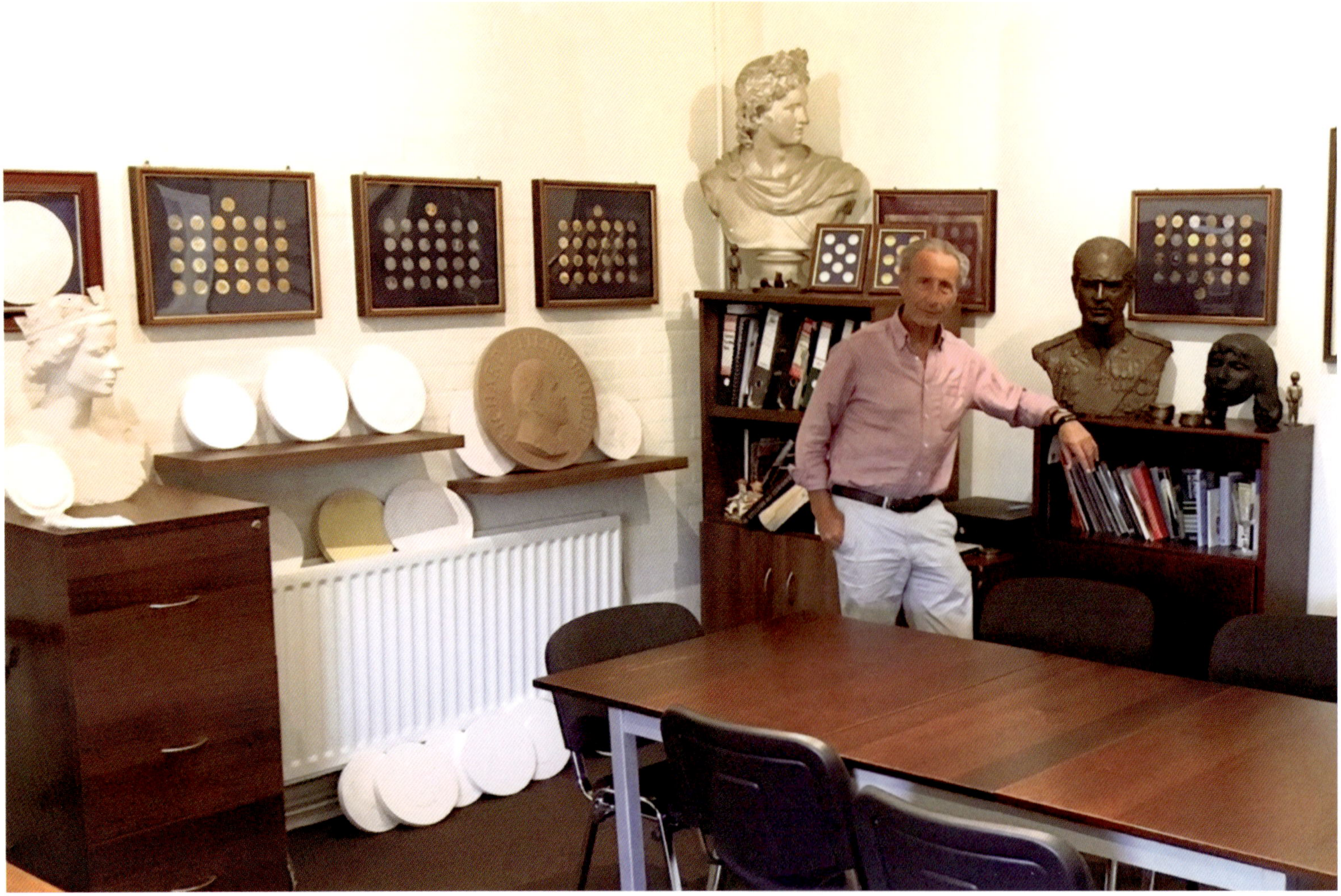

Raphael in his office

very well, having spent all his student years there, and likes to recruit many of his workers locally. The Mint is approached through a courtyard in the middle of which stands a tall mimosa tree that flowers spectacularly every year. Raphael had the tree planted when he first acquired the site, and the exotic appearance of the mimosa, as un-English as its owner, brightens the industrial surroundings. The tree is an important talisman, perhaps having a symbolic relationship to the Tree of Life that figures in so many of his paintings. The courtyard that surrounds it is lined by the low narrow buildings that were once small industrial workshops for local craftsmen. Derelict when Raphael bought them, their labyrinthine passages are now restored to house the complex machinery of minting.

In Raphael's airy office, the walls and glass cabinets display a visual history of both the Mint and of Raphael's life and career as a sculptor. There is plenty of greenery, a tribute perhaps to his gardener daughter Laetitia, whose book *The Virgin Gardener* stands on one of the cabinets. On another stands a bust of Laetitia, opposite a photograph of his wife, Marillyn. Copies of his portrait busts of the Queen and the Duke of Edinburgh are also here. The walls of the office are crowded with framed sets of medals and coins and, among them, various certificates. These include his 1961 National Diploma in Design, showing Modelling and Sculpture as his main subject, with Terra Cotta as his additional subject. Framed documents record his 1979 election as a Fellow of the Royal Society for the Encouragement of Arts, Manufactures and Commerce, and his 1984 election as a Fellow of the Royal Society of British Sculptors. On another wall hangs an architect's drawing of Brentwood Cathedral, where Raphael executed a major sculptural frieze denoting the fifteen Stations of the Cross.

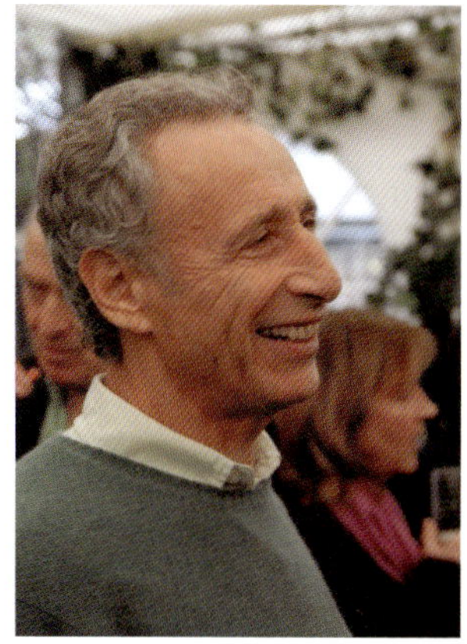

Raphael

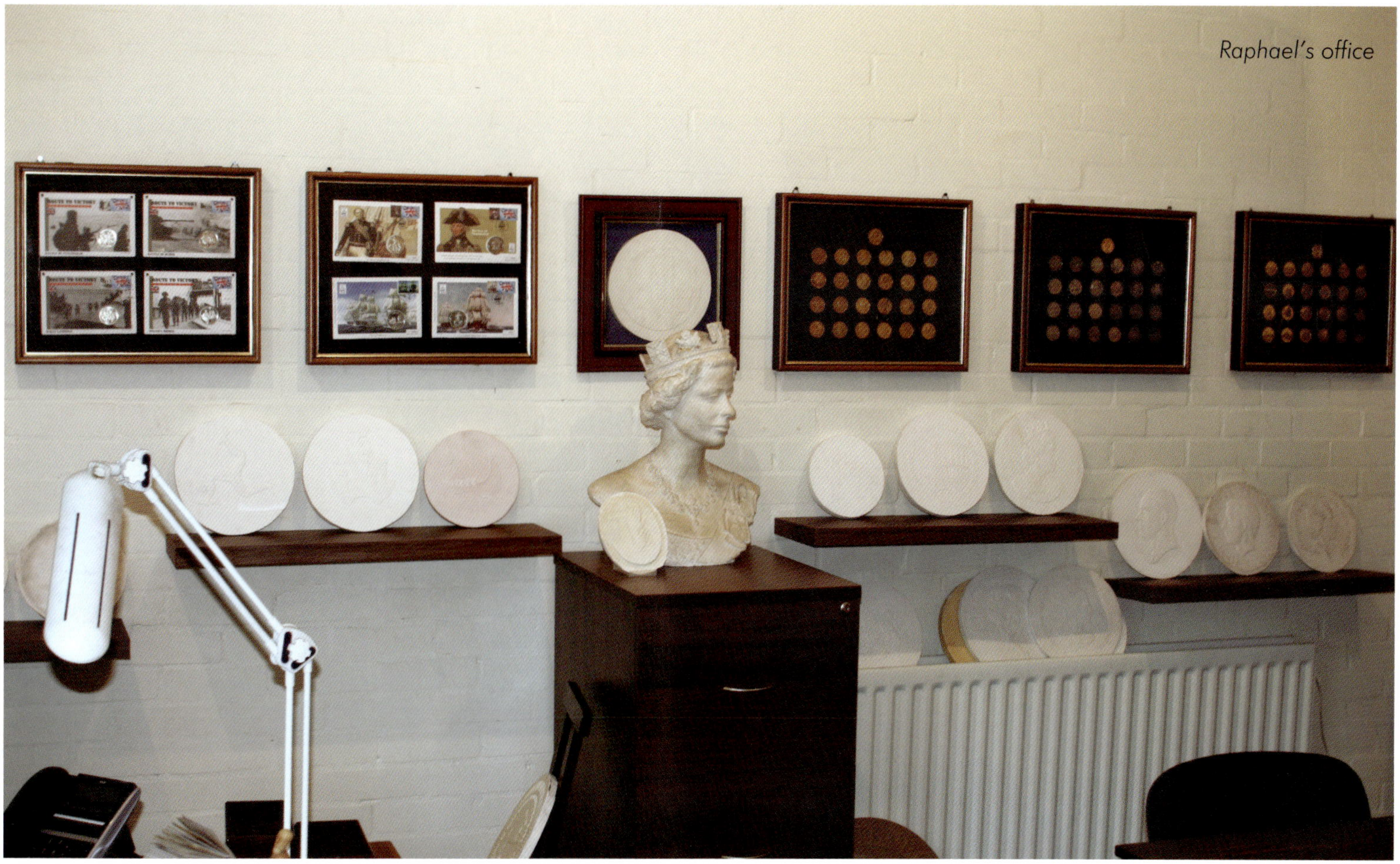

Raphael's office

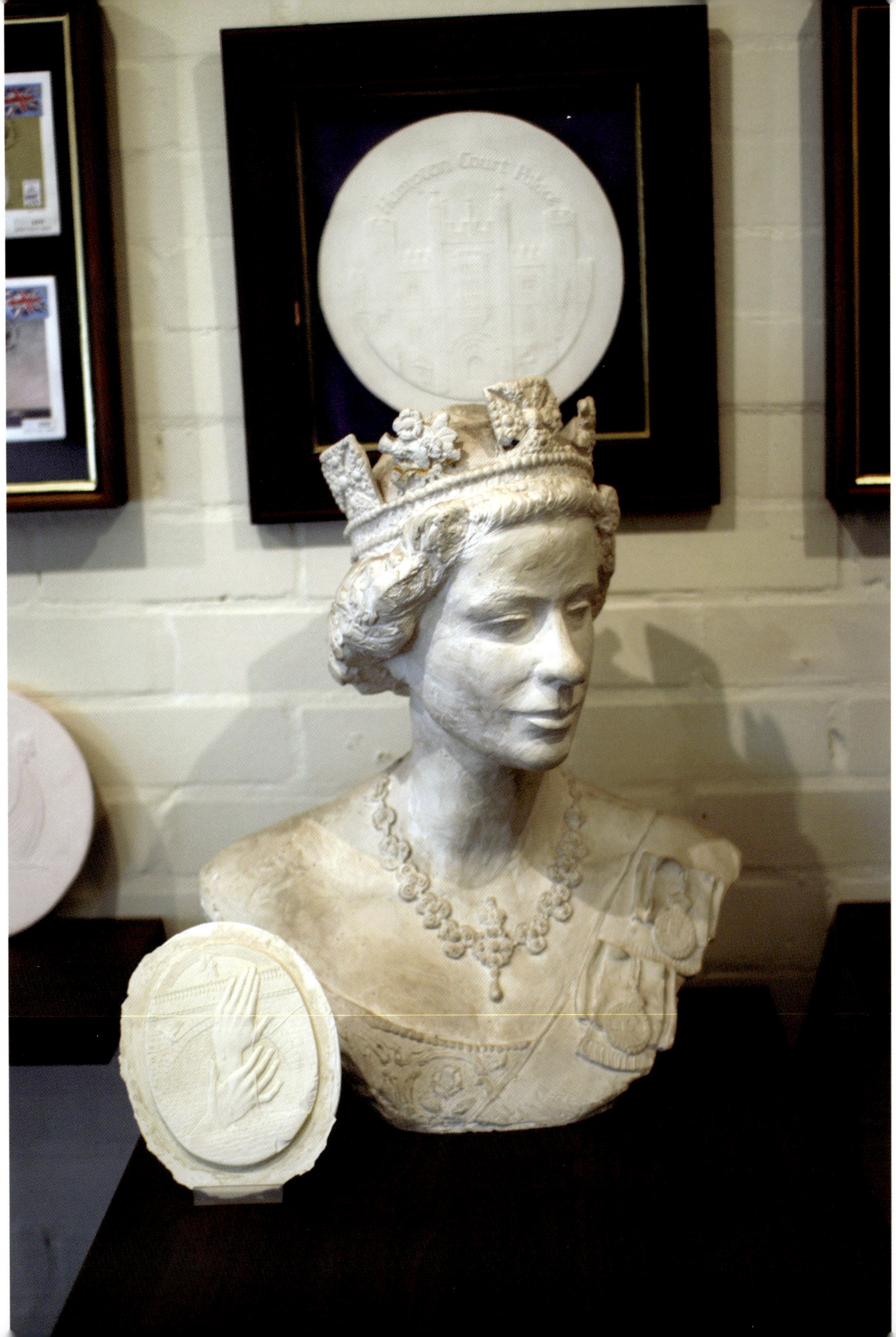

Plaster cast of H M Queen Elizabeth

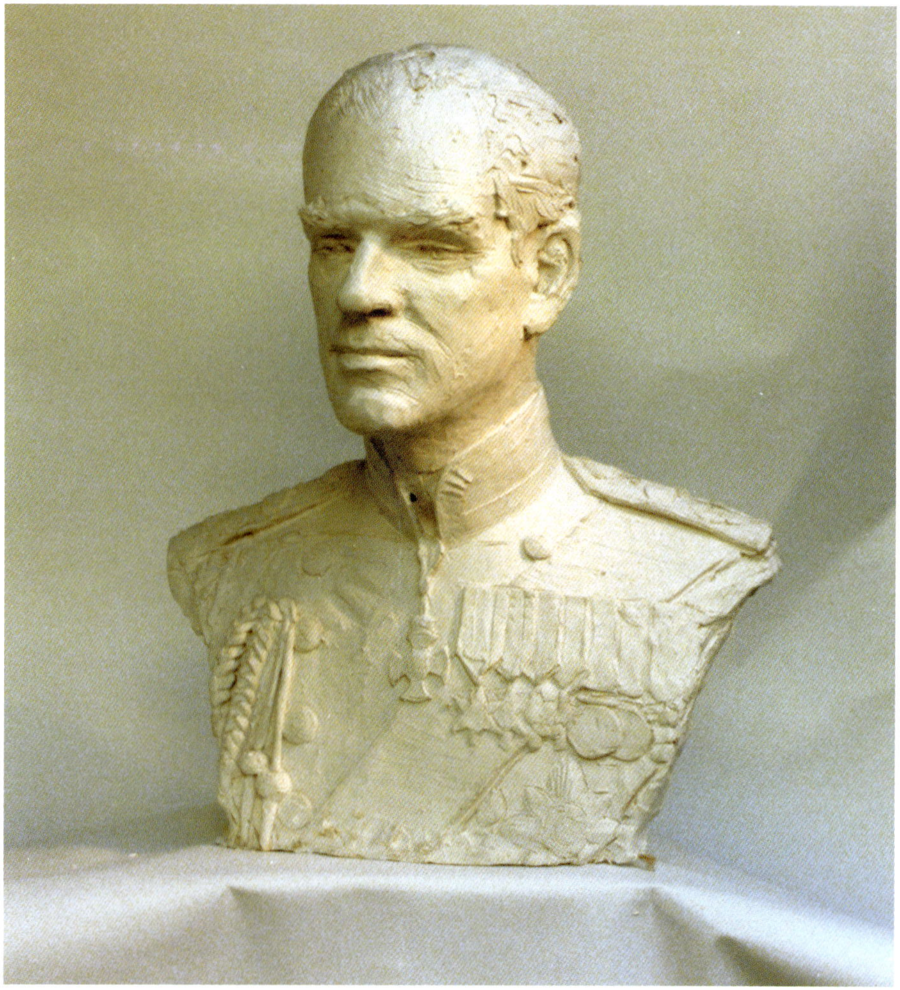

Plaster cast of Prince Philip

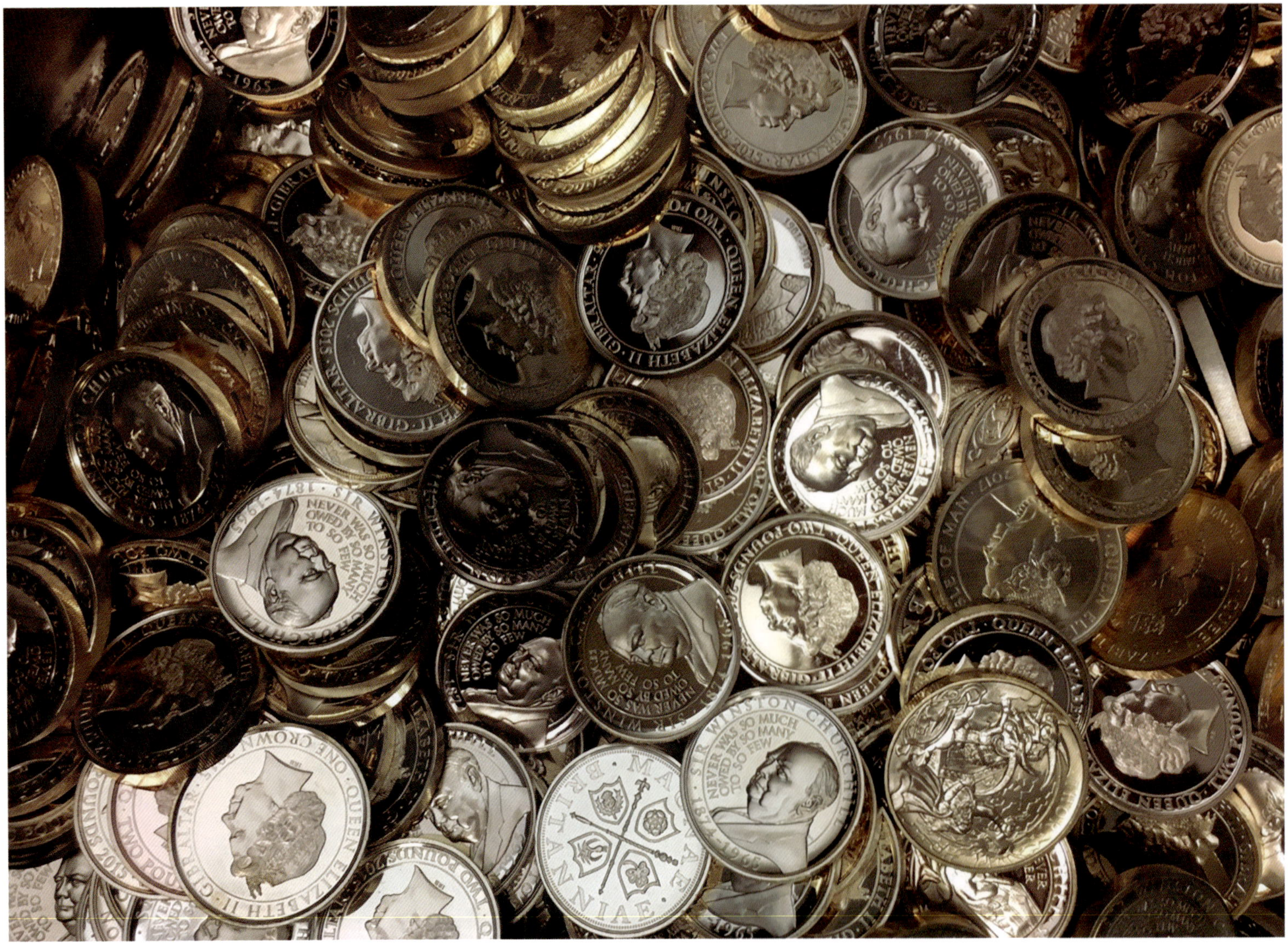
SIR WINSTON CHURCHILL
NEVER WAS SO MUCH
OWED BY SO MANY
TO SO FEW

Coins

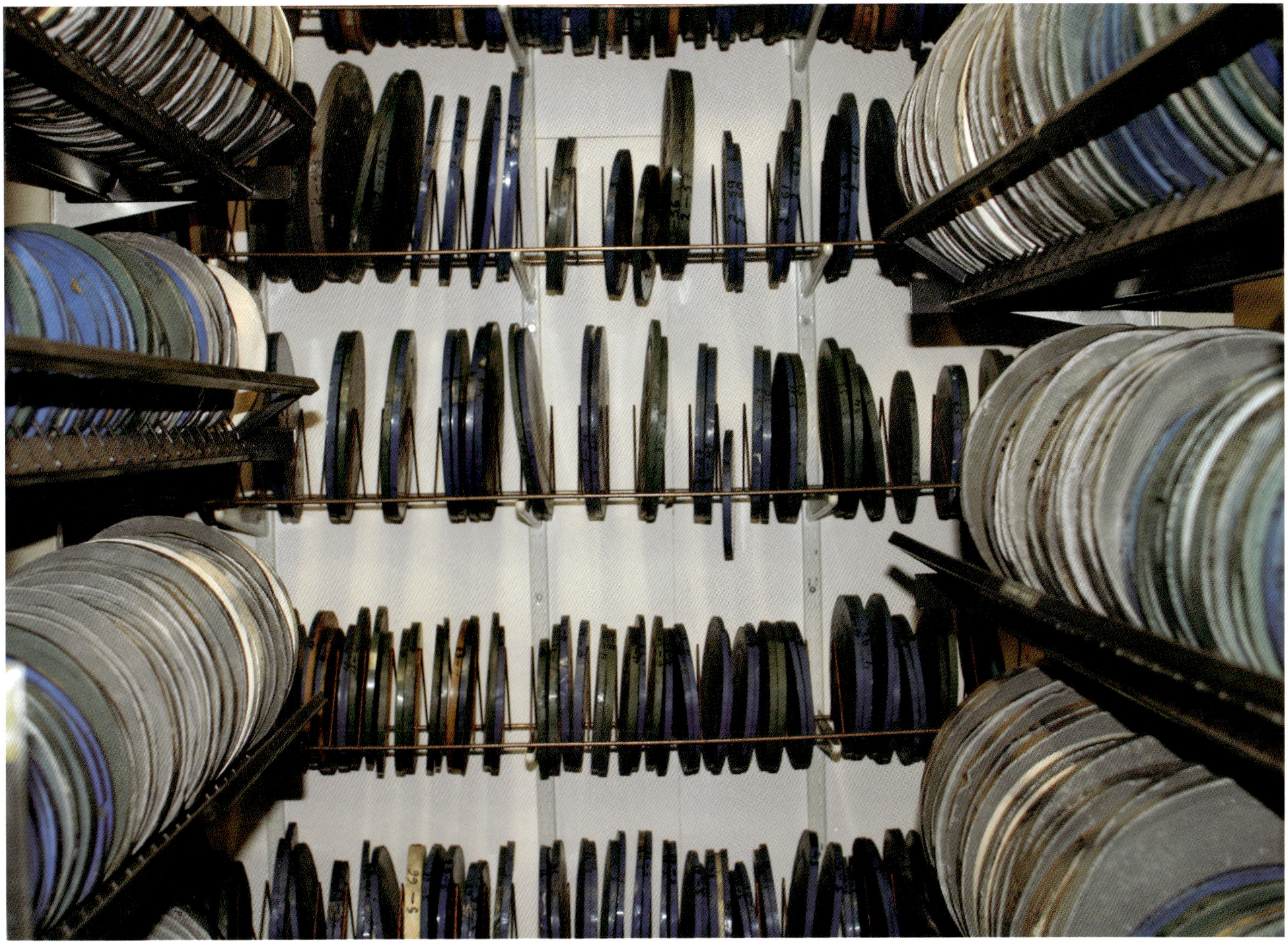

The archive room

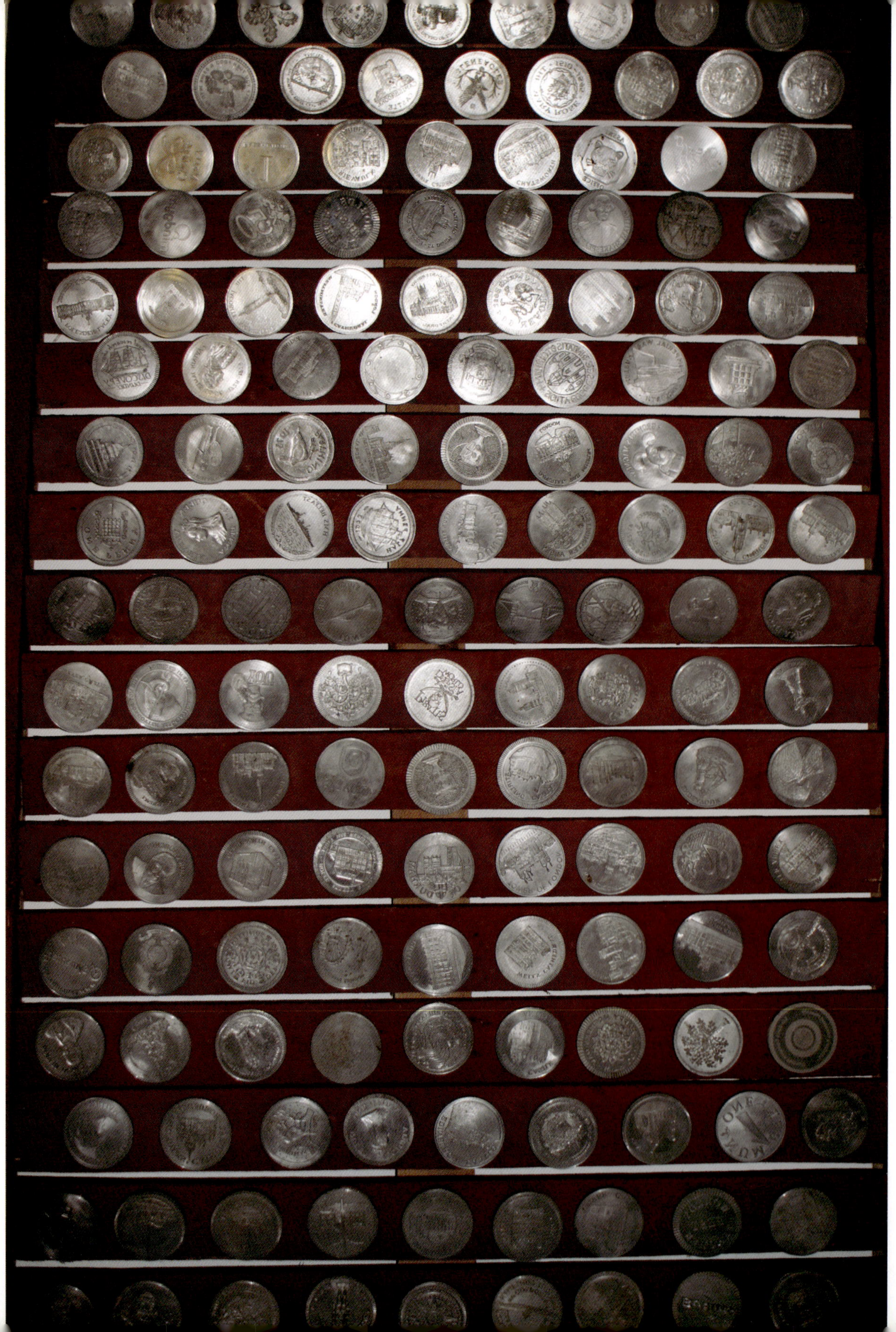

Left: An array of dies

Opposite: A selection of dies

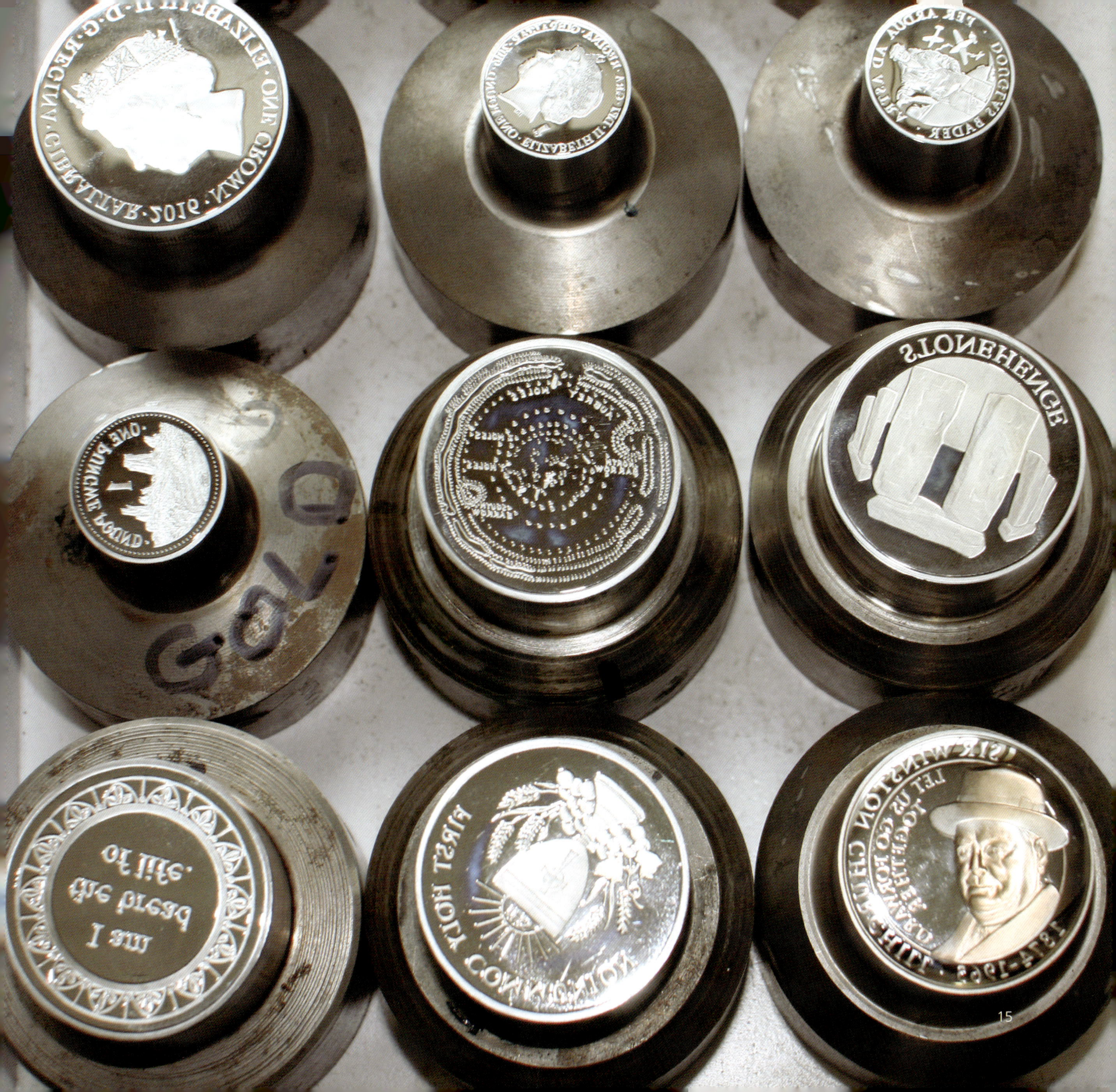
ONE CROWN · 2016
ELIZABETH II · D · G · REGINA
GOLD
STONEHENGE
I am the bread of life.
FIRST HOLY COMMUNION
SIR WINSTON CHURCHILL
1874–1965

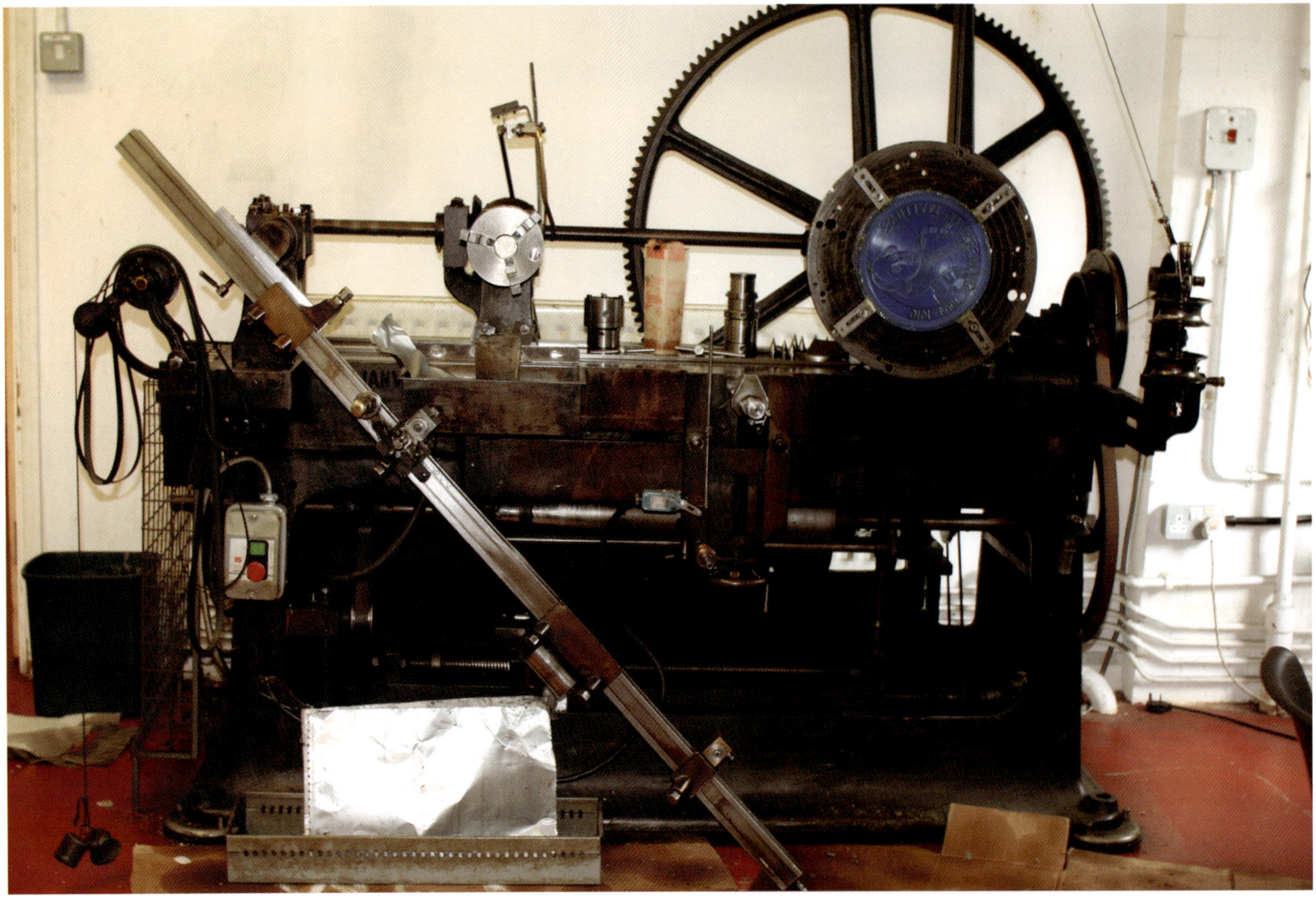

Janvier Reducer Die Cutter

Between the certificates are framed sets of coins. In pride of place is the 1985 set of British legal tender – the £1, 50p, 20p, 10p, 2p and 1p coins – with Raphael's effigy of the Queen's head on each. Winning the competition to portray the Queen for the new British and Commonwealth currency was a breakthrough moment in his career, significantly raising both his profile and that of the Mint. Work began to flow his way. Forty years on, Tower Mint has produced an enormous number of medals commemorating all sorts of occasions, from the Queen's Silver and Golden Jubilees to heroic victories of the past. On the office tables a tactile selection of dies shows the intricate negative designs from which the positives are struck.

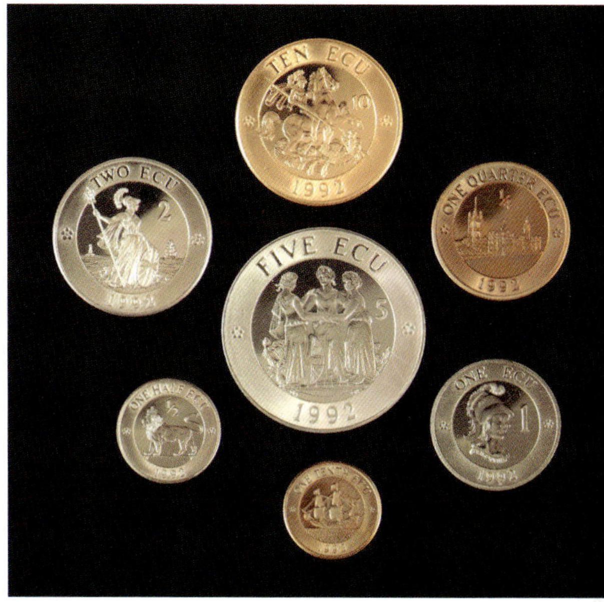

Ecu coins

A walk through the connecting rooms of the Mint reveals the complex processes of minting, with an impressive collection of machinery in noisy action. There are stores of the various metals in use, from base to precious. A hygienically separated area houses foiling and embossing presses for stamping designs onto chocolate blanks. Nearby are stores of top quality chocolate blanks imported from Belgium, and personalised packaging for the chocolate coins. A huge storeroom archives over thirteen thousand hand-sculpted plaster and resin moulds with the original designs from which all the dies are cut. These are filed by subject-matter for potential re-use. In another room the master dies made from the resins are assembled.

Raphael started minting commemorative medals with a single press, the 19th century Heaton press, purchased from the Royal Mint's scrap auction after its move to Wales. His son David recalls those first days. 'I well remember the old flour mill in Greenwich where the Mint started. I remember as a boy being in the back of the car with my father making deliveries to royal palaces. It was very much a one-man band.' As the business began to prosper Raphael acquired other second-hand machines such as the beautiful old Janvier reducer die-cutter from Paris. Raphael was then approached to design and produce a pattern for an Ecu coin for use as possible European currency. The ECU (European Currency Unit) was conceived as a monetary unit but never became legal tender, and was eventually replaced by the Euro. Interestingly, the acronym ECU was formed from English words, but was also the name of an ancient French coin – one reason for the name 'Euro' which replaced it, because it did not favour any single language. Tower Mint's ECUs are now collector's items.

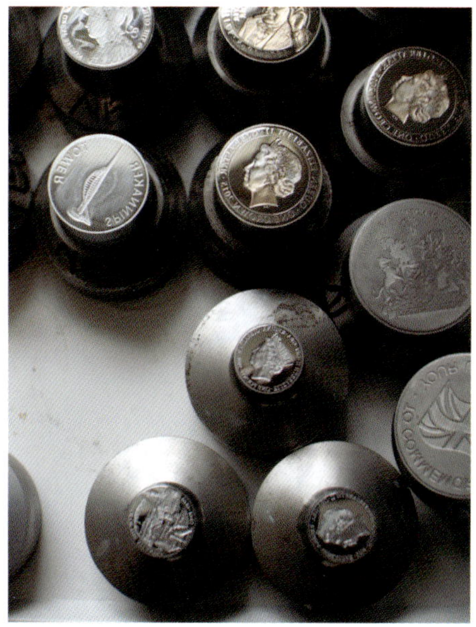
Dies

The Mint is busy all year round. There are always deadlines to meet, as well as occasional glitches to sort out, but Raphael and his staff are unflappable. The difficulties they have surmounted over the years have formed them into a close-knit unit. The story of the evolution of Tower Mint, from its first home in Greenwich with just one press, is a compelling one. No less compelling is Raphael's own story, and his unusual progress from boyhood in Palestine to his present high-profile position as a sculptor and minter. Both stories are intimately connected.

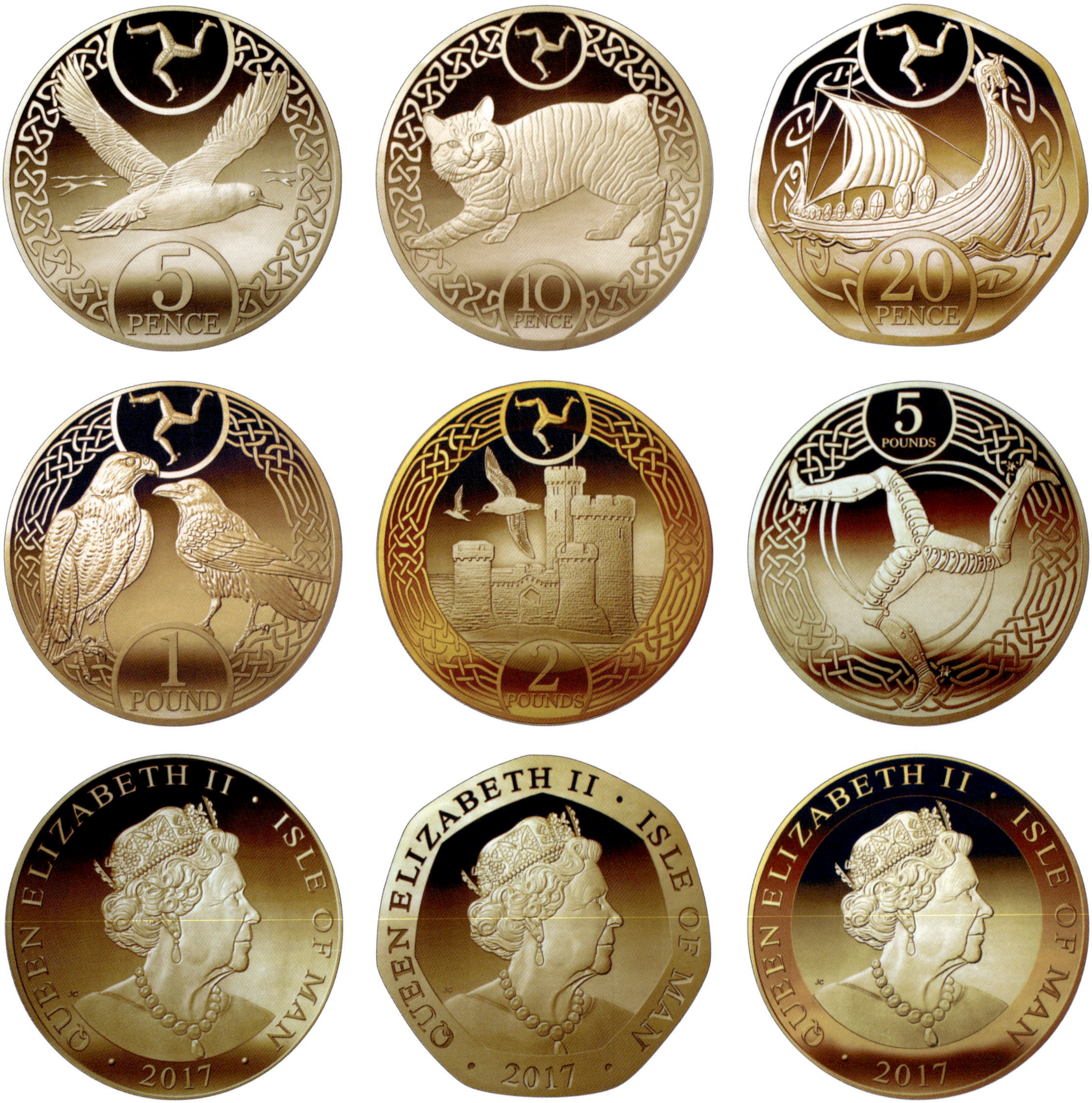
5 PENCE
10 PENCE
20 PENCE
1 POUND
2 POUNDS
5 POUNDS
QUEEN ELIZABETH II · ISLE OF MAN · 2017
QUEEN ELIZABETH II · ISLE OF MAN · 2017
QUEEN ELIZABETH II · ISLE OF MAN · 2017

Opposite: Isle of Man new coinage 2017

Right: Old metal weighing scales

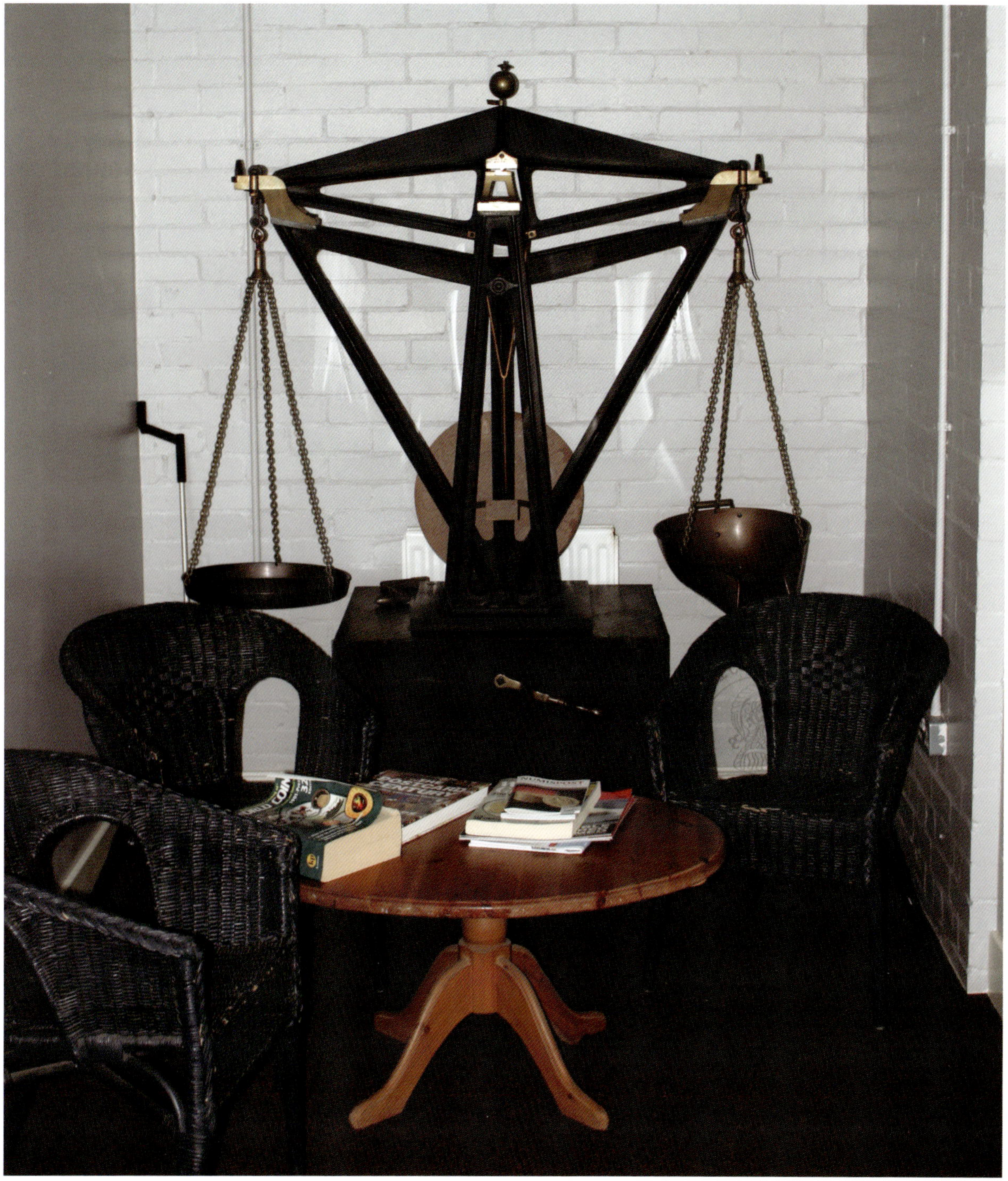

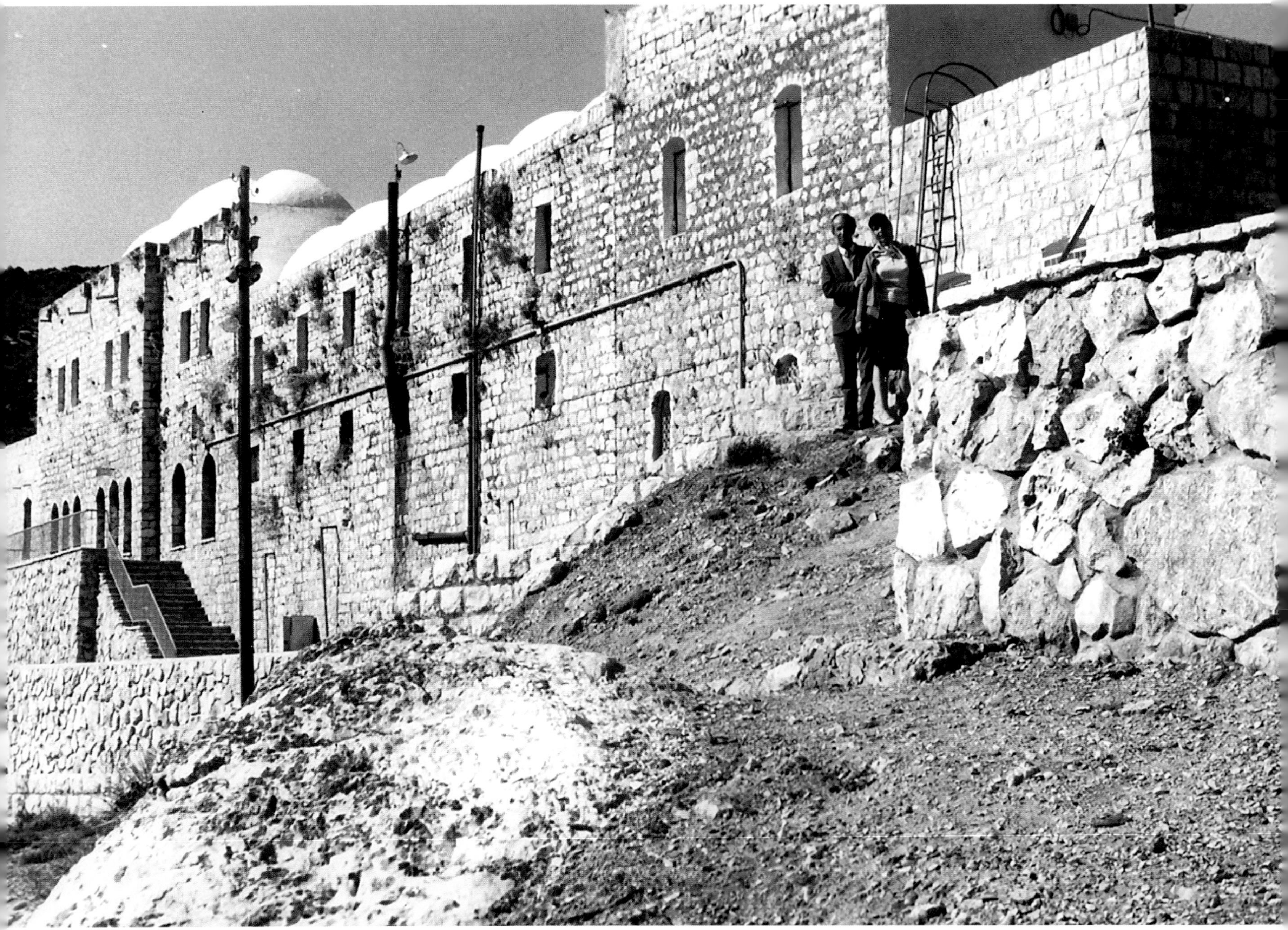

City walls, Palestine

Chapter 2

Prospects in Palestine

THE MIXTURE OF personalities in Raphael's parentage and grand-parentage was far from ordinary. In Jewish circles his grandfather on his father's side was an important man, the influential Sephardic Rabbi, David Hay Edery (also spelt Ederi or Edrei). Edery, of Moroccan origin, was born in 1888 in Safed, a small village in northern Palestine, in the mountains of Upper Galilee, looking east towards the Golan Heights, north to Lebanon, west to Mount Meru, and south to Tiberias and the Sea of Galilee. Safed had been founded in 70AD, and by the 16th century had become the spiritual centre of the Jewish world, where many famous scholars and mystics had congregated after escaping the horrors of the Spanish Inquisition. Coming from Morocco and Southern Spain, most of the Jewish inhabitants were Sephardi and brought Sephardic principles with them. It was in Safed that the first printing press in the Middle East was set up, and, in 1578, the first book in Hebrew printed. Now part of Israel, Safed is one of the four Jewish holy cities, along with Jerusalem, Hebron and Tiberias.

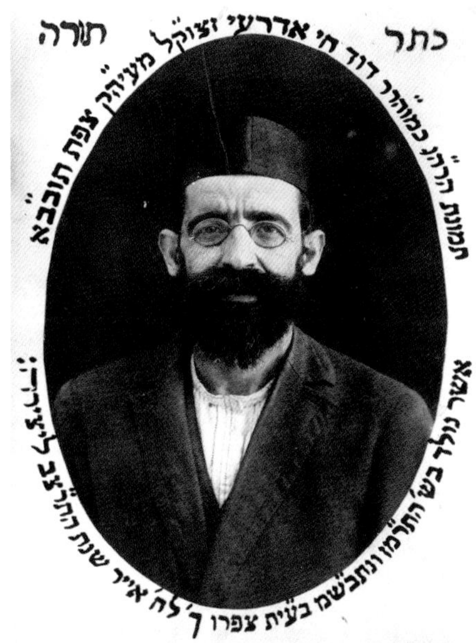

Rabbi David Hay Edery

Raphael's grandfather, Rabbi David Hay Edery, was himself the son of a rabbi. He had become a kabbalist, committed to teaching the inner meaning of the Hebrew bible, where many words are believed to contain esoteric messages. Kabbala had emerged in 12th-13th century southern Spain and France and was reinterpreted in the Jewish mystical renaissance of 16th century Palestine. Edery followed the missionary tradition of the Jewish teachers, who travelled widely to promote Sephardic principles. An important destination for their proselytism was Russian Turkestan, the huge area that now includes the separate states of Turkmenistan, Kazakhstan, Uzbekistan, Kyrgyzstan and Xinjiang. Particularly important was the Emirate of Bukhara, situated on the Silk Road, from early times a centre of trade, scholarship, culture and religion. The first Sephardic teachers arrived in Turkestan in 1896 and flourished, spreading their influence across three major settlements: Russian Turkestan, Eretz Israel (The Land of Israel), and the Emirate of Bukhara, where the oldest and most traditional group was concentrated. In Turkestan their Sephardic identification had no real factual basis but had been inculcated into the community by the persuasive teaching of Rabbi Joseph Maman who had come to

Bukhara from Safed in 1793, the first person from Eretz Israel to arrive there. Rabbi Maman came originally from Tetuan in Morocco but spent the rest of his life with the Bukharan Jewish community.

Many of the teachers from Safed had broad travel experiences. Raphael's grandfather Rabbi David Hay Edery had been to Kurdistan and Georgia, before going, at the age of twenty-four, to Russian Turkestan to help create a more modern educational framework. The teachers who had no relatives there were given lodgings by local businessmen, and Edery was given a full pension by the Reuvenoff family in Tashkent. He was a major contributor both to the Jewish community in Turkestan and also to Safed, as a paper delivered at the Fifth International Colloquium in Jerusalem in 1984 made clear. 'David Hay Edery became influential in public life after his teaching career. He was addressed in Turkestan as "Zion"... He was recognised as an outstanding religious authority during the years 1914-19. The religious rulings he wrote in Turkestan were published in Safed in 1922 upon his return from Russia. During the Russian Revolution of 1917 he organised Zionist activities in Turkestan and established the first religious Zionist party in Tashkent... Having become one of the leaders of a Zionist cultural association, "Tarbut", he was persecuted by the Bolsheviks and sometime later returned to Eretz Israel.' [1]

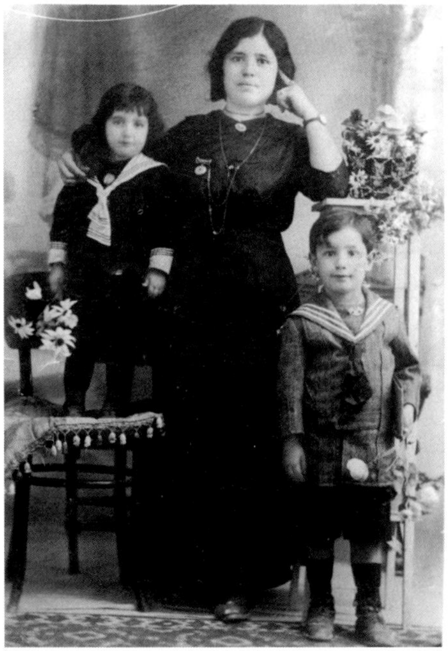

Malka Mamman

Edery worked as a missionary teacher all his life, dying in 1932 while on mission in Sefrou in Morocco. He was multi-lingual, speaking Hebrew, Arabic, Russian and some French, and had travelled widely, including making trips to Lebanon and France. Somewhere along the way he had acquired a British passport that was later to prove extremely useful to his family. He was married to Malka Mamman, probably a descendant of the famous Rabbi Joseph Maman, whose origins were Moroccan and whose father was also a rabbi. David and Malka had five children, the eldest of whom, and the only boy, was Samuel Maklouf, Raphael's father, born in Safed in 1911. The four girls Rebekka, Shoshana, Margalith, and Simcha followed in that order. Besides this Palestinian family, Edery was also reputed to have another family in Russia.

Rabbi Edery's son, Samuel Maklouf, was a deep disappointment to his father. From early on Samuel was anti-religion. He rebelled against the rabbinical teachings and religious traditions of his forebears and dropped the surname Edery, probably for its religious associations as well as for its common occurrence in Safed. As a young boy he was sent to *kheder* – the children's school – and was intolerant of the teaching there. On Saturdays nobody was allowed to tear a leaf off a plant, or point at the moon. Samuel grew up to become a bit of a playboy – dashing and adventurous, highly sociable but also a bit of a dreamer; an emotional man who laughed and cried easily, but was not at all self-critical. As a child he had survived an attack of meningitis and could recall his fever being so severe that the damp cloths his mother used to cool him down made steam rise from his forehead. Perhaps because of this he was spoilt. He was clever

Samuel with tank in Palestine

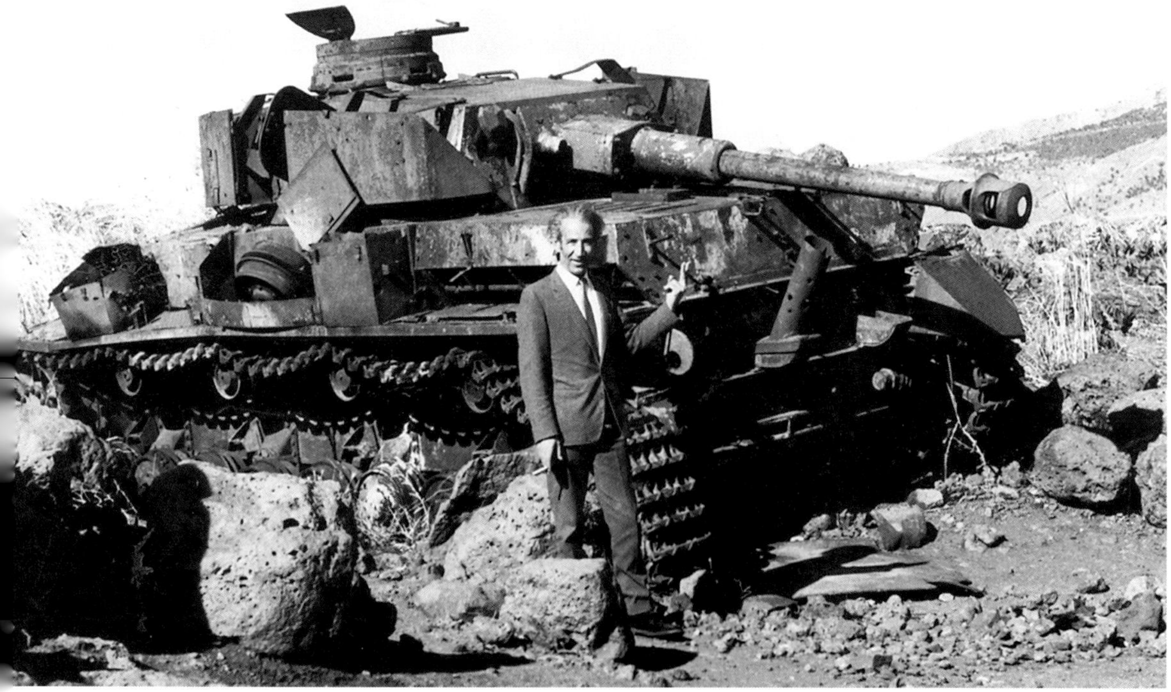

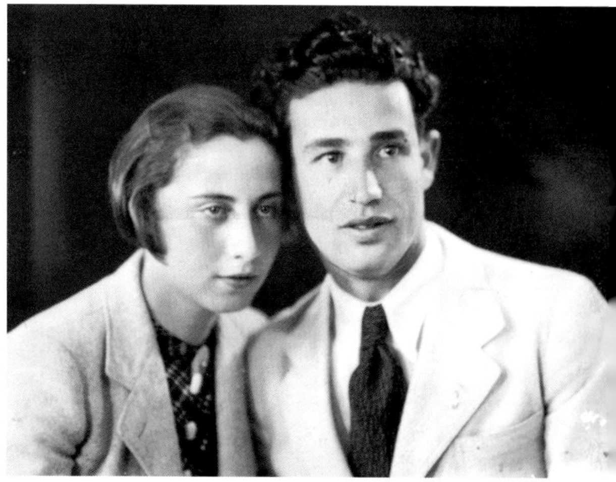

Leonie and Samuel

enough to win a scholarship to Paris to study medicine, but was soon packed off back home after setting his hotel lodgings alight while having a smoke.

During the 1930s Samuel made a living by dabbling in antiques. It was in Tel Aviv that he met and fell for a young German girl, Leonie Loeb, recently arrived in Palestine. There was, it seemed, an immediate spark – an attraction of opposites - between the dark, handsome Samuel and the blue-eyed Leonie. Samuel spoke no German, Leonie spoke no Hebrew, but they were able to converse with each other in French. They were married in a registry office in 1937. On December 10th that year their eldest child Raphael was born. Over the years they had five other children: Esther Ruth, Joseph, Alisa, Peter, and Hannah.

Raphael's mother, Leonie Loeb, was born on 20 November 1915 in the city of Saarbrucken, situated close to Alsace on the German/French border, in Napoleonic times a part of France. Her parents, Leo and Frieda Loeb, born in 1876 and 1885 respectively, were Ashkenazi Jews. Leo was one of eight brothers, the children of Jewish horse traders

Clockwise from left: Arie, Frieda, Samuel, Leonie, Lilli, Moses

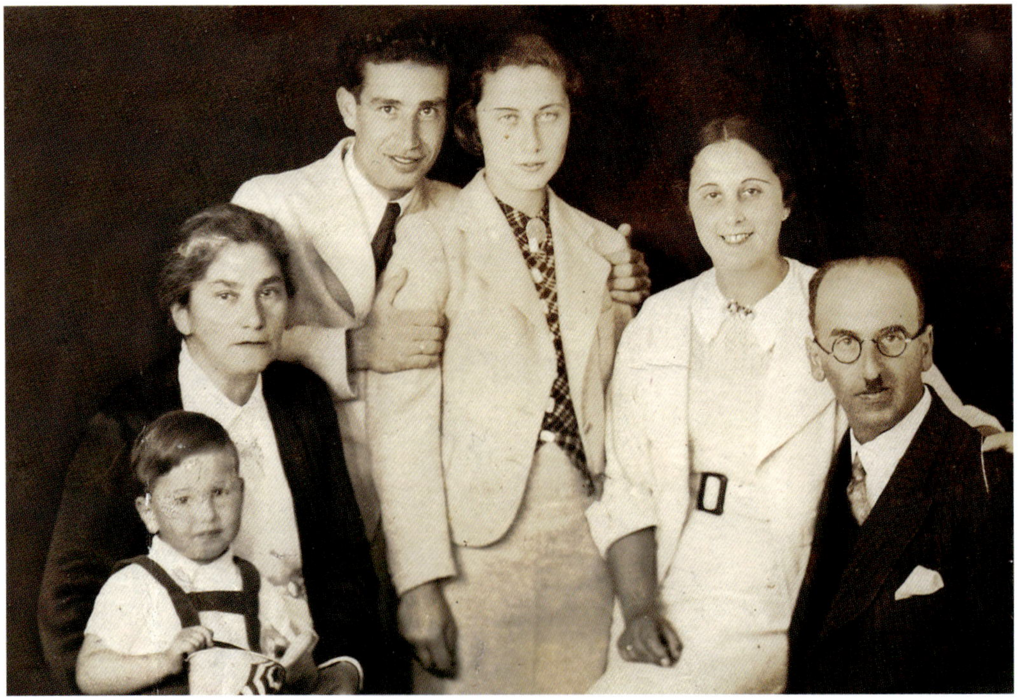

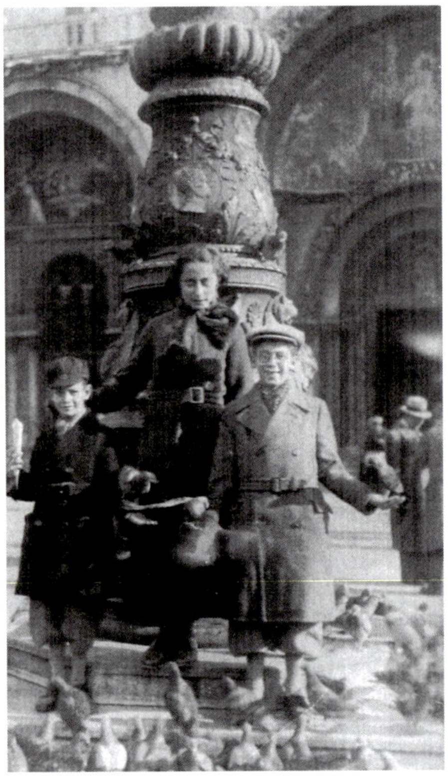

Leonie in Venice

and merchants originally from the Rhineland. All eight brothers served in the German Wehrmacht in World War I, fighting mainly in Russia or Poland. Leo was wounded and died in a war hospital on the Russian front in October 1915, a month before his younger daughter Leonie was born. Although his elder daughter Lilli (born 1905) would remember her father, Leonie never knew him. By all accounts he was a handsome man. In 1904 he married Frieda Vollmer. Frieda had had a typically German upbringing, but, having read Hitler's book *Mein Kampf,* was daunted by its message. The rapid rise of antisemitism after Hitler became Chancellor weakened her allegiance to Germany. However, such was the efficiency of the German government that the army pension she received after her husband's death continued right through the 1920s and 1930s, enabling her to bring up her two daughters in relative comfort.

Since World War I Saarland had been under French administration, but in 1935 a Plebiscite was held, offering the population the choice of remaining within the French economy or returning to Germany. The majority of the people voted for Germany. Those against were permitted to leave the country with their possessions but without any money. It was at that time that most of the Jews emigrated. Leonie, however, had already left the country. She went first as a nanny to Venice and then on to Palestine. Her mother paid her fare, and Leonie marked her departure from Germany in 1934 by sending a postcard to her mother in Saarbrucken. Soon afterwards Frieda followed her daughter to

Palestine. Lilli had already married in Germany, but she and her husband, Moses Eisenmann, with their small son Arie, joined Frieda in Palestine. They settled in Ramathaim, a small village north-west of Tel Aviv.

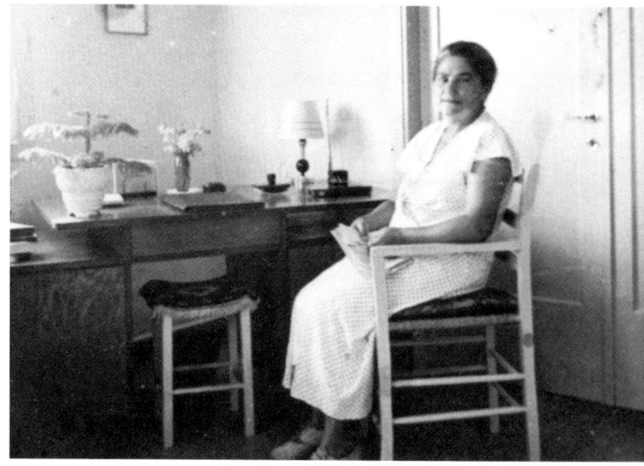

Frieda Loeb

The whole family spoke only German. They were observant Ashkenazi Jews, very religious and also superstitious. Raphael recalled that during a ferocious storm, with thunder and lightning, his terrified grandmother declared 'God is angry with us'. They lived in a newly built house, with running water, wooden floors, and glass fitted in all the windows. During the 1940 Italian bombing of Tel Aviv and Haifa, Raphael remembered his mother putting tape on all the windows to stop them shattering. Frieda's German habits made it difficult for her to adjust to the very different life in Palestine. The Middle-Eastern climate presented a challenge, with the orange trees in her Ramathaim garden needing constant watering.

There could hardly have been more of a mismatch in character between Frieda's daughter Leonie and Samuel Maklouf. Leonie was European in outlook, Samuel was Oriental. Although both had their own particular talents, these made an awkward combination. Leonie was typically German in her love of order, 'a fascist in the kitchen' as her daughter Ruth recalled. Samuel was by nature volatile and nomadic, always keen to move on, believing the grass to be greener on the other side. Although he was dextrous, able to 'make something out of nothing' he was far from being a steady earner. Money was tight, and for much of the time the couple lived apart, unable to look after their children who were constantly separated and moved around, either taken by Samuel to live with one of the relatives or sent off in a taxi to a children's home. During the war, when the German Army was moving east and getting dangerously close, Raphael and Ruth – as children with British passports - were briefly evacuated to Cyprus. Meanwhile, while Samuel was away on his adventures, Leonie made a home with her mother in Ramathaim.

Raphael liked living with his other grandmother Malka in Safed, because she was not as strict as Frieda and he preferred her food, based on olive oil, to Frieda's rich creamy cakes. Malka's house was at the very bottom of the village, near the well that served as the whole village's water supply. She lived side by side with the Arabs, speaking Arabic and living just like them. Raphael has vivid memories of Arab women with pots on their heads carrying water from the well.

In the village the women did all the work while the men sat in cafés and talked about politics and football, or sat on cushions while the women ground the coffee. Only one family possessed a radio and everyone would crowd outside their house to listen to the news. The village had lots of steps, and when Raphael tripped on them and dislocated his arm, he was attended by an Arab doctor. Whenever he was at home his father would take

Clockwise from left: Ruth, Samuel, Raphael, Alisa, Joseph

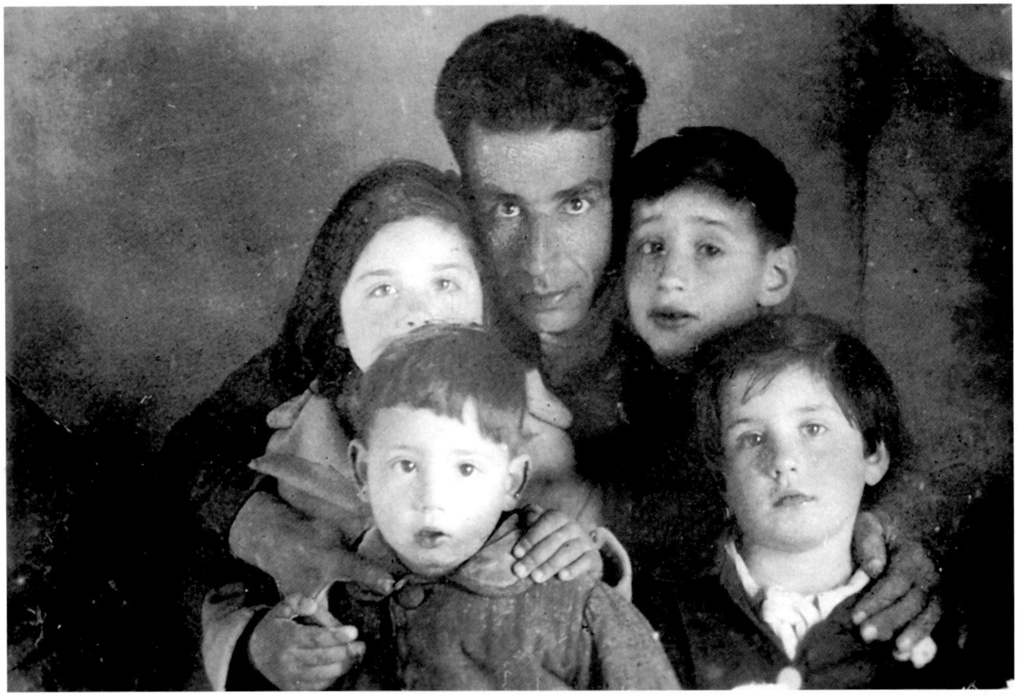

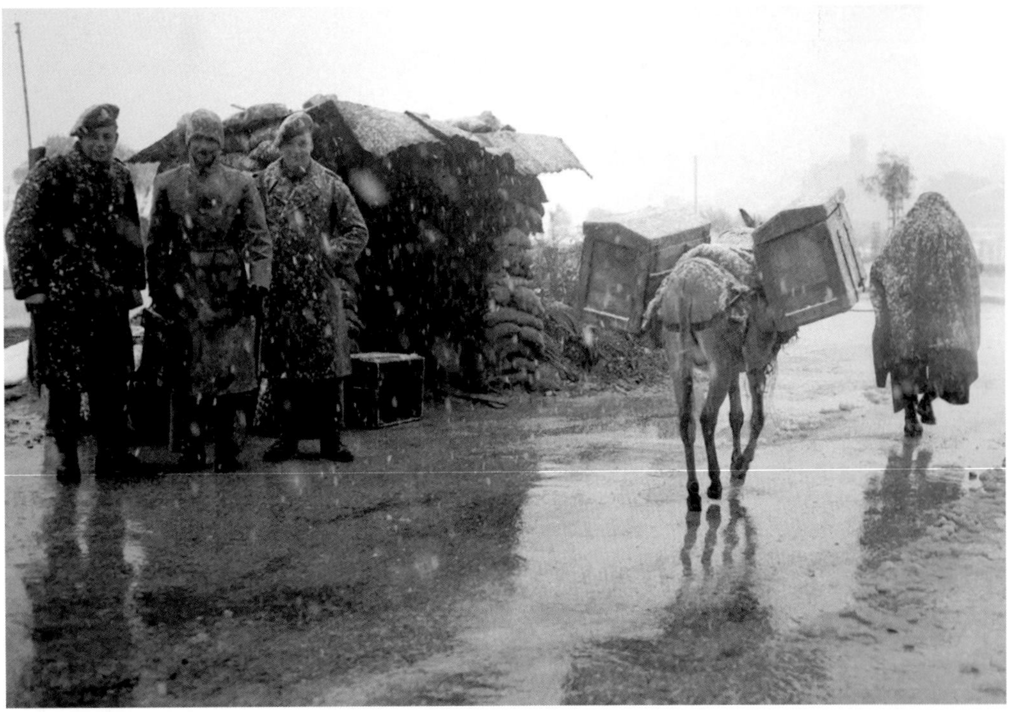

British troops at a road block in Palestine late 1947

Raphael to a *hamam* to wash, or to the barber, whose many mirrors were polished to a brilliant shine.

Raphael showed an early interest in drawing, and also made small sculptures out of wet sand. He and Ruth would dawdle on the way to school, often arriving with objects they had collected. Hordes of refugees were passing through Safed, very poorly dressed in rags, stopping at the well for water. In Ramathaim the British soldiers were much in evidence with their tents pitched around. They were building a bridge nearby and enlisting the Arabs to work for them. The 'tommies' had soft white bread and tinned pineapple, which the children particularly loved, and they would barter pitta bread and watermelons in exchange for these special goods.

In 1939, before the outbreak of the war, Samuel had decided to start a new life and try his luck as a travelling salesman in Australia. He had no job to go to, but took with him a consignment of Egyptian lucky charms to sell in the Australian outback. Grandmother Frieda paid the fare for the couple and their two-year-old son to take a ship to Perth. One of Raphael's earliest memories is of being so hot on board ship that he was put in a bucket on deck to cool down. His sister Ruth was born in Perth in 1939. The Australian venture turned out to be a failure, and within the year the family returned to Palestine, where both Joseph and Alisa were born.

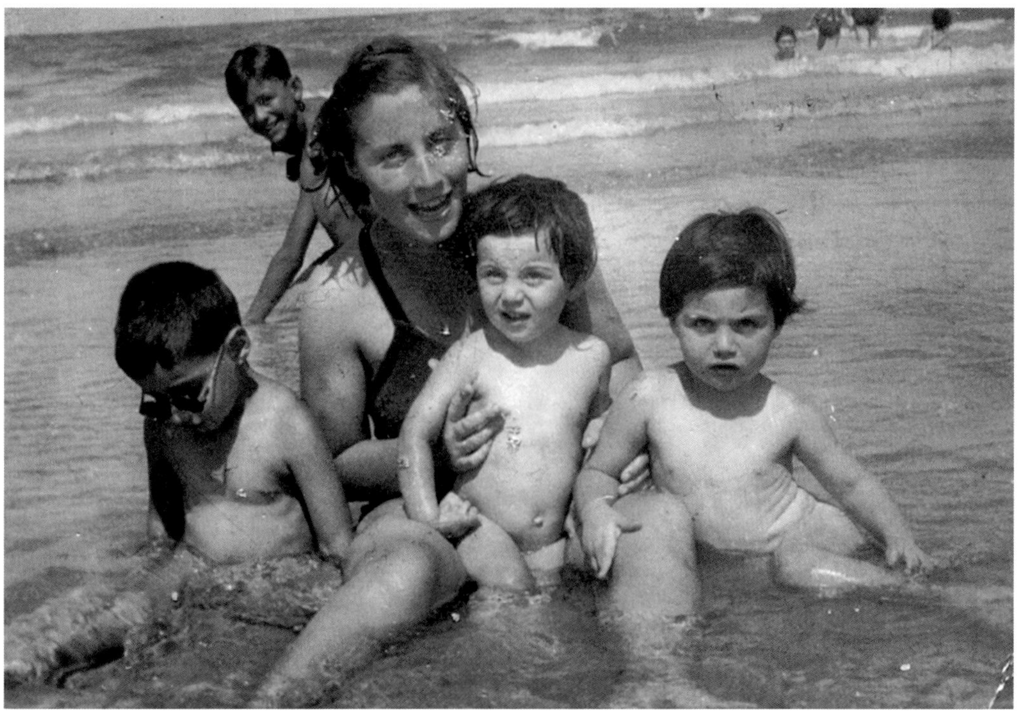

Clockwise from left: Raphael, Leonie, Alisa, Ruth

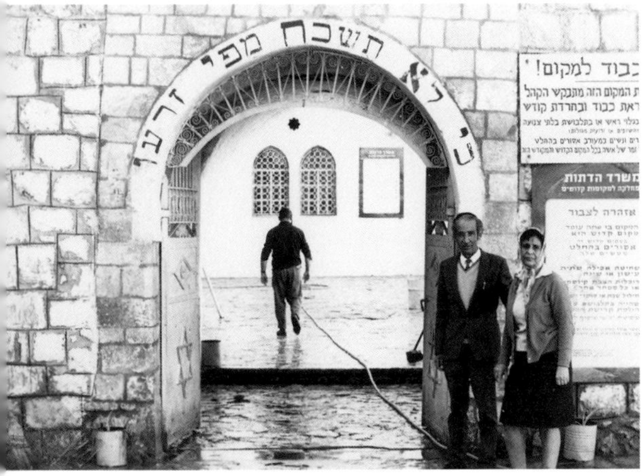

Archway, Palestine

The situation in Palestine was changing radically. Three developments had at first advanced the Zionist cause: the Balfour Declaration of 1917, proposing the establishment of a national home for the Jewish people; the 1919 Paris Peace Conference where Chaim Weismann, leader of the Zionist delegation, had presented a map of the proposed homeland; and the acceptance of the 1922 League of Nations Mandate for Palestine. However, when, in the White Paper of 1939, Neville Chamberlain abandoned the idea of establishing a Jewish Commonwealth, tension between the British and the Jews increased. At the outbreak of war it seemed that Churchill, a long-term Zionist sympathiser, might rescind the White Paper, and for a brief period there was close British-Jewish cooperation. As news of Nazi persecution reached them, many Jews wanting to fight the Nazis joined the British Army. The British Army also trained Jewish groups of volunteers, young men from kibbutzim who took on military training while working part-time at farming. Samuel Maklouf was also apparently among those who worked for the British Army.

Under the Mandate there were about ten thousand British service personnel in Palestine, but by the end of the war their numbers had increased tenfold. The Arab Legion, commanded by General Glubb Pasha, was formed, and the Transjordan Frontier Force was formed to prevent illegal immigration. It was this issue of immigration that soured a previously good relationship. Thousands of refugees from all over Europe were desperate to get to Palestine, but with Italy's entry into the war in 1940 bringing the conflict closer to the Middle East, the British tried to enforce strict immigration quotas so as not to antagonise the Arabs. The sinking of the ship The Struma in 1942 did most damage, turning the Zionists against Britain. The *Struma*, carrying Jewish refugees from Romania, was denied entry and sank in the Black Sea, drowning all but two of its passengers.

In an attempt to lift the restrictions on Jewish immigration underground movements such as the Irgun and the Stern Gang began harassing British forces, and by the end of the war the British position had become untenable. The fate of thousands of Holocaust survivors in displaced persons camps aroused public opinion, including that of America, against their immigration policy.

In May 1948 the British Mandate over Palestine expired. The Jewish People's Council gathered at Tel Aviv Museum to approve a proclamation declaring 'the establishment of a Jewish state in Eretz-Israel, to be known as the State of Israel'. This accepted as a pragmatic solution to political and demographic issues the partition of the previous British mandate into independent Jewish and Arab states.

For the Maklouf family, life in Palestine had become increasingly tense. After the death of Leonie's mother Frieda Loeb in 1944, and with little prospect of a peaceful coexistence

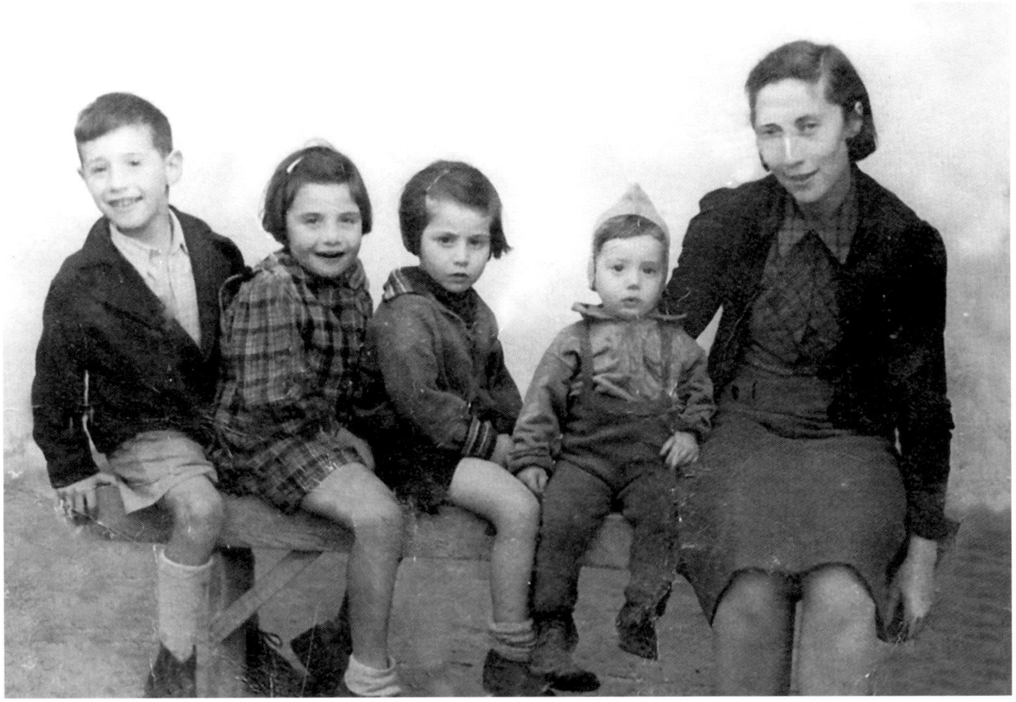

From left: Raphael, Ruth, Alisa, Joseph and Leonie

between Jews and Arabs, the Makloufs decided to leave the country. By the time the State of Israel was founded they were already in England. Luckily the family had British passports, and several German relatives in London to whom they could turn. And, most importantly, in England they could arrange treatment for Raphael's eye condition, contracted during an early attack of measles. Throughout his childhood in Palestine his eyes constantly watered, forcing him to wear dark glasses and keep his head down to avoid the bright Middle Eastern sunlight.

In 1946 Samuel and Leonie flew to London ahead of their children, and later that year Raphael and Ruth were put on a plane by Aunt Lilli, and by themselves flew to London, via Malta and Paris. When they stopped in Paris, the city was deep in snow. Neither child had seen snow before, and they collected some in a tin to take with them on the plane to show to their parents. They were met with more snow when they arrived in London. Leonie, fearful that the children would find the harshness of the climate a shock, had knitted woollen pixie hats to keep their ears warm.

Post-war London was a grey, cold place. Raphael and Ruth had left the heat and the brilliant light of Palestine for a battered and depressed city, and the coldest English winter for many years.

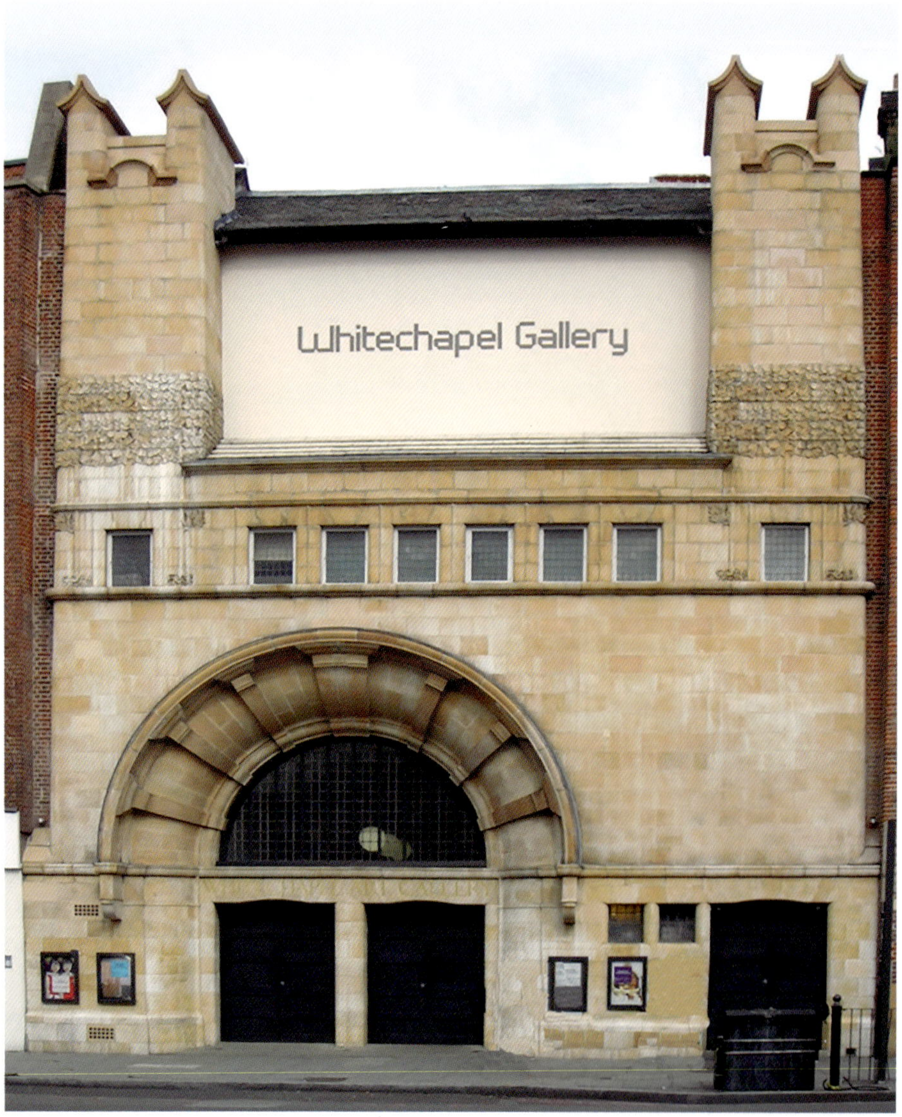

Whitechapel Gallery

Chapter 3
British Beginnings

IN STARTING A new life in Britain, the Maklouf family were greatly helped by relatives already in the country. Although three of Samuel's sisters had married Israelis and remained in Israel, his sister Rebekkah had met and married a British soldier, Harry Burnett. Burnett served several army postings abroad, but ended up with his family in Stoke-on-Trent. Three of Leonie's German relatives had moved to London before the war: Eva Altmann, a doctor, who lived in Highgate and was married to Ken Alberman, owner of the cosmetic company Innoxa; Ella Vollmer, who lived in a flat in Swiss Cottage surrounded by the heavy German furniture she had brought with her on leaving Germany; and Martha Kahn, who lived in north London with children she had adopted. To the Makloufs, therefore, London had seemed the obvious place to settle, despite the post-war depression. In the winter of 1946 Samuel and Leonie found their first home, a damp little house in Bulwer Street, Shepherds Bush, opposite a farrier who shooed rag-and-bone men's horses. They later found lodgings in the Mile End Road, backing onto a graveyard in a Spanish-Portuguese settlement of Sephardic Jews. Samuel set up as a market trader in the vicinity.

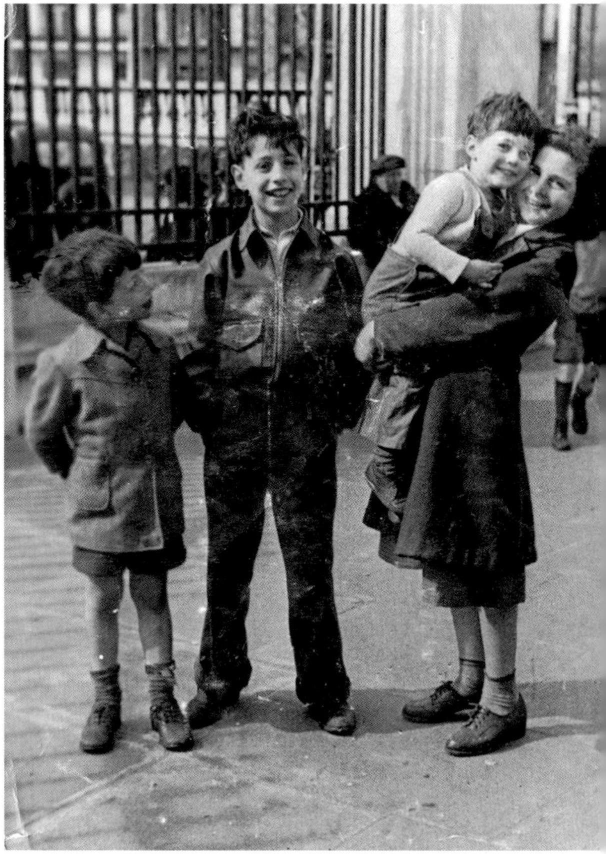

From left: Joseph, Raphael, Ruth holding Peter, in London

Raphael's eye disease was a chronic problem and, now in Britain, a possible cure for it was quickly found. He was examined at Moorfield's Eye Hospital in London, where a course of radium treatment was proposed. For this to be implemented Raphael was sent as a boarder to a specialist children's eye hospital - White Oak Hospital in Swanley, Kent.

White Oak Hospital had been established in 1903 by the Metropolitan Asylums Board for the treatment of London's poor law children suffering from ophthalmia and other diseases of the eyes, skin and scalp. It operated for almost fifty years, and was closed down in 1950, shortly after Raphael left, presumably superseded by the recently founded National Health Service. The hospital was designed to cater for around three hundred children, boys and girls, who boarded in separate units. Thirty cottages surrounded the central administration block, each accommodating twelve children and a house-mother.

White Oak Hospital

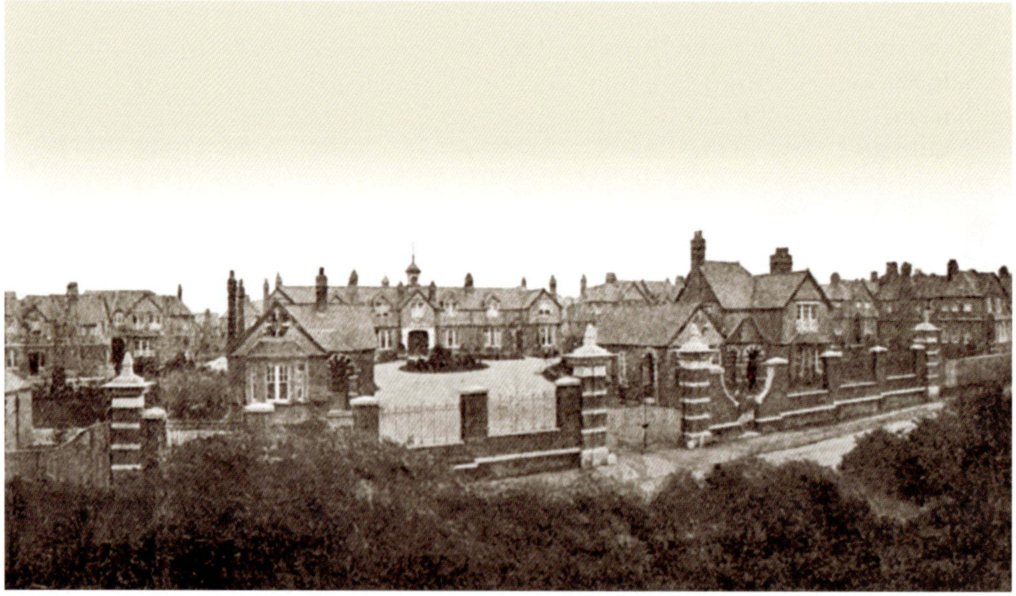

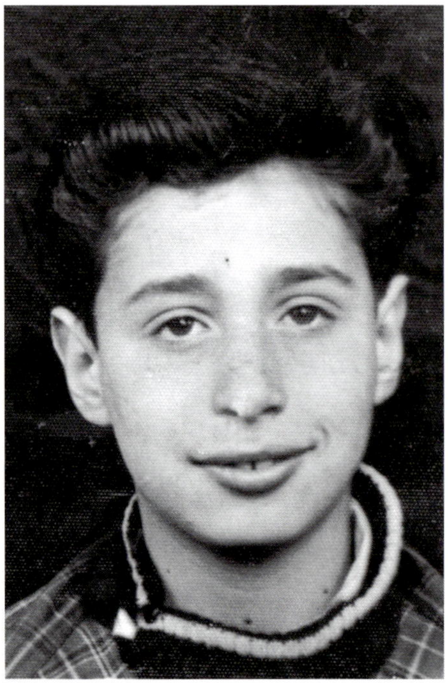

Raphael

Siblings were not allowed to visit, and parental visits were strictly limited to no more than an hour a week. Some of the patients suffered terribly from homesickness, but Raphael, who was quite accustomed to being moved to different places, simply accepted it as part of normal life. As he recalled, 'it was an amazing experience for me. I hardly spoke English. I was the only foreigner. Nobody came to visit me. Because it was for people with eye problems there was no reading or writing, but they had an art room with clay and pottery.' [1] For the next two years the hospital became his home. At first he did not understand any of the activities, particularly the morning assembly with hymn singing. With no doubt the best of intentions and because Raphael seemed so lost, his matron decided to ask a local rabbi to come and visit. The rabbi was an Ashkenazi Jew with twirly locks and a long beard, and he appeared at bedtime when the boys were tucked up in their dormitory. Looming over Raphael's bed, he launched into a list of all the things forbidden to a Jewish boy, including eating bacon – something Raphael had already been quite happily doing.

This visit from the rabbi had unpleasant consequences, as Raphael can remember in detail. 'The next morning we all went down as usual to play football below the orchard, but in the orchard the boys pounced on me, one on each arm, two on each leg, and two of them climbed a tree and pelted me with apples, shouting "that's what you did to Jesus". I knew it was something to do with the rabbi's visit, and I said to the matron that I didn't want him to come any more. Although it was done in fun, it made me feel completely different from the others.' [2]

Although there were no official lessons at the hospital there was an ordered daily regime, with morning assembly, queueing for medicines and daily injections, and games in the yard. In the summer there were picnics outside, with soggy sandwiches and hot tea. For Raphael the art room became something of a refuge. 'I started making little clay caricature portraits of the nurses and the boys. There was a woman in charge who said "these are wonderful"'. Raphael's confidence grew, as well as his ability to speak English and adopt such English habits as making beds with 'hospital corners'. After two years he left White Oak hospital with his eyes cured.

Back with his family in the Mile End Road, Raphael found himself in the midst of a huge Jewish community, but, like his father, he was very anti-religion and took no part in the religious practices. Instead he frequented the Beaumont Hall Youth Club where he painted or played table tennis. Only ten minutes walk away was the Whitechapel Art Gallery, which had an upstairs Art room for local children. On Saturday mornings Raphael went there to paint or work in clay. The woman in charge there, Sonya Hansford, was particularly struck by the small clay models that he was making. His terra cotta sculpture of three street musicians was much admired, and figured in an exhibition in the Whitechapel's gallery. A picture of this sculpture was printed in the local newspaper.

As Raphael reminisced, 'I can't remember going to school at all. I was fourteen and had it in my head that I wanted to do more little sculptures, and I spent all my spare time at the Whitechapel. The woman in charge there, Sonia Hansford, thought that I ought to go to art school. She took me on the bus all the way to Camberwell School of Art, carrying my portfolio and an orange box full of my little models. She obviously didn't ring up beforehand or find out anything about the school because she went in the front door to the Secretary's office. It wasn't term time, but in the office there were these men standing about – Leonard Daniels, Joe Dixon, and Karel Vogel, Head of Sculpture. I was wearing shorts and she just barged in, saying "You must look at this boy's work". I remember them looking at it in stony silence, and then Vogel said "he has a primitive talent". At that time there was a Junior School there and they took me in.' [3]

Camberwell School of Arts and Crafts (now Camberwell College of Art) was unique in welcoming into its fold any young person with no money and little academic education but who showed obvious talent. It had been founded in 1898 as a technical institute, sharing its site in the Peckham Road with the South London Gallery. Both the school and the gallery were the fruits of an artistic movement in Camberwell that had been supported by the painters Edward Burne-Jones, Lord Leighton, Walter Crane and George Frederick Watts. The school aimed to give 'the best artistic and technical education to all classes in the district', originally concentrating on specific trades such as

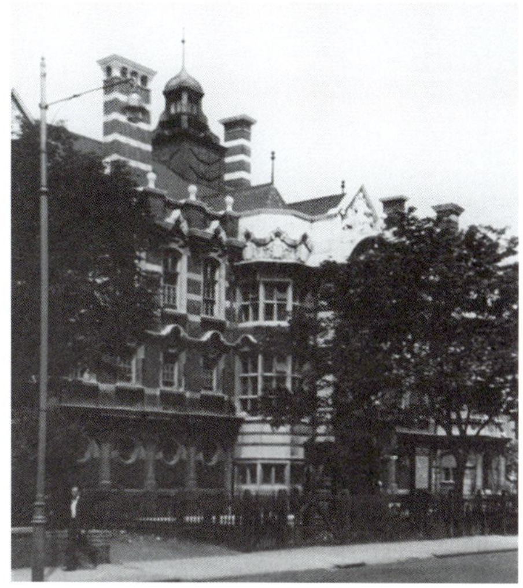

Front view of Camberwell School of Art and Crafts, 1952 (Photo ccourtesy of A. Miller)

Reproduced by kind permission of Geoff Hassell and the publishers of his book Camberwell School of Arts & Crafts – Its Students & Teachers 1943-1960, *published by the Antique Collectors Club in 1995*

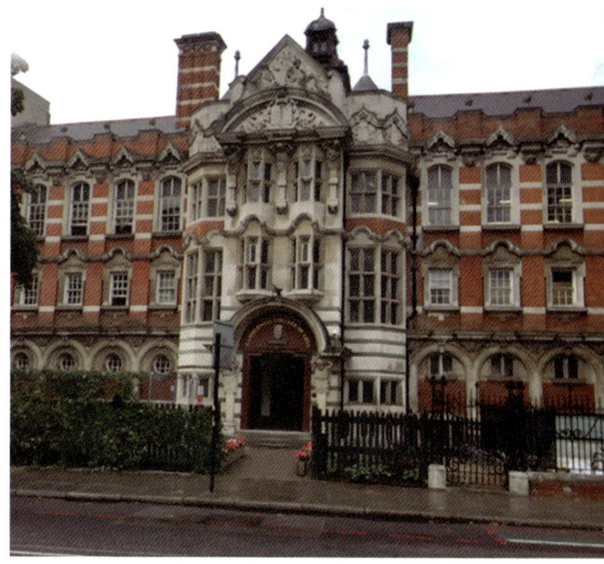

Camberwell College of Arts today

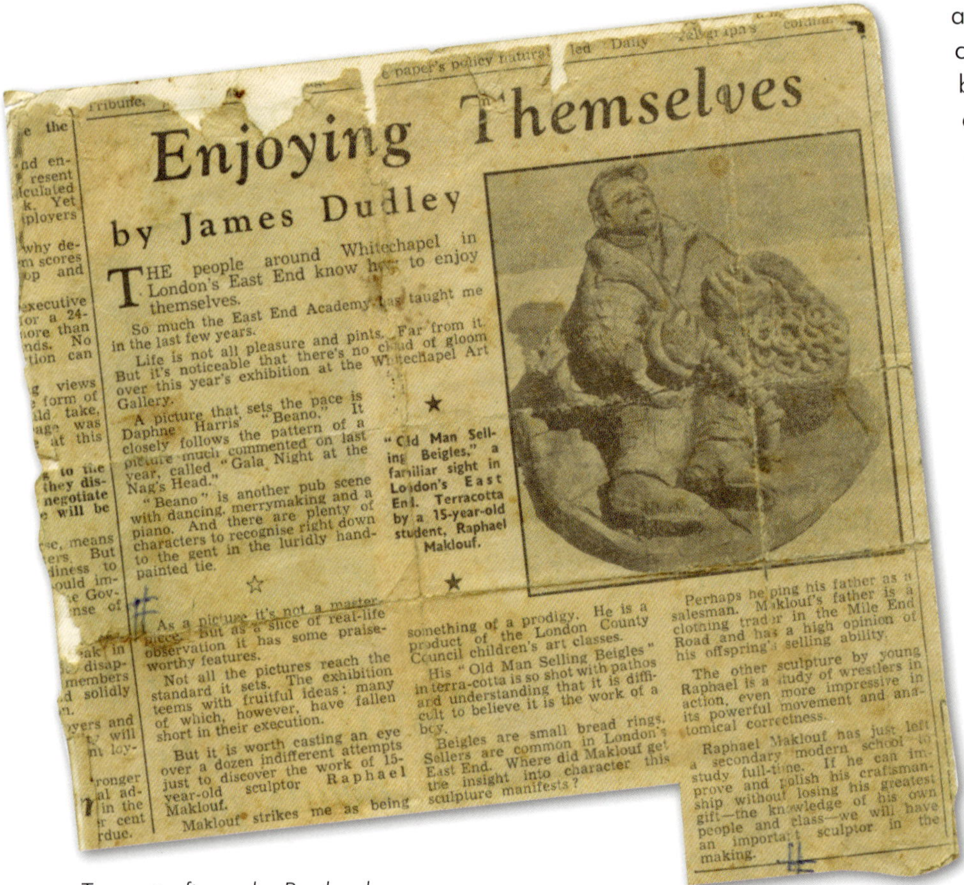

Enjoying Themselves

by James Dudley

THE people around Whitechapel in London's East End know how to enjoy themselves.

So much the East End Academy has taught me in the last few years.

Life is not all pleasure and pints. Far from it. But it's noticeable that there's no cloud of gloom over this year's exhibition at the Whitechapel Art Gallery.

A picture that sets the pace is Daphne Harris' "Beano." It closely follows the pattern of a picture much commented on last year, called "Gala Night at the Nag's Head."

"Beano" is another pub scene with dancing, merrymaking and a piano. And there are plenty of characters to recognise right down to the gent in the luridly hand-painted tie.

☆

As a picture it's not a masterpiece. But as a slice of real-life observation it has some praiseworthy features.

Not all the pictures reach the standard it sets. The exhibition teems with fruitful ideas: many of which, however, have fallen short in their execution.

But it is worth casting an eye over a dozen indifferent attempts just to discover the work of 15-year-old sculptor Raphael Maklouf.

Maklouf strikes me as being something of a prodigy. He is a product of the London County Council children's art classes.

His "Old Man Selling Beigles" in terra-cotta is so shot with pathos and understanding that it is difficult to believe it is the work of a boy.

Beigles are small bread rings. Sellers are common in London's East End. Where did Maklouf get the insight into character this sculpture manifests?

Perhaps helping his father as a salesman. Maklouf's father is a clothing trader in the Mile End Road and has a high opinion of his offspring's selling ability.

The other sculpture by young Raphael is a study of wrestlers in action, even more impressive in its powerful movement and anatomical correctness.

Raphael Maklouf has just left a secondary modern school to study full-time. If he can improve and polish his craftsmanship without losing his greatest gift—the knowledge of his own people and class—we will have an important sculptor in the making.

★

"Old Man Selling Beigles," a familiar sight in London's East End. Terracotta by a 15-year-old student, Raphael Maklouf.

Teracotta figure by Raphael

architecture, cabinet-making, embroidery, wood carving and wood block cutting. By 1908 new buildings had been erected to accommodate more classes, including Typography, Plumbing and Brickwork. Further extensions housed Drawing and Painting rooms, as well as Wood and Metalwork, Pottery and Sculpture. By 1920 a Fine Art Department had been created and the courses included Textiles, Printing, Bookbinding, Design and Illustration. In 1938 William Johnstone was appointed Principal and he started bringing in practising artists, rather than trained teachers, to his staff. Johnstone had himself trained in Paris in the atelier of André l'Hôte and had noticed how the presence of practising artists inspired the students.

During the first years of the war the school was closed and the juniors evacuated to Kent, but when the bombing became less of a threat it reopened. Johnstone already had some fine painters, including Lawrence Gowing, Sam Carter and John Dodgson, on his staff, and in 1942 he appointed Victor Pasmore as Head of Painting. Pasmore, who had 'resigned' from the army as a conscientious objector and had spent six months in jail, had no formal art training, but was at that time a lyrical figurative painter with exquisite taste. He in turn brought in practising artists to teach, among them William Coldstream, Claude Rogers and Joe Dixon. Pasmore, Coldstream and Rogers, the three founders of the pre-war Euston Road School, initiated an exciting period for Fine Art at Camberwell, and it was in this stimulating atmosphere that Raphael now found himself.

In the Painting and Sculpture Schools the Life Room played a central role, and every student was expected to do some work from the live model. Models were at a premium. The 'career model' Quentin Crisp gave an amusing account of his experiences at various art schools, including Camberwell, the last art school at which he posed. 'When I was first a model total anonymity was deliberately preserved. I was called 'Model' and addressed the teachers as 'Sir'.... Some teachers, arriving in the Life Room would say "Stay put as you are. That's it for the day, everybody." Others, handling my limbs with the least possible carnality, would rearrange them with some secret theory of aesthetics.

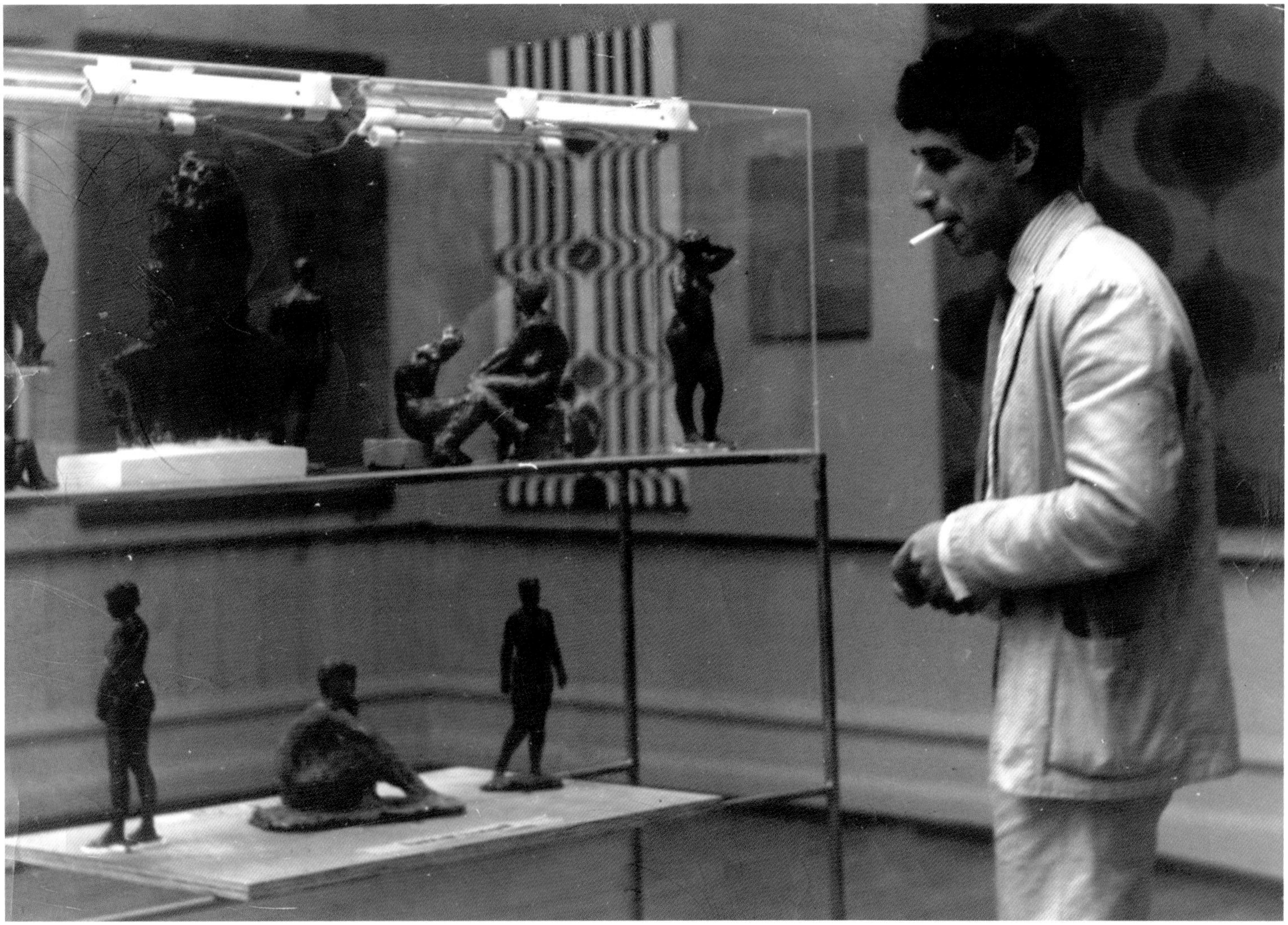

Raphael exhibiting his bronze figures at the South London Art Gallery

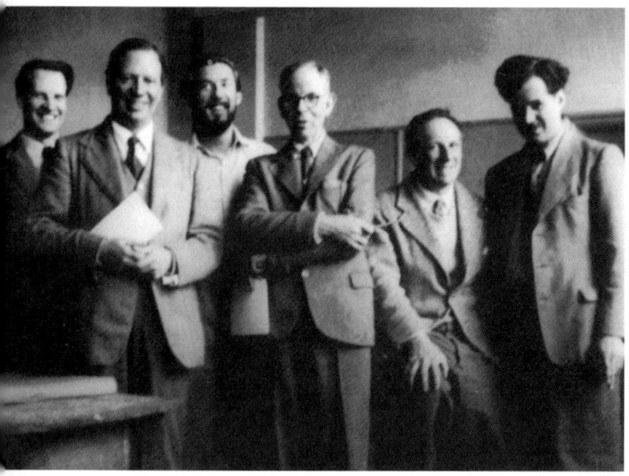

From left to right: Geoffrey Monk, Leonard Daniels, John Brason, Gilbert Spencer, Karel Vogel and Joe Dixon, c.1953

Reproduced by kind permission of Geoff Hassell and the publishers of his book Camberwell School of Arts & Crafts – Its Students & Teachers 1943-1960, *published by the Antique Collectors Club in 1995*

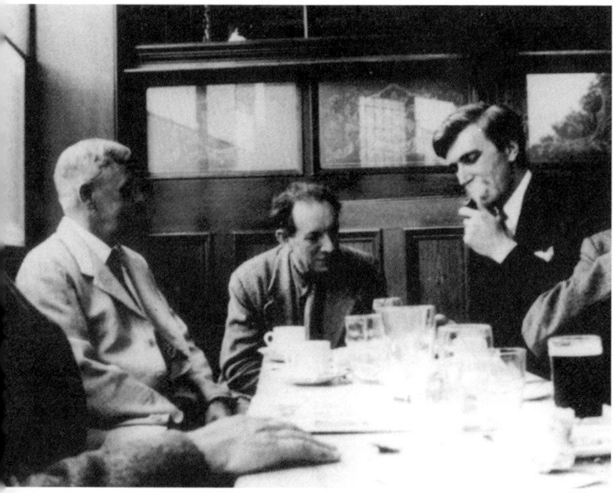

From left to right: Michael Rothenstein, R.V. Pitchforth, Karel Vogel and Richard Macdonald, Walmer Castle pub, Camberwell, c.1953

Reproduced by kind permission of Geoff Hassell and the publishers of his book Camberwell School of Arts & Crafts – Its Students & Teachers 1943-1960, *published by the Antique Collectors Club in 1995*

The most difficult Master for whom I ever worked was a Mr Rogers. When I flung an arm into the air, he reeled backward, crying "What on earth are you doing now?" He didn't approve of posing and wanted me to look like an ordinary mortal.' [4]

At the same time as the Fine Art Department was created, Camberwell's Junior School was established, taking children from the age of thirteen and providing not only a general education but also specialised art courses. The Junior School survived for almost forty years, closing in 1958, by which time Raphael was a part-time lecturer in the Senior school, having been through seven years of education there.

In 1951, when Raphael had first appeared at Camberwell as a boy, the three men he happened to meet were Leonard Daniels, who had served as a war artist and had in 1948 succeeded Pasmore as Principal; Joe Dixon, who joined Camberwell in 1949 and over the next thirty years held various positions including Senior Lecturer, Head of Department and eventually Vice-Principal; and Karel Vogel, a Czech refugee from Nazism, who in 1948 was appointed Head of the School of Sculpture. Both Joe Dixon and Karel Vogel were to play important parts in Raphael's life.

Effectively Raphael's education began at Camberwell. At first he commuted by bus from the Mile End Road to the Junior School. The focus for the juniors was on drawing and painting, but they also studied a mixture of disciplines including Puppetry, for which they made marionettes and held puppet shows. In those post-war years anyone entering the school was expected to pass School Certificate, usually with Art as part of the package. In practice there was a great deal of flexibility, with such a wide age range of students, ex-servicemen in their twenties mixing with teenagers, Raphael being one of the youngest. One of the tutors, Gordon Scott, took Raphael under his wing and gave him one-to-one lessons in reading and writing English. The curriculum, which led to the National Diploma in Design (NDD), followed up Junior School with a two-year Intermediate course of general studies. These included Life Drawing, Painting, History of Art, Anatomy, Architecture, Fashion Design, Lettering, plus a craft such as Pottery. Gilbert Spencer, Stanley Spencer's brother, was then Head of Painting, and Stanley, a small man with a high-pitched voice, would occasionally appear to give criticisms.

Not only was Camberwell Raphael's primary place of education, it became his home from home. Throughout his childhood he only infrequently shared a home with his parents, having been constantly moved around to different places. He confessed that he hardly knew his mother. In his first years at Camberwell it was Joe Dixon who filled the parental role. He was enormously kind to him, and for long periods Raphael lodged with him and his family in his Putney house.

Raphael with Karel Vogel's Head of Learie Constantine

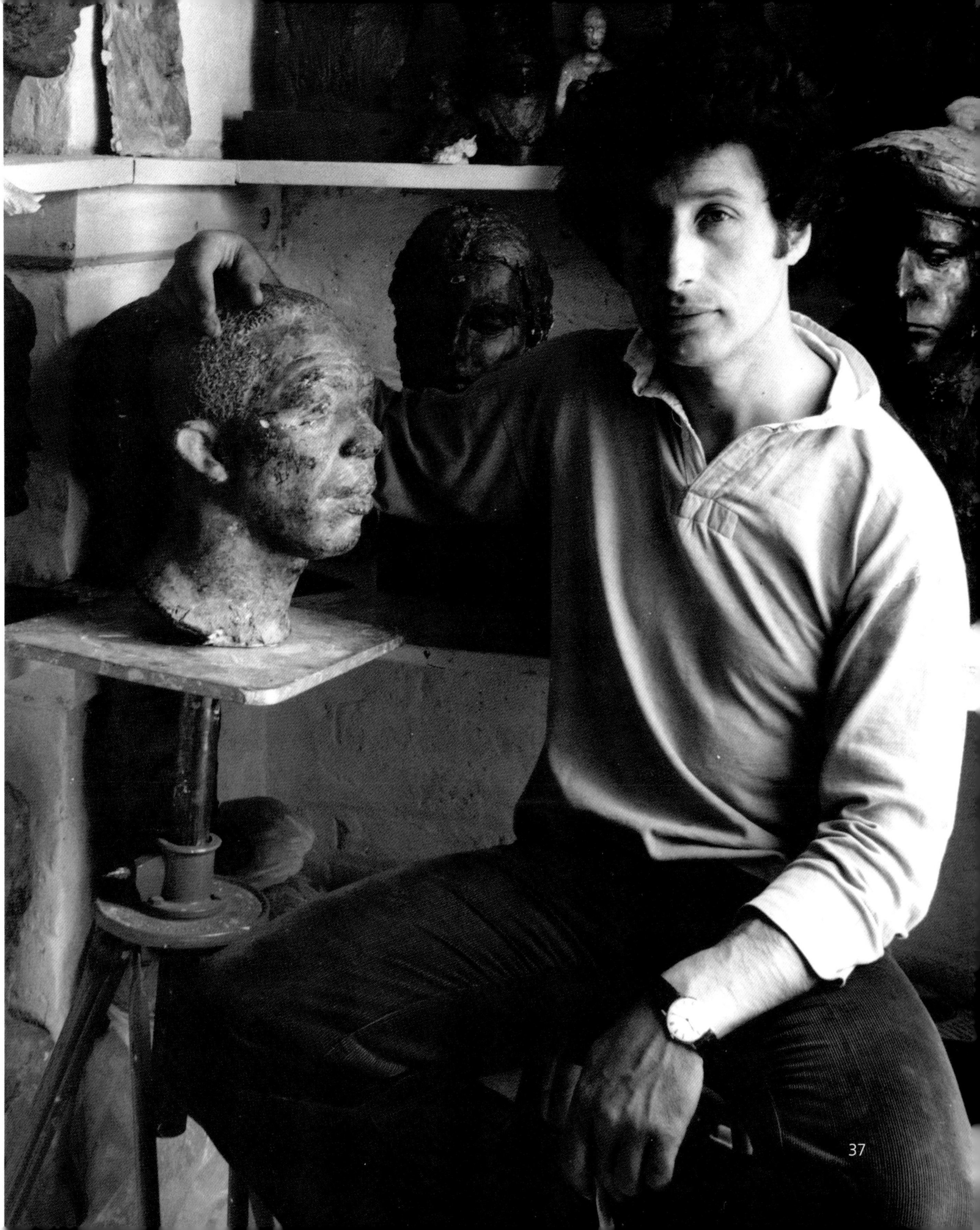

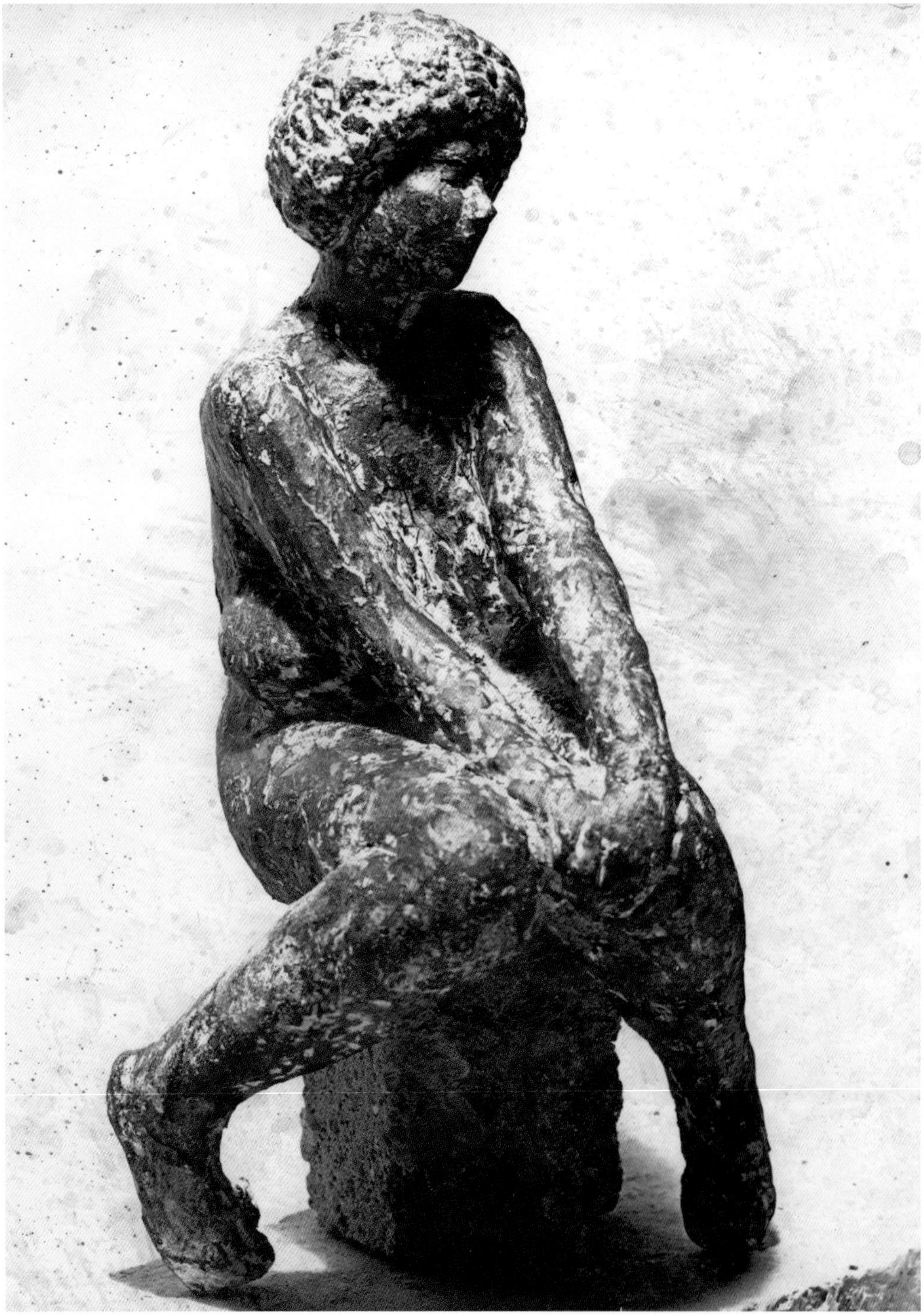

The model Adesina – bronze

Joe Dixon, the son of a stonemason from Lancashire, had won a scholarship to the Royal College of Art, and from there a travelling scholarship to Europe. He had arrived at Camberwell in 1949 immediately after travelling in Italy, his favourite country. He remained at Camberwell for the next thirty years, holding various positions including Senior Lecturer, Head of Department, and eventually Vice-Principal. As Raphael said, 'he and his wife were wonderful people, very generous – their door was always open. Joe loved making his own wine. He wasn't religious – he was very left-wing - but he was a real Christian. His wife used to sing hymns to the radio's accompaniment. They had a son who was born deaf and dumb. When I went to Camberwell I had a London County Council Grant and I had never had so much money in my life. I didn't know anything about money or banks, and Joe helped me set up a bank account with Barclays. He actually ran the school and organised everything for everyone.' [5]

Whereas Joe Dixon was a substitute father for Raphael, Karel Vogel was a grandfather figure who gave him a sense of security. He was also the most important influence on the future direction of his artistic life. Vogel was born in Czechoslovakia in 1897 and studied Classical Archaeology and History of Art at the University of Prague and Sculpture at Prague Academy of Fine Arts, continuing his studies in Vienna. He enjoyed a considerable reputation as a sculptor in his own country and made many fine portrait heads there, including one of Oscar Kokoschka. When Hitler's armies advanced into Czechoslovakia he and his wife decided to emigrate to England, to try to establish himself as a British sculptor. At the outbreak of war he was interned as an émigré alien but soon released, taking up teaching posts at Oswestry and Liverpool art colleges. In 1948 Vogel was invited to join the staff at Camberwell and within a few months was appointed Head of the Sculpture School. A highly intelligent man and an excellent lecturer, he influenced a whole generation of students.

In Raphael Vogel found just the sort of talented, malleable boy to whom he could pass on his knowledge and beliefs. It was clear to all the other sculpture students that Vogel adored him. Along with another favoured student, Michael Snowden, Vogel christened the two promising young sculptors the two Archangels – Raphael and Michael. In Jewish angelology Raphael is the affable Archangel who helped Tobias on his travels. Milton called him a 'sociable spirit'. As Archangel Raphael, Raphael Maklouf, sociable, open and friendly to all, was well-named.

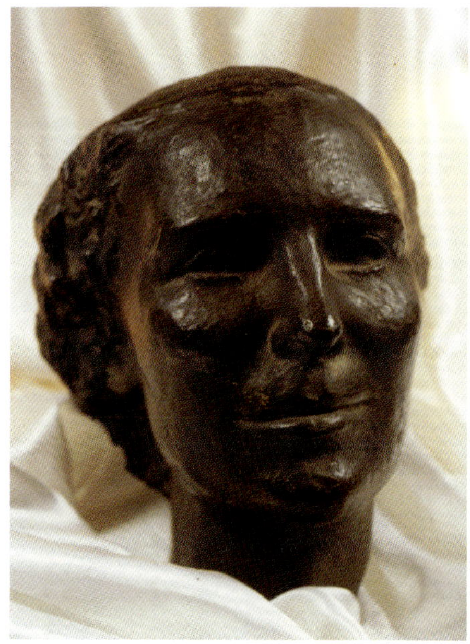

Karel Vogel. Helen Watson, bronze, courtesy of Lesley South

Reproduced by kind permission of Geoff Hassell and the publishers of his book Camberwell School of Arts & Crafts – Its Students & Teachers 1943-1960, *published by the Antique Collectors Club in 1995*

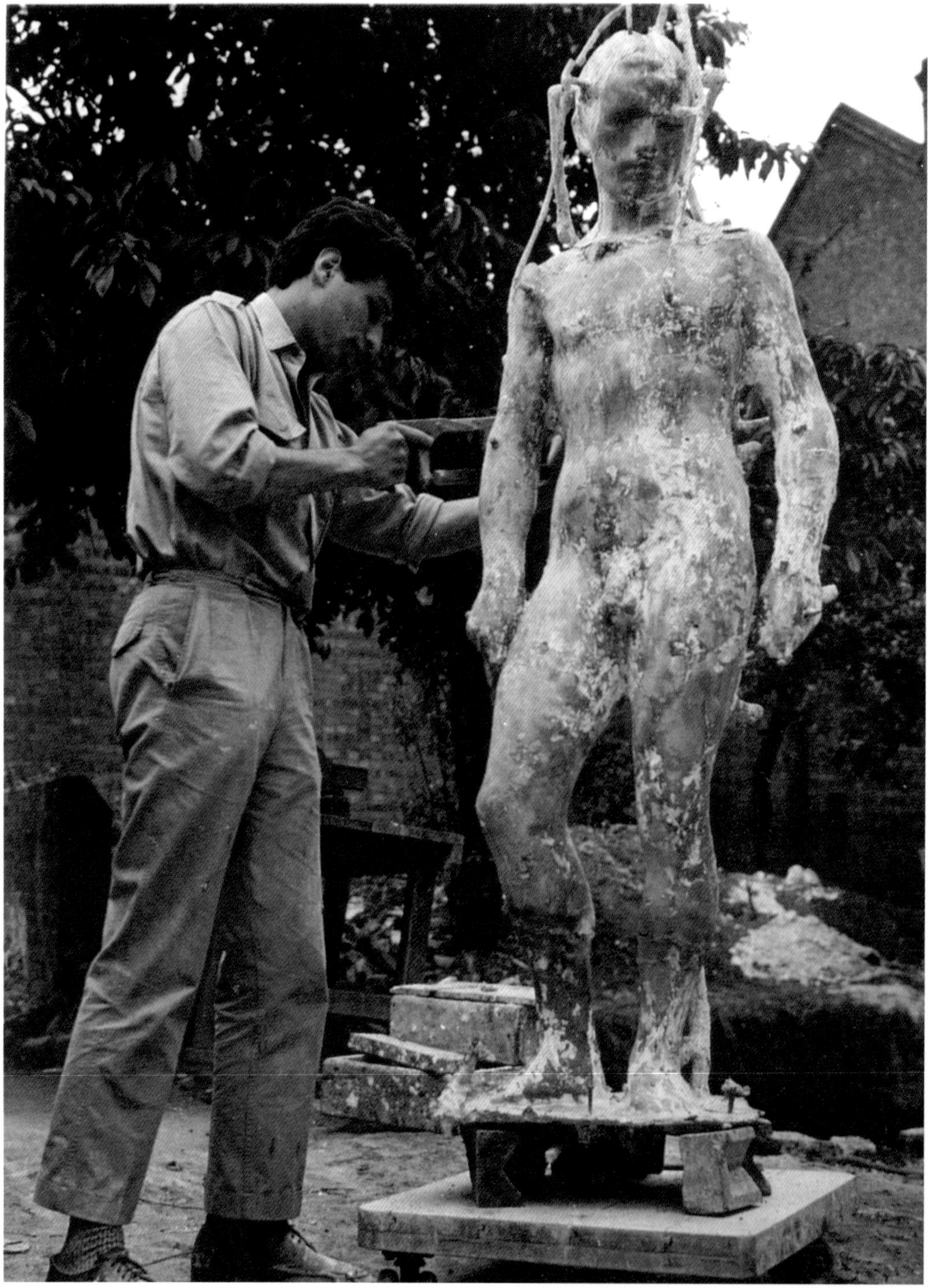

Chapter 4

The Archangel's Apprenticeship

CAMBERWELL SCHOOL OF Arts and Crafts became Raphael's home from home. His London County Council Grant covered his living expenses and all materials in the college were free. After a year sharing digs in New Cross, he moved to a flat at No 50 Peckham Road, which he shared with fellow student Michael Snowden and a succession of others. The flat was directly opposite the Sculpture School, and with the Janitor's connivance, they made some wax impressions, cast an extra set of keys to the Sculpture studios, and learned how to switch on the heating. The two archangels, Raphael and Michael, worked in the big studio seven days a week as well as most evenings, when they usually persuaded another student to pose for them. They had complete freedom to do what they wanted, and the prevailing ethos at Camberwell encouraged them to work with a passionate intensity - an almost religious zeal. Raphael remembers that time with some nostalgia. 'We got the keys and worked there at weekends. The library down the road had books and LP records. I used to get long operas because my hands got too clayey to change the records. I got very fond of music from listening to music while working. I never found other recordings as good as the ones that I used to listen to again and again.' [1] There were also three local cinemas, and Raphael was able to indulge his love of films. Watching films, particularly Westerns, had been an important part of his early education, when, for the princely sum of one-and-sixpence, he could spend a whole day at the cinema.

In the 1950s British art schools were wonderful places, filled with practising artists who provided both inspiration and a liberal education. The emphasis was not on academic teaching, but on encouragement to study by looking at paintings and sculpture. Raphael spent hours exploring the London galleries. He copied Rubens's *Judgement of Paris* in the National Gallery, and even a small tapestry in the Victoria and Albert Museum. Camberwell benefited from a starry cast of tutors. The Painting tutors included Michael Salaman, Chris Pemberton, Chris Chamberlain, Dick Lee, Euan Uglow, Tony Eyton and Claude Rogers. The tutors would all congregate after hours at the Walmer Castle, a pub at the end of the road. As Raphael reminisced, 'there was a foundry for casting sculpture

Opposite: Life size bronze

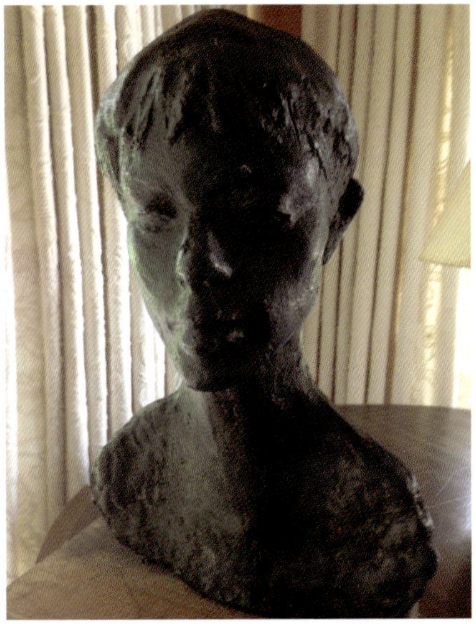
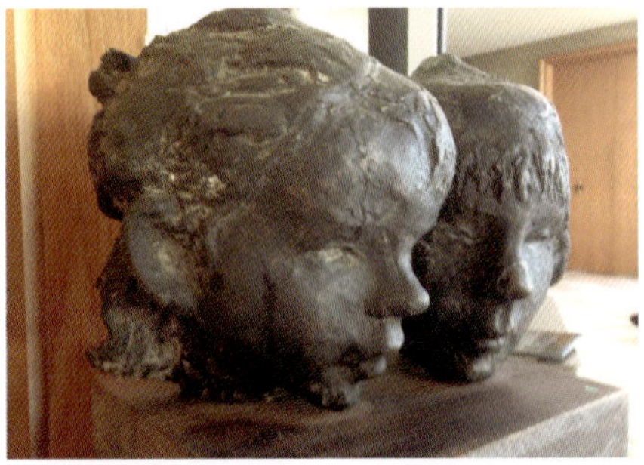
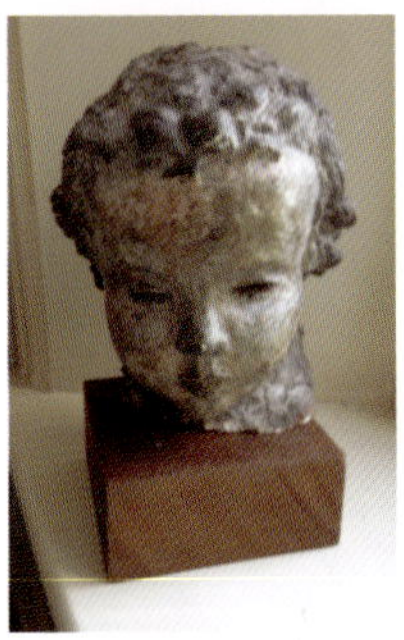
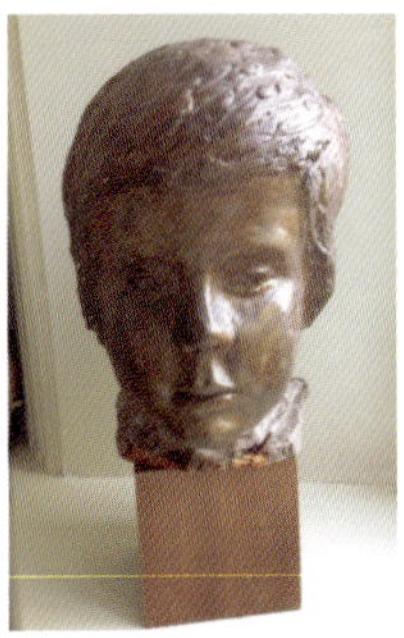

Top: Head of Olivia Scully
Centre: Heads of Kirsten and Nadine
Above: Alexander and Arabella

– at that time it was the only art school in the country to have one – and the Pottery was superb. Lucie Rie taught there, and when Hamada came I sent all my students to go and listen to him. It was a once in a lifetime chance.' [2]

For the sculpture students the influence of Karel Vogel was paramount. Like most of the other tutors, he was a practising artist who worked alongside his students and whose method of work could therefore be seen by all. Before arriving in London Vogel had worked in Prague, where much of his pre-war sculpture was displayed. He had managed to escape the Nazis on the pretext of holding an exhibition in London, and had brought his life-size standing nude *Klare* with him. This eventually found a home outside the South London Gallery but has now disappeared. In order to make a living when he first arrived in England, Vogel worked for Royal Doulton, making ceramic figurines for them. As he established himself in Britain, he participated in many exhibitions, including the two Battersea Park Open Air exhibitions of 1951 and 1960. He contributed three large reliefs for the Pavilion of Power and Production for the 1951 Festival of Britain exhibition, in which other major sculptors, including Henry Moore, Jacob Epstein, Frank Dobson, Georg Ehrlich, Lynn Chadwick, Reg Butler, and Eduardo Paolozzi, played a part. Vogel's commissions in England included a figure study in St Peter's Square in London and a figure group in Harlow New Town. Two of his last portrait heads featured Alec Guinness and his Camberwell colleague Claude Rogers. Many of Vogel's drawings were exhibited at the Leicester Galleries, and, after his death, a retrospective exhibition staged by the Arts Council, was held at the South London Gallery in December 1962, then toured the country in 1963. In the catalogue's Foreword, his fellow expatriate Ernst Gombrich wrote: 'He knew how to open his students' eyes to the individuality of the model and make them forget their own mannerisms...If there is one word that more than others sums up this quality that gives unity to his work it is poise.' [3]

Vogel had apparently been disappointed not to be taken on by the Slade School because he felt he deserved the best students in the country. He was therefore determined that his Camberwell students should turn out to be better than all, special and different. In the Sculpture School he was an absolute dictator. A highly intelligent and cultured man, he was fond of opera and used to hum the arias from his favourite works. Students were encouraged to destroy their work, remodel, destroy and remodel to achieve a finished piece. Vogel could be destructive in his criticisms, sometimes gouging with his scalpel right through a student's work. Using a cigarette holder, he smoked all the time, as did many of the students, who rolled their own cigarettes to make each packet go further. Vogel was intrigued by this, and one day announced 'Klara was making cigarettes for me last night but she couldn't get as many out of a packet as you do'.

The students addressed him as Dr Vogel, and he was particular about this title. Michael Snowden remembered a fellow student, Richard Cowdy, helping to cast Vogel's large figure for St Peter's Square in *ciment fondu*. The piece required an inordinate amount of anatomical pushing and pulling, and when Cowdy loudly complained, Vogel responded 'Do not raise your voice at me – I am the Doctor here.' Although his commitment was to teach four days a week, he was in the Sculpture School five days a week, setting the poses and working alongside the students, talking as he worked. Everybody worked from the model, and Vogel made them start by drawing the pose from every angle – profile after profile, front, side, back and three-quarter views. He was dismissive of examinations and did not run specific courses, but taught the practicalities of modelling in clay, from the initial armature to mixing the plaster, casting and firing. The idea was to prepare students for making a living from their work. Getting a likeness was important, as was anatomical accuracy. As Snowden remembered, 'we had a studio set aside for teaching Anatomy, with a skeleton and a 'muscle man' – a flayed standing figure. Those, and Wolfe's *Anatomy*, were the sources of our information. Vogel would point out the structural rhythms of the figure and explain how, if one took half of the pelvis and put the two halves together, they made a figure of eight. His teaching relied on the insights to be gained by comparison. At any one time there would be fifteen to eighteen students working from the model in the large studio. When he was asked why the students were all doing the same subject, he replied 'Of course they are doing the same thing. They learn from each other. If they were doing different things they would not learn." Vogel encouraged learning by practice and despised exams. One year everybody failed the Art History exam.' [4]

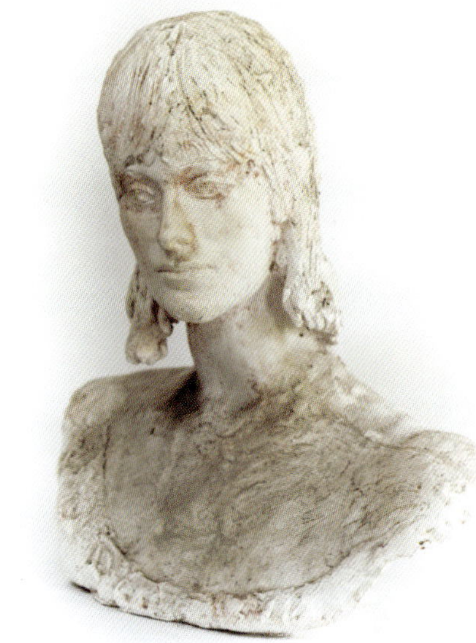

Original plaster model of Sophie
Photo by Kirsten Scully

The sculpture of the ancient Greeks was Vogel's touchstone, and he focused on male youth, particularly favouring the physical manifestation of the transition between childhood and adulthood. As Michael Snowden remembered, 'his teaching was based on drawing, like teaching people to read. He believed that reading from Nature was a lifetime study, and that objectivity precluded any mannerism. He liked naturalism in art as in life, and when I recall his treatment of the work of many different students, I believe that feeling was at the core of his teaching.' At heart a Romantic, Vogel's delight in the look of the world and particularly the human form, underpinned all his work. When, in his early sixties he was stricken with multiple sclerosis, he would sit in a wheelchair and draw, singing to himself. He died at the age of sixty-four. On the last day of his life he was brought into Camberwell in his wheelchair. His students were only later aware that he had come to say goodbye. He died by assisted suicide, with Joe Dixon at his bedside. Afterwards one of the younger students, Brindsley Tyrrell, remarked 'now there is no one left to say how beautiful it all is'. [5]

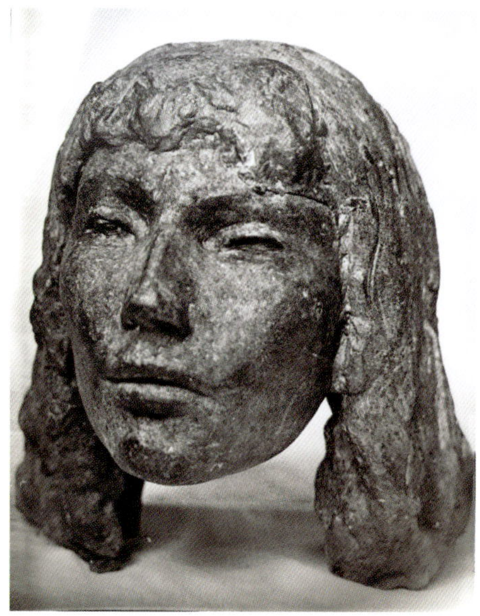

Bronze head of student

One of his students, Teresa Fawcett, found the atmosphere in the studios, and Vogel's overbearing presence, extremely oppressive. For her the studio was 'a frozen space, in which normal rules did not apply. We always worked from life – that's what we all did. We always had professional models but we all modelled out of school. We worked all

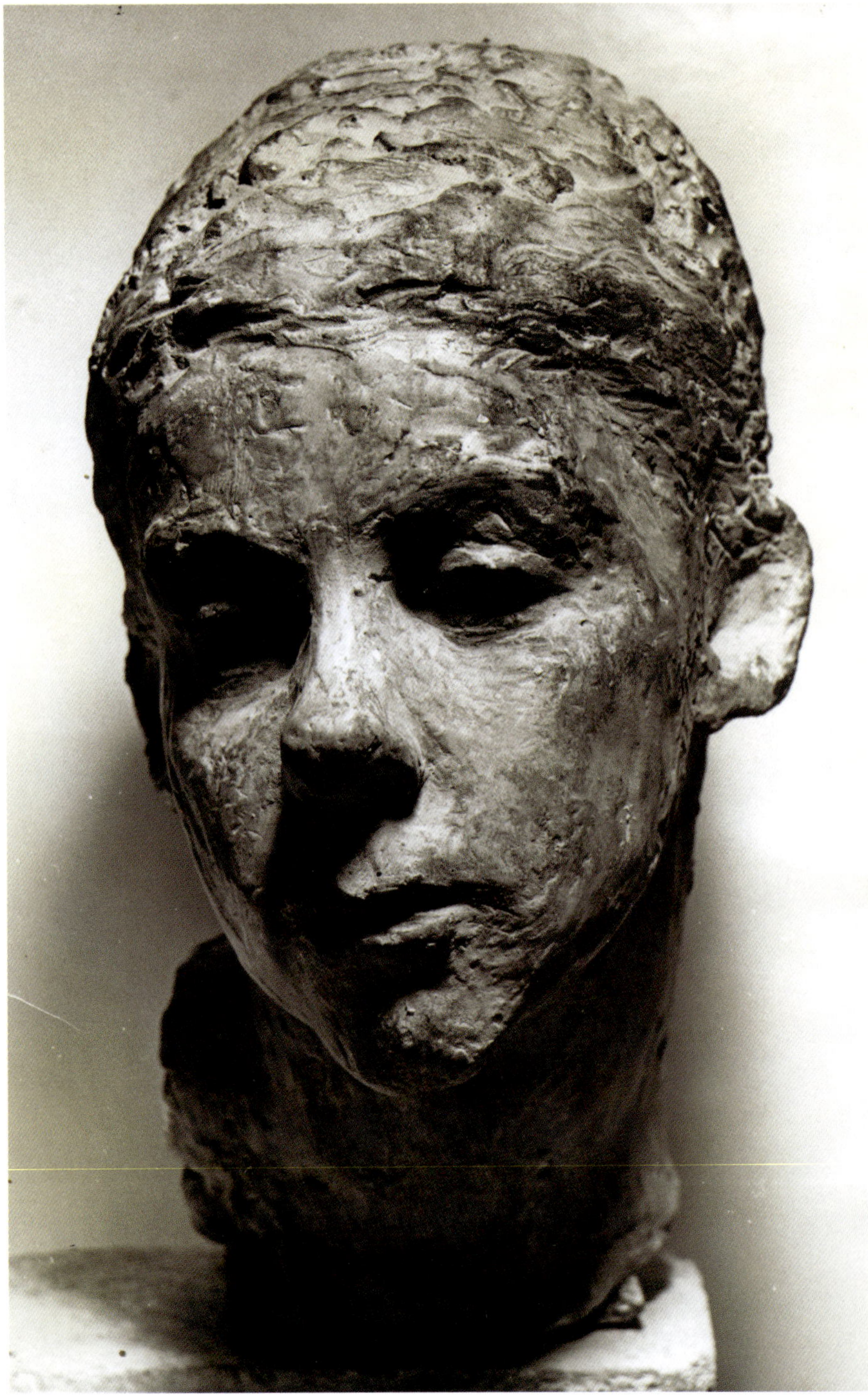

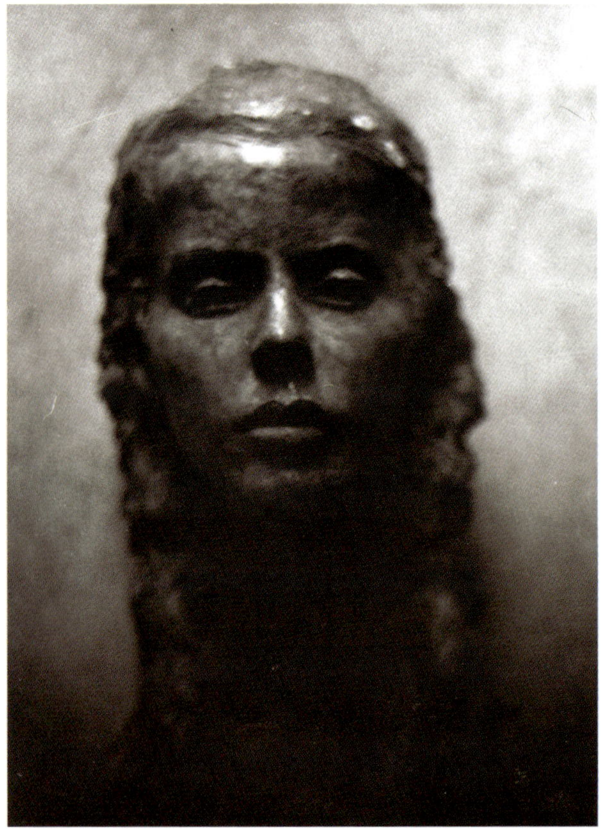

Above: Head of fellow student Ann Napier

Left: Head of fellow student Anne Whipp

Opposite: Bronze casting at Camberwell

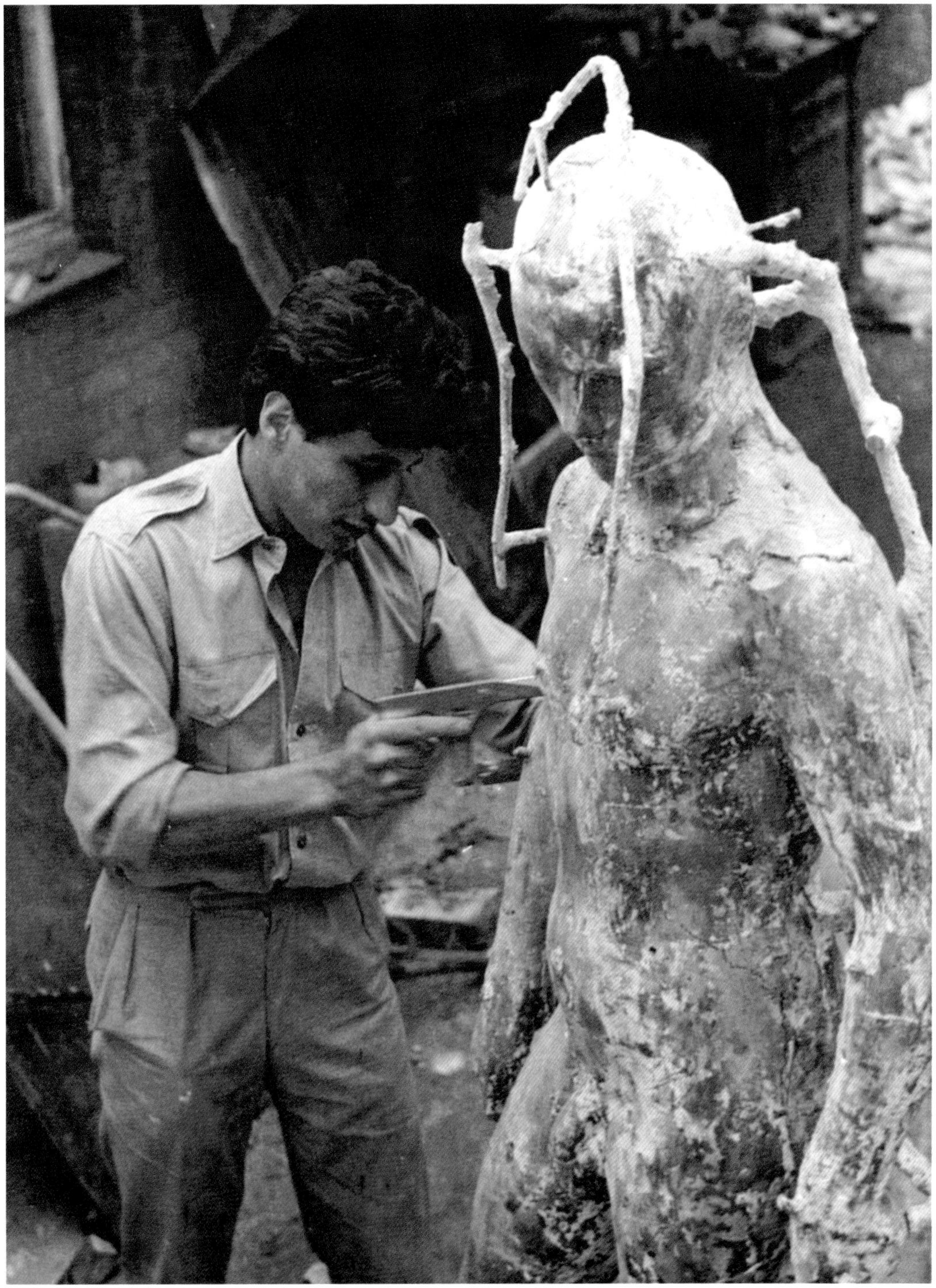

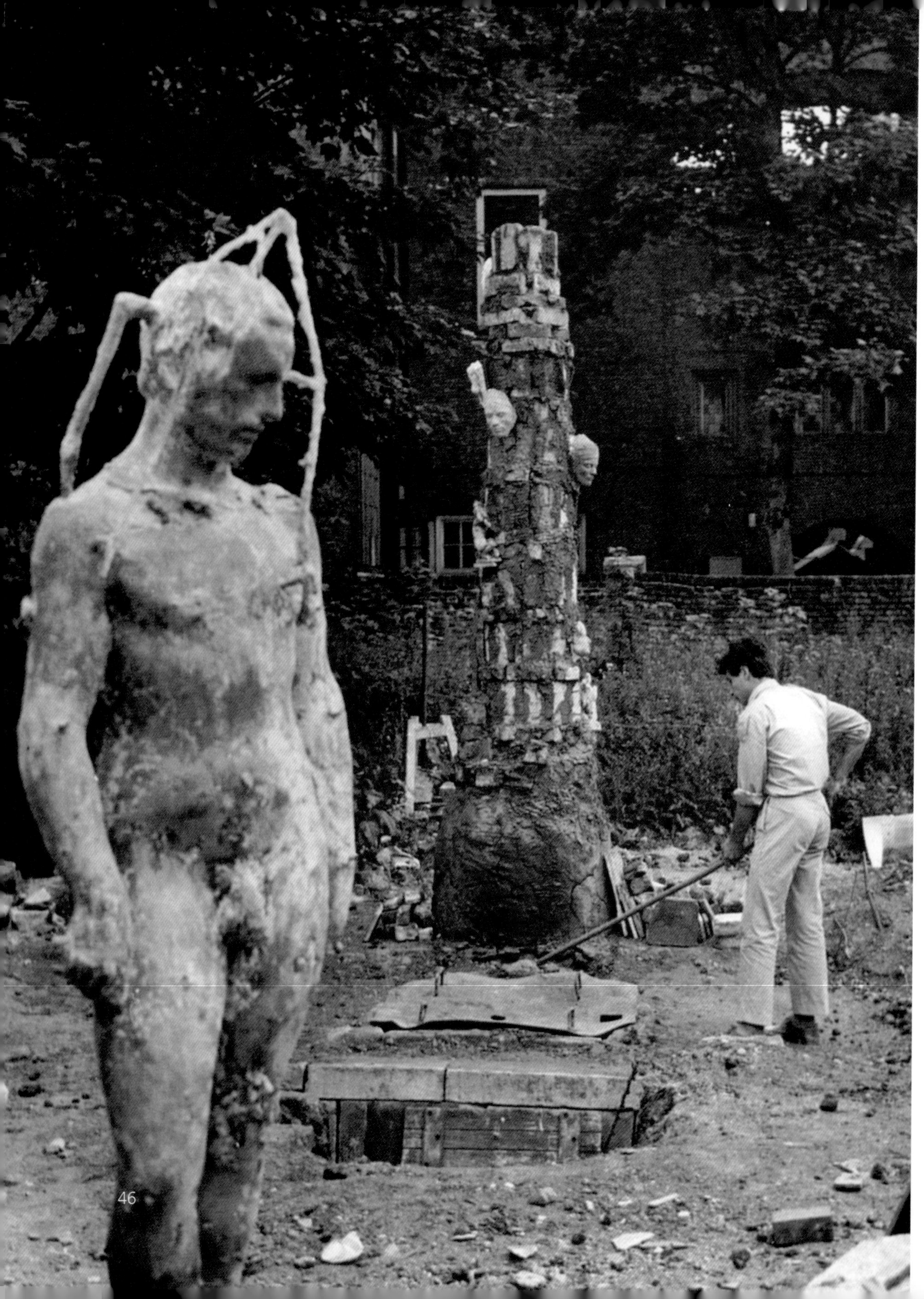

Left and opposite: Casting of Raphael's life size bronze figure at Camberwell

Opposite, bottom right: From left: Michael Snowden, Nigel Konstam, Mike Gillespie, Sidney Shepherd, Giacomo Baragli

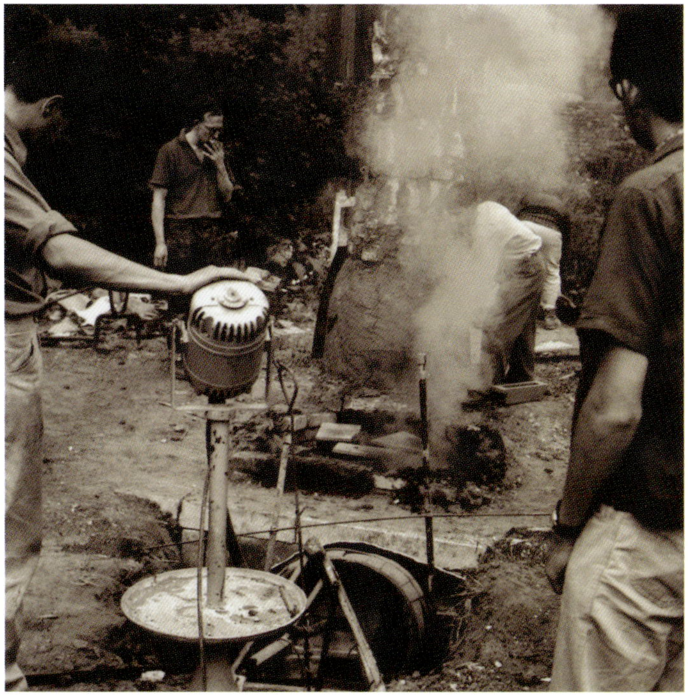

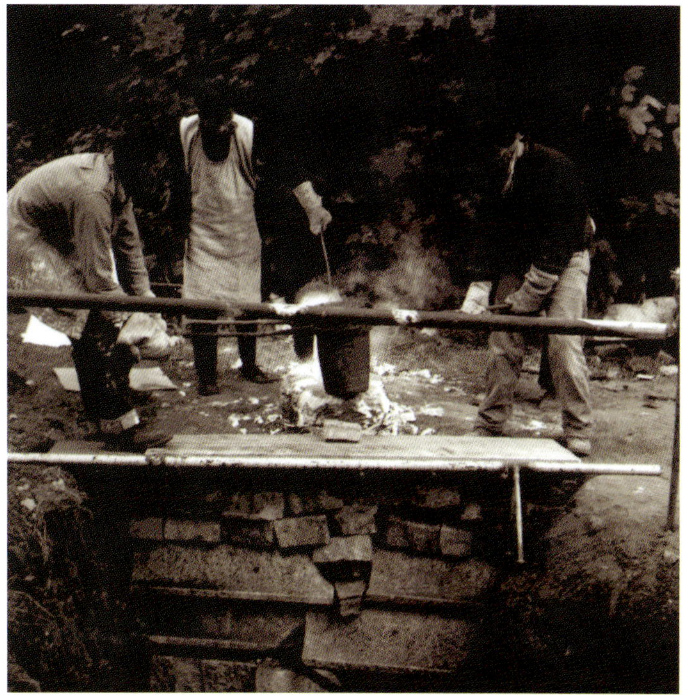

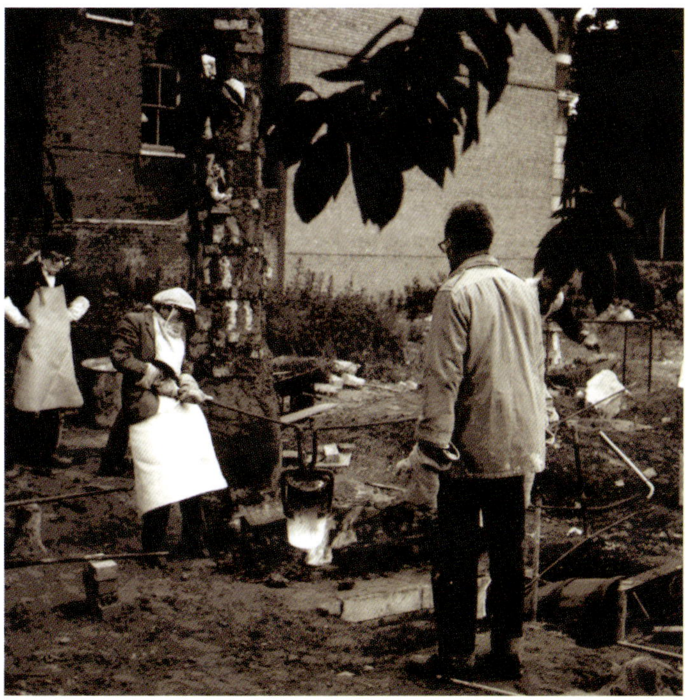

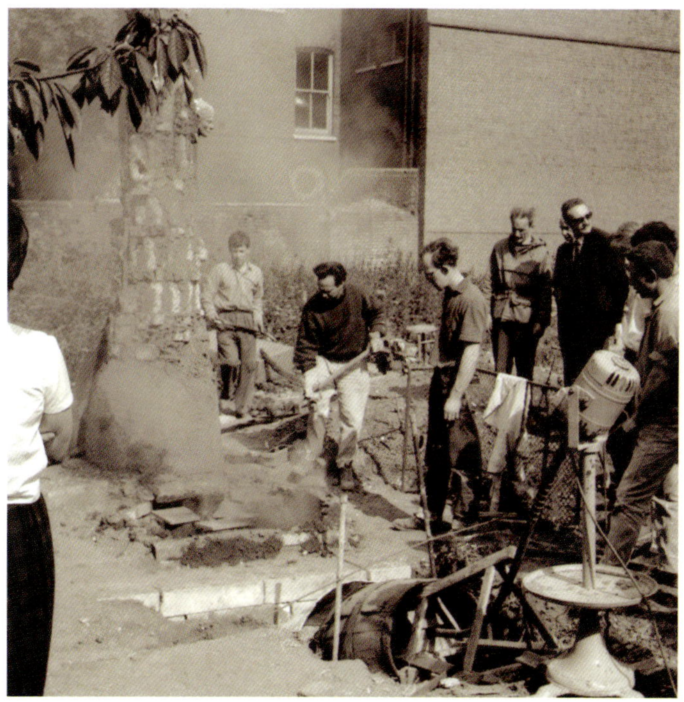

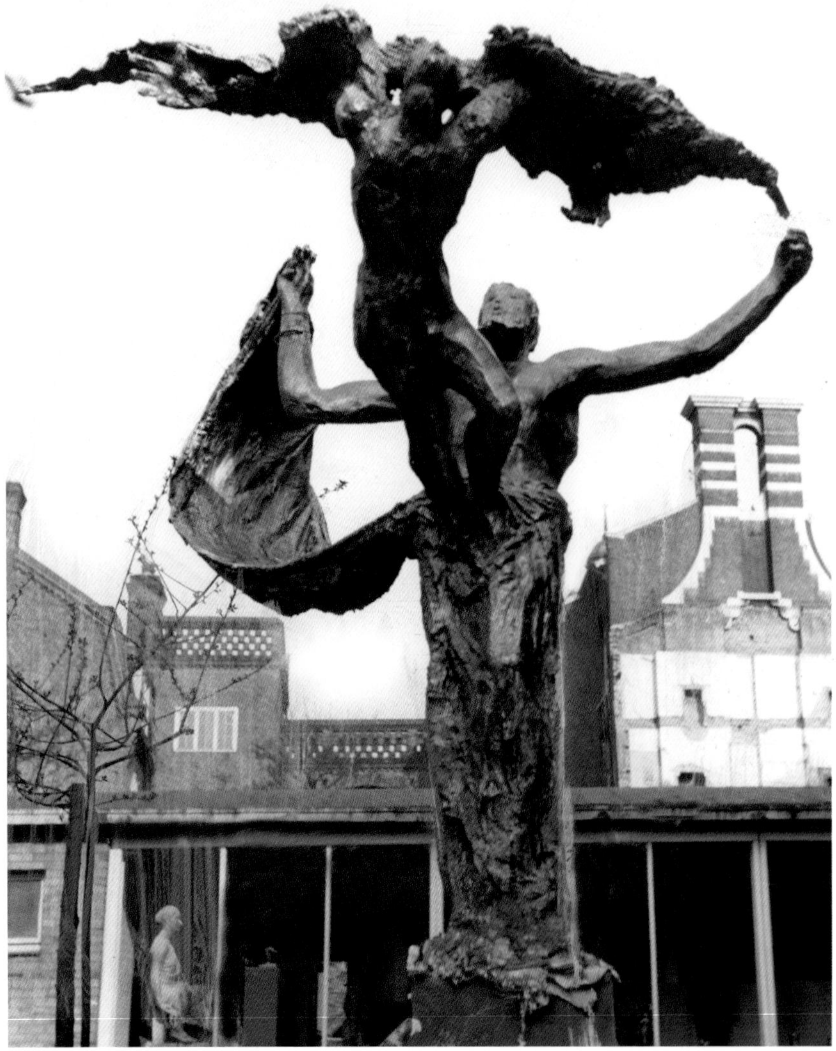

Daedalus and Icarus

Opposite: The Sacrifice of Isaac

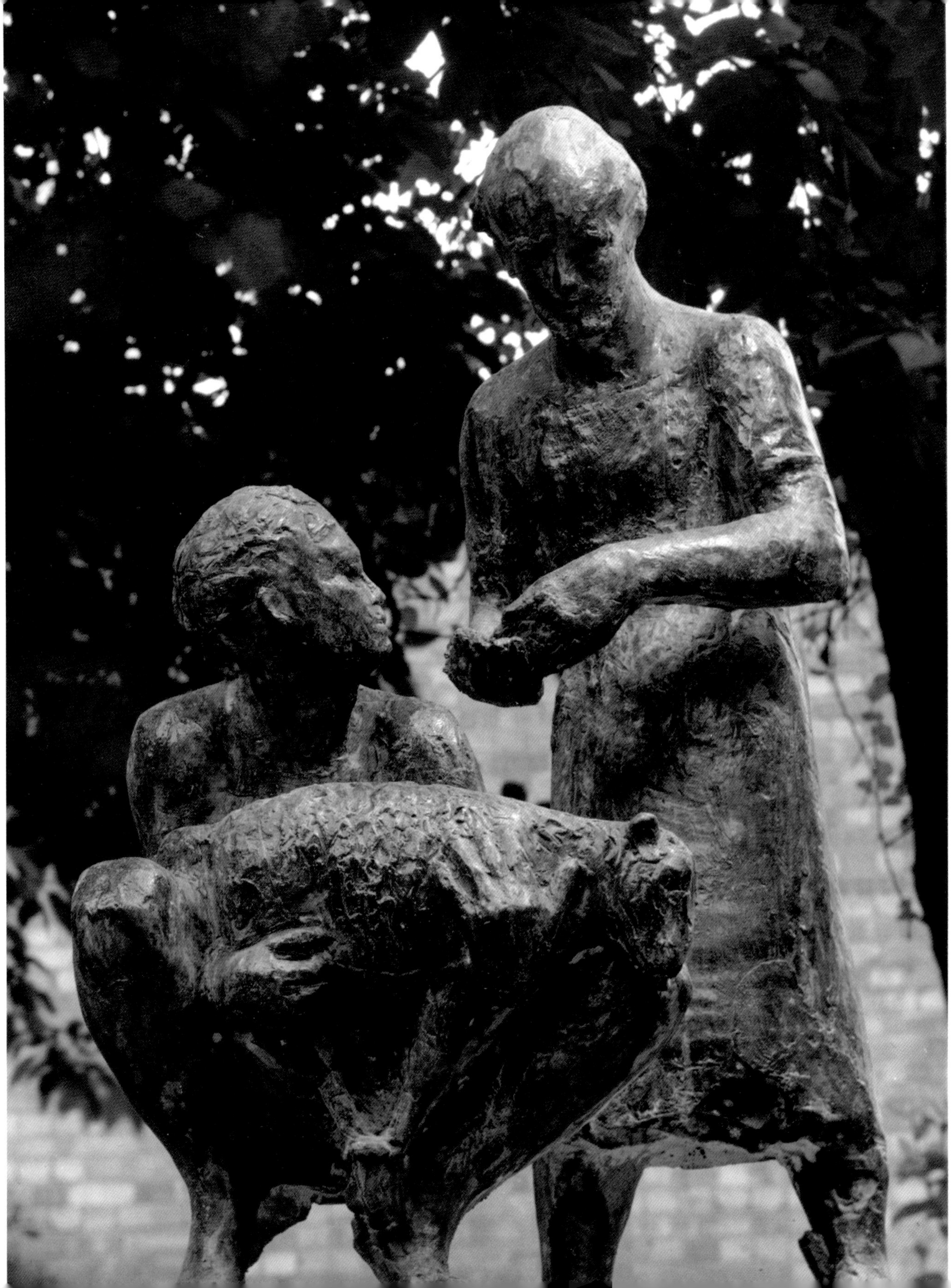

Bronze figures

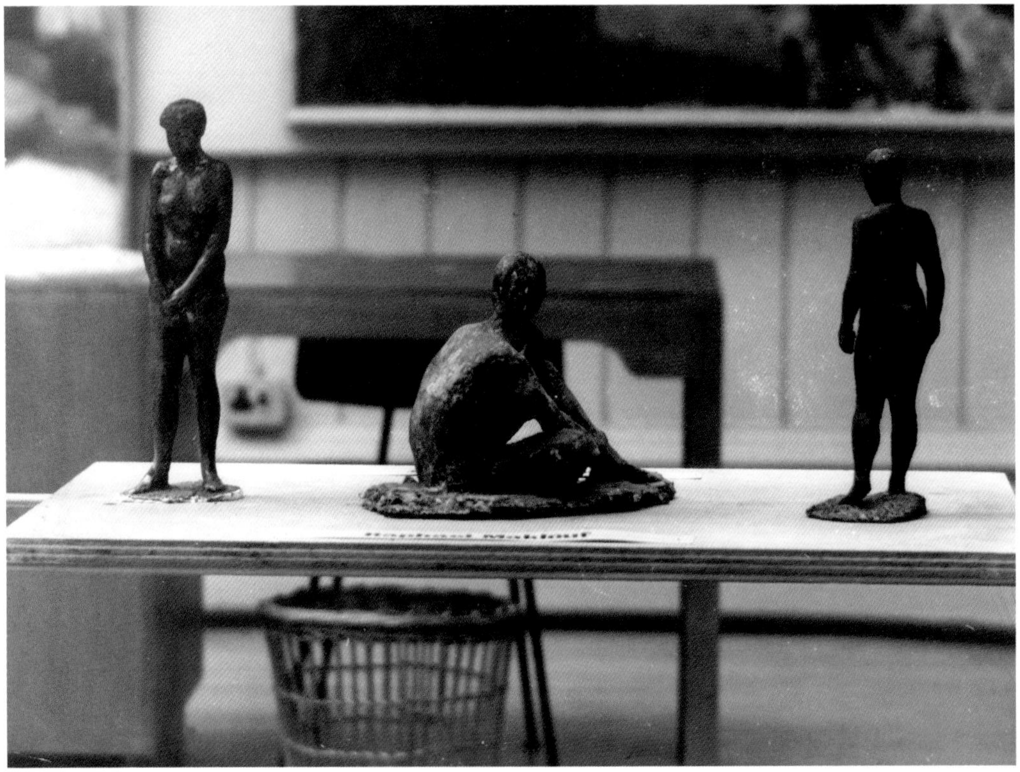

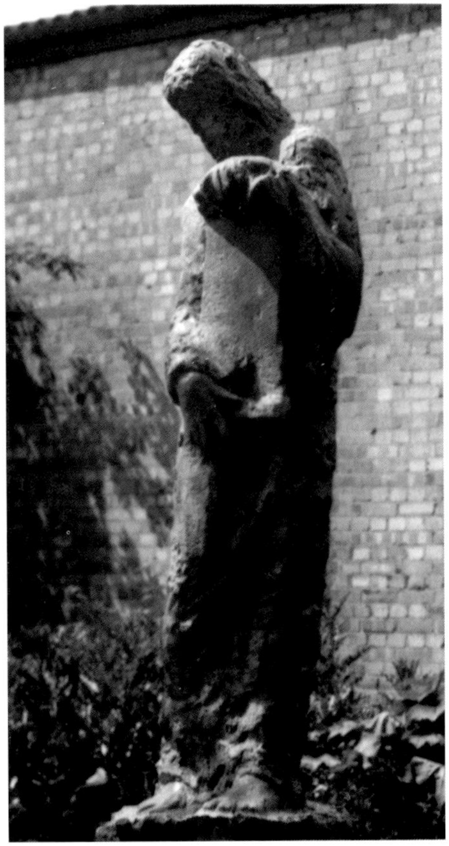

Moses

hours of the day – it was expected. I now think it was stultifying – we should have taken time out. Nobody went anywhere.' [6]

Vogel liked his modelled figures to have a smooth naturalistic surface. He tended to idealise the human figure and selected a handsome boy for his model of Adam. It was Teresa who posed for the figure of Eve. Vogel encouraged his students to work life-size and was contemptuous of the half-size figures made by students from other colleges. However, as Raphael recalled, it was compulsory for all sculpture students in the country to do a half life-size figure for the Diploma. 'Everyone had to do it. Goldsmiths students came to Camberwell to use our model. I was fascinated by how different they were. All their figures had little flakes on, Epstein style, whereas we had smooth surfaces. Once done we had to take our work to a central place where everybody's work was collected. When we got there I found even more bizarre differences in the way people worked.' [7]

Although Raphael was heavily influenced by Vogel's teaching, his own work differed in some ways from those of others, as Michael Snowden recalled. 'When I first met Raphael he came in as somebody from the Intermediate Course. We shared a flat at New Cross

Small bronze

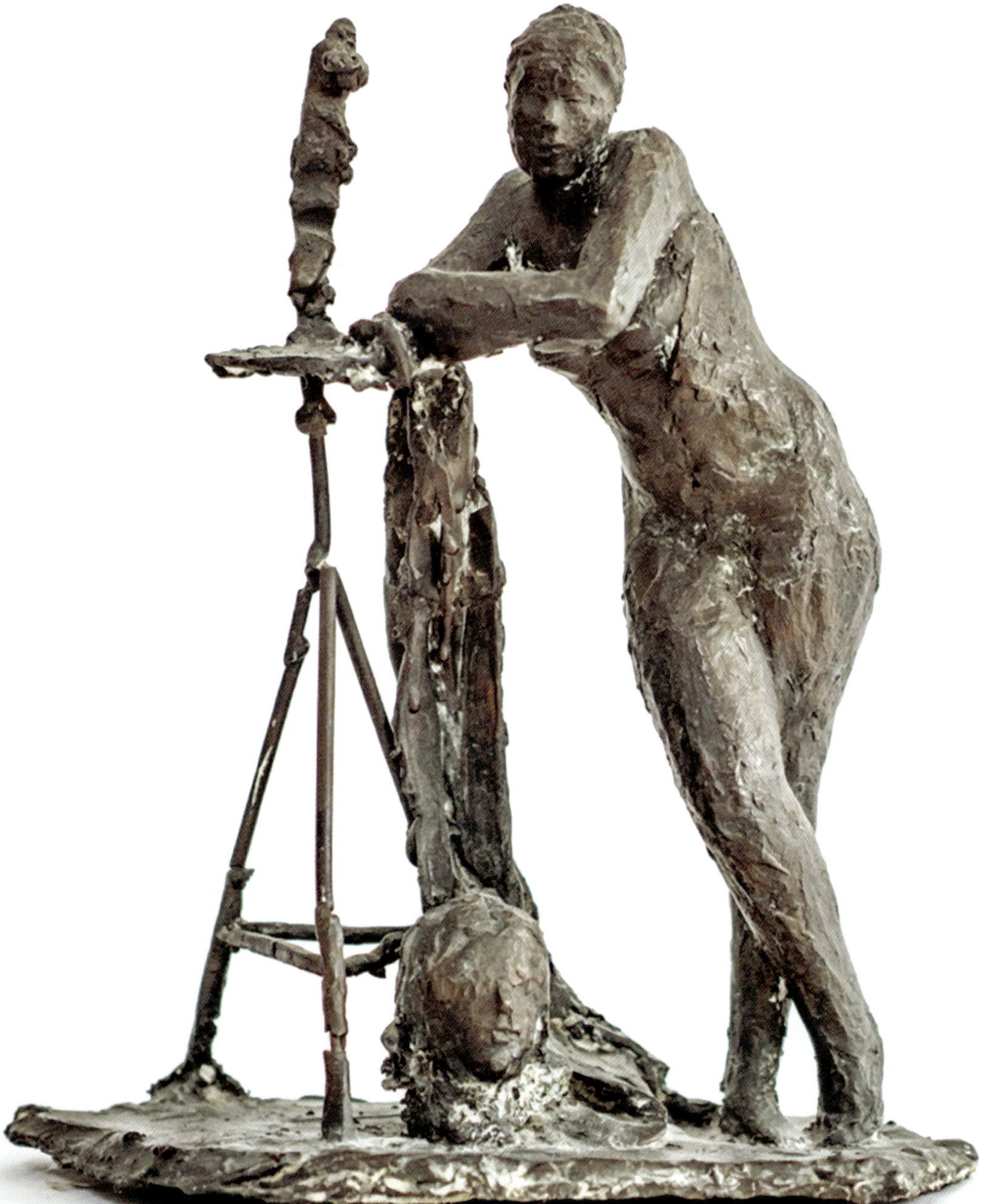

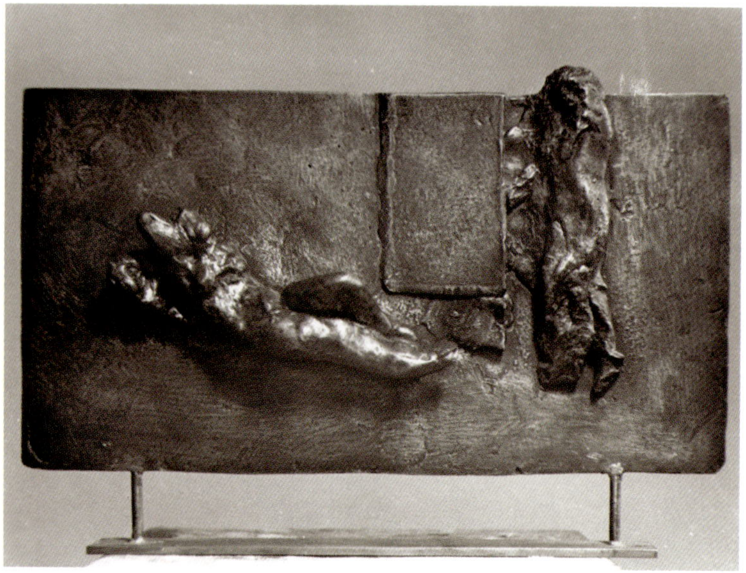

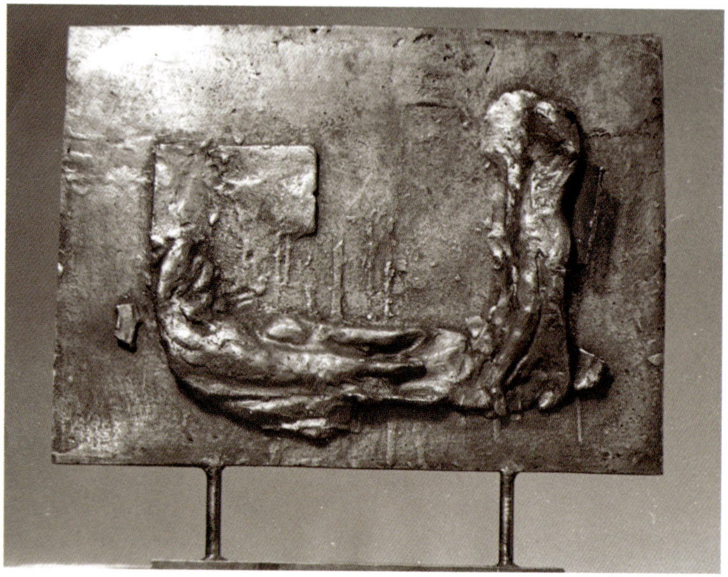

Above: Reclining Venus I and II

Right: Bronze, Girl swinging a child

Below: Seth Cardew, fellow student

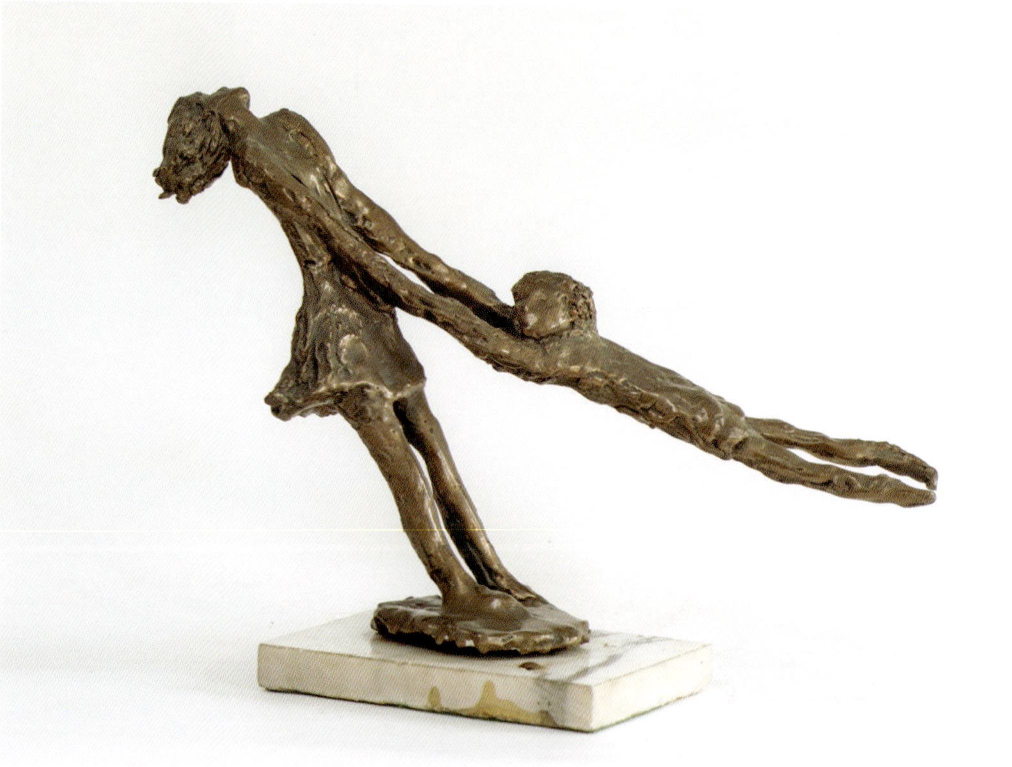

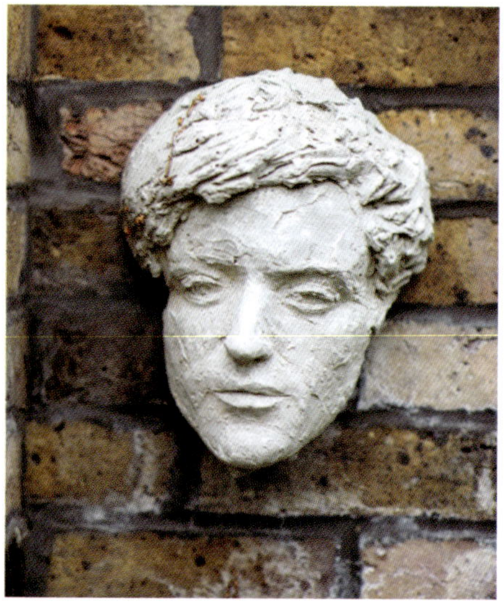

where we had a sort of lunch club across the road. His work had a pictorial quality all his life – he manipulated the surfaces.' Raphael acknowledged this: 'Different artists work in different ways. My muse is Painting, which I do for personal reasons. The other side is more practical, working to commission. If it hadn't been for Vogel's personality, I probably would have gone to the Painting School, although I am not a colourist. It's what I call Painting-Sculpture. Carving didn't come naturally to me, but modelling did. With carving you can't change things, but with clay you can change things in a second. But the problem with having a model is that in the end one becomes a slave to it. I was not trying so much to copy the model as to get the mood. I did a whole series from imagination, relating to my paintings.' [8]

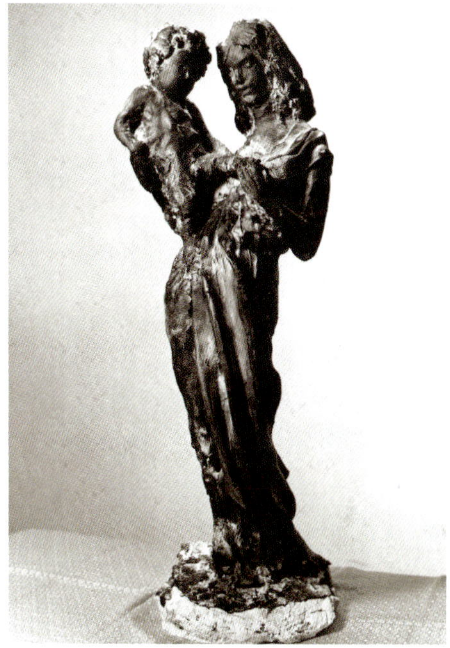

Madonna and Child in bronze at New Malden Church

However, at Camberwell it was figurative sculpture – and the sculpting of the human figure – that ruled the day, and the teaching in those years has served its sculptors well. Raphael, along with Michael Snowden and another Camberwell contemporary, Nigel Konstam, has continued the tradition inculcated by Vogel. Snowden has carried out numerous public commissions in Scotland, including portrait busts of the Scottish poets. As he now says, 'the profile of sculpture has risen hugely in my lifetime. The amount of public sculpture all over Britain is amazing. A lot of it is very bad but at least it's put up.' Nigel Konstam, similarly, has received many public commissions, including portrait busts of King Carlos I and Queen Sofia of Spain. He has also maintained a parallel career as an Art Historian and teacher. His book, *Sculpture – The Art and Practice of Sculpture (Collins 1984)*, gives a detailed analysis of carving, modelling, and casting figure pieces.

Although Raphael spent most of his time within the grounds of Camberwell, he kept in touch with his family living nearby. Michael Snowden recalled an occasion when Raphael enlisted him to help his father, Samuel Maklouf, whose business was not going well. A market trader, Samuel sold anything from carpets to jewellery, and he had two suitcases full of costume jewellery to dispose of. Michael and Raphael helped him and a fellow trader set up their stall in an outdoor market. 'As salesmen those two men were operative geniuses. Raphael's father told us to take the earrings off the cards and spread them out. People would search for the matching earrings and buy them when they found them. We laid some out on velvet and priced them double. Those were the ones people bought. As soon as they sold we took some more from the bottom of the pile and laid them out, putting higher prices on them. They all went.' [9]

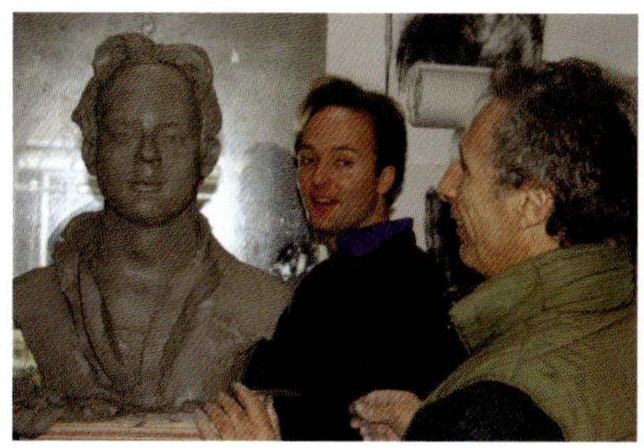

Raphael modelling head of Rupert Shaw

Apart from occasionally helping his father, Raphael spent all his days at Camberwell. Vogel believed that three or four year's study was not long enough for his prize students to develop their own work, and he persuaded the Principal to give his two Archangels well-paid part-time teaching jobs. The two of them shared the work. They also shared the Saturday morning classes, which the local youth attended. At first they asked them to make models of saints. Then they had the ambitious idea of getting the children to make

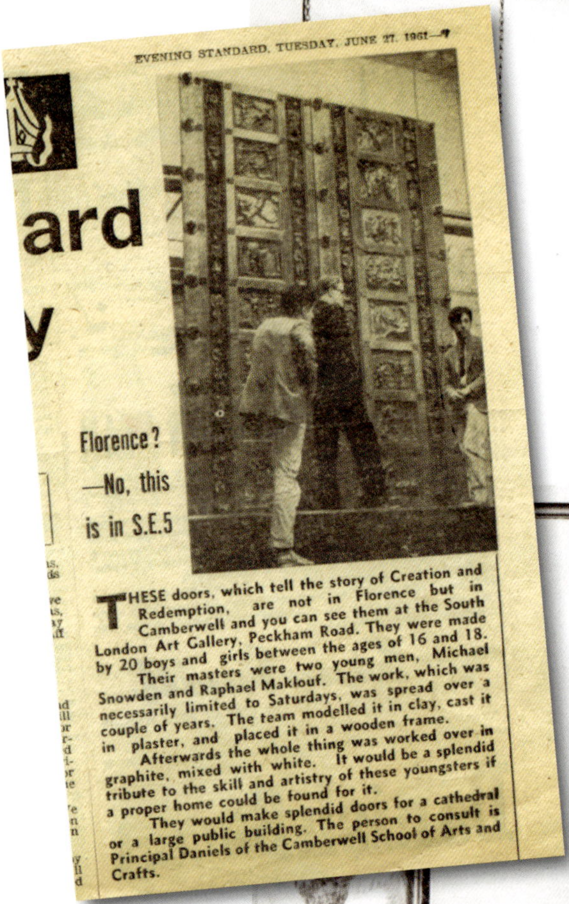

EVENING STANDARD, TUESDAY, JUNE 27, 1961—7

ard

y

Florence?
—No, this
is in S.E.5

THESE doors, which tell the story of Creation and Redemption, are not in Florence but in Camberwell and you can see them at the South London Art Gallery, Peckham Road. They were made by 20 boys and girls between the ages of 16 and 18.

Their masters were two young men, Michael Snowden and Raphael Maklouf. The work, which was necessarily limited to Saturdays, was spread over a couple of years. The team modelled it in clay, cast it in plaster, and placed it in a wooden frame.

Afterwards the whole thing was worked over in graphite, mixed with white. It would be a splendid tribute to the skill and artistry of these youngsters if a proper home could be found for it.

They would make splendid doors for a cathedral or a large public building. The person to consult is Principal Daniels of the Camberwell School of Arts and Crafts.

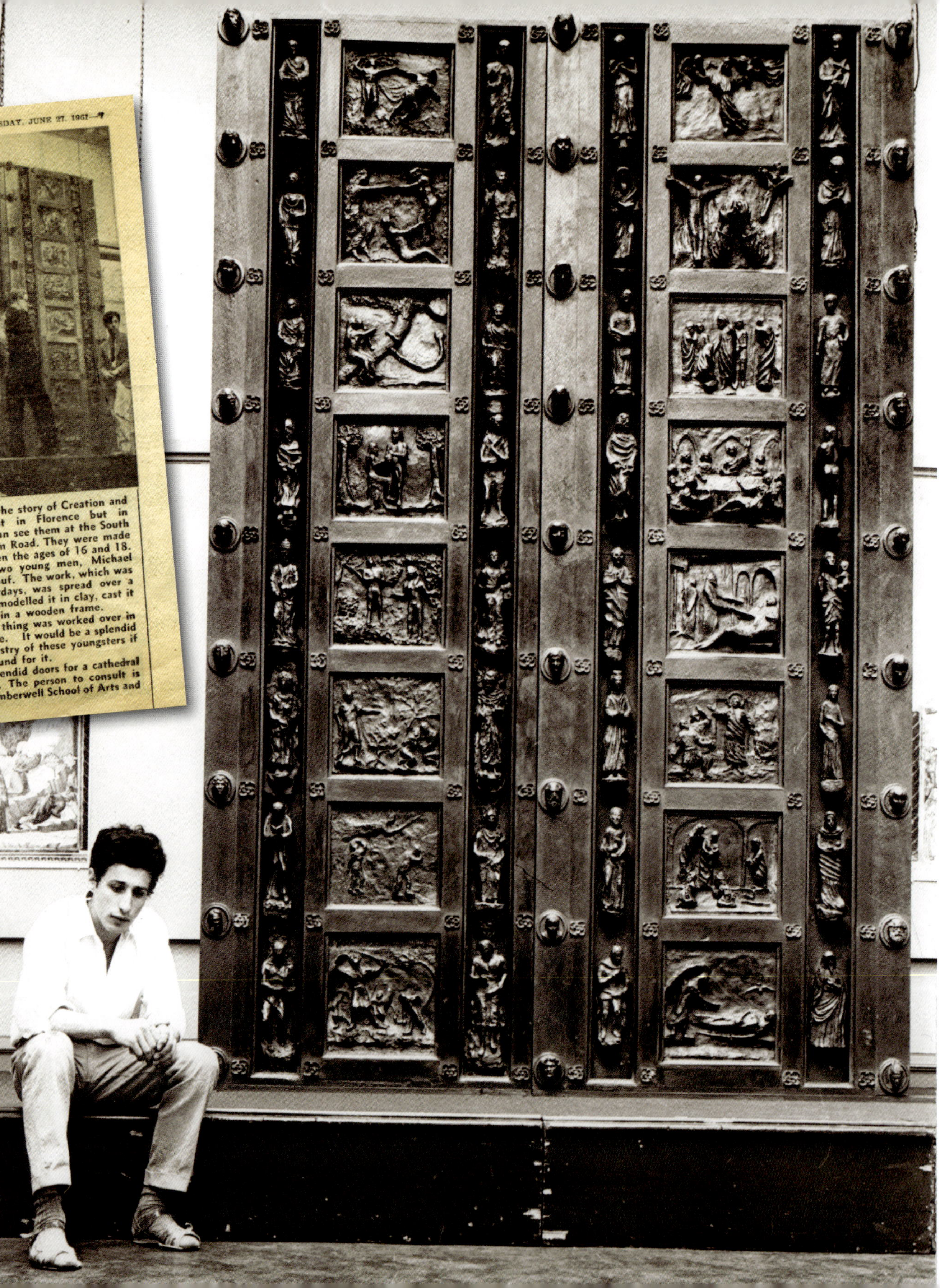

panels of religious subjects to be assembled into huge doors, rather like Ghiberti's doors for the Baptistry in Florence. These doors were a triumph, making headlines in the local press. An article in the Evening Standard entitled *Florence – No, this is in SE5!* trumpeted their appearance on the scene. 'These doors, which tell the story of Creation and Redemption, are not in Florence but in Camberwell... They were made by 20 boys and girls between the ages of 16 and 18. Their masters were two young men, Michael Snowden and Raphael Maklouf. The work, which was necessarily limited to Saturdays, was spread over a couple of years. The team modelled it in clay, cast it in plaster, and placed it in a wooden frame. Afterwards the whole thing was worked over in graphite, mixed with white... It would be a splendid tribute to the skill and artistry of these youngsters if a proper home could be found for it. They would make splendid doors for a cathedral or large public building.' [10]

The Saturday morning classes had another surprising outcome, as Raphael remembered. 'One day the local vicar, the Reverend John Nicholls, walked in and asked if anyone could help him out with St Giles Church. During the war a bomb had hit the church and the statue of St Christopher in a niche had fallen over and broken. The vicar asked if someone would be willing to mend it. The original was carved, but I decided to sculpt it and then cast it in cement to look like stone. In order to make the cement look patinated I got a whole lot of rusty nails and iron and mixed the rusty water with the cement. It turned out exactly like the original.' [11] This sculpture commission, accepted by Raphael, who admits to never having refused a commission, was to have important consequences.

After seven years at Camberwell, however, Raphael began to feel restricted. 'Karl Vogel kept me at Camberwell when I should have flown the nest. He was a bitter man, and always felt that the British establishment was a closed shop. He was anti the abstract sculpture of the Henry Moore, Reg Butler type. He believed in the academic tradition – working from life. I worked from life all the time – always from the model – and so did my friend Michael Snowden. We had been indoctrinated to see through his eyes – it was like a religious sect. His view was that Art should be hand crafted. When all my friends were going to the Royal College etc Vogel said "don't go". Teresa Fawcett did a summer school abroad with Manzù and when she came back Vogel completely ignored her. Some of my more mature friends thought I was barmy to stay with Vogel, but he was a grandfather figure to me, gave me a sense of security, and gave me a job.' [12]

Beneficial or not at the time, the imperative to work – and work hard – modelling the figure from life was to stand Raphael in very good stead later on. But he was somewhat distracted by the arrival of an attractive new student who had appeared in the Painting School. Her name was Marillyn Lewis.

Opposite: 'The Gates of Paradise' created in Saturday morning classes with Michael Snowden

Life size Madonna and Child in Ciment Fondu

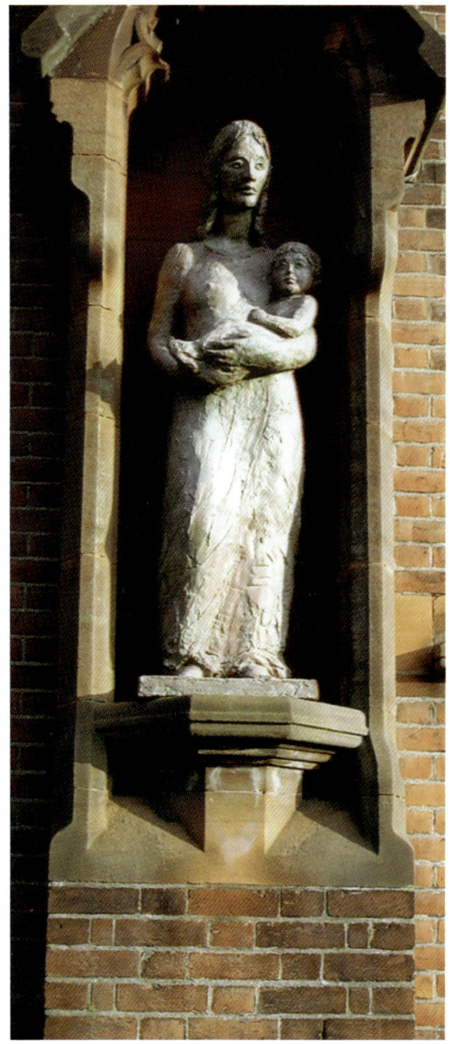

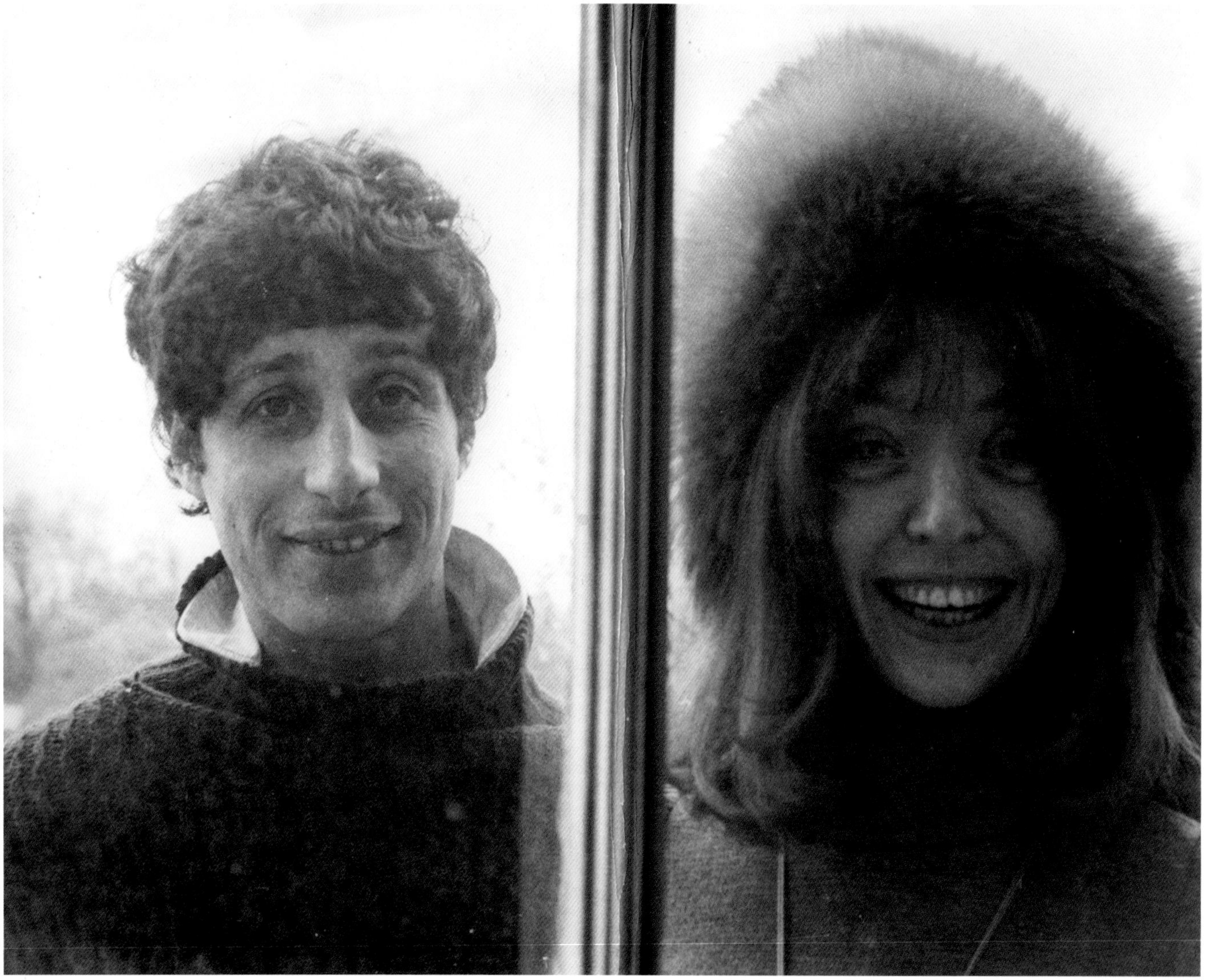

Raphael and Marilyn (photograph by Gaila Clarke-Hall)

Chapter 5
The Pursuit of Love

MARILLYN ARRIVED AT Camberwell in 1959 via Finishing School in France and a year at Trinity College Dublin. 'I had decided to leave Trinity College Dublin having spent just a year of a degree course in Spanish and English Literature. It was somehow not the way I wanted to go. I decided I would like to explore my interest in pottery. It was suggested that I should go to Camberwell. I had never even heard of Camberwell, but when I arrived in South London I just walked in to the Art School. It was already the middle of the term but that did not seem to trouble Philip Matthews, who thought the best idea was for me to enrol full time on the Intermediate Course. Such was the informality of admission procedures to art schools at that time! The Intermediate Course included pottery as well as Life Drawing, Lettering, History of Art, Printmaking – an array of subjects leading towards a specialist subject of either sculpture or painting. I loved being there, especially in the pottery studio. Lucy Rie was teaching there, as was Ian Auld, and "Frenchy" (Miss Honorora French) was in charge of the kiln. She dressed like a bird of paradise in exotic colours and managed to keep an unruly group of students under control. Ian Godfrey was a great friend and life was full of laughter. The Painting School, where I did my NDD, was very "Camberwell", still under the spell of Sir William Coldstream. The emphasis was on drawing from life, everything plotted and measured with no interest in feeling. The models' poses were anti-glamorous.' [1]

Former student David Hepher gave a vivid description of the prevailing atmosphere: "Camberwell stopped one dead in one's tracks and made one look at the real world very hard. It was a very perceptual school, perhaps too much so. Cézanne was God and there was a general mistrust of twentieth century art. That was its strength, blinkered, narrow, but sound. Its failure was to place too big a burden of the achievements of the past onto its students' heads and I think this often stifled and inhibited those who passed through. The mores of Euston Road could so easily turn into a sort of constipated morality.' [2] For Marillyn, the upsides outweighed the downsides. 'There were some amazing people teaching there – Robert Medley, Head of the Painting School, whose mellifluous voice used to float around the studios; Anthony Fry, a figurative painter who rejoiced in light and

Lilla Robertson, Marillyn's grandmother painting in Hong Kong

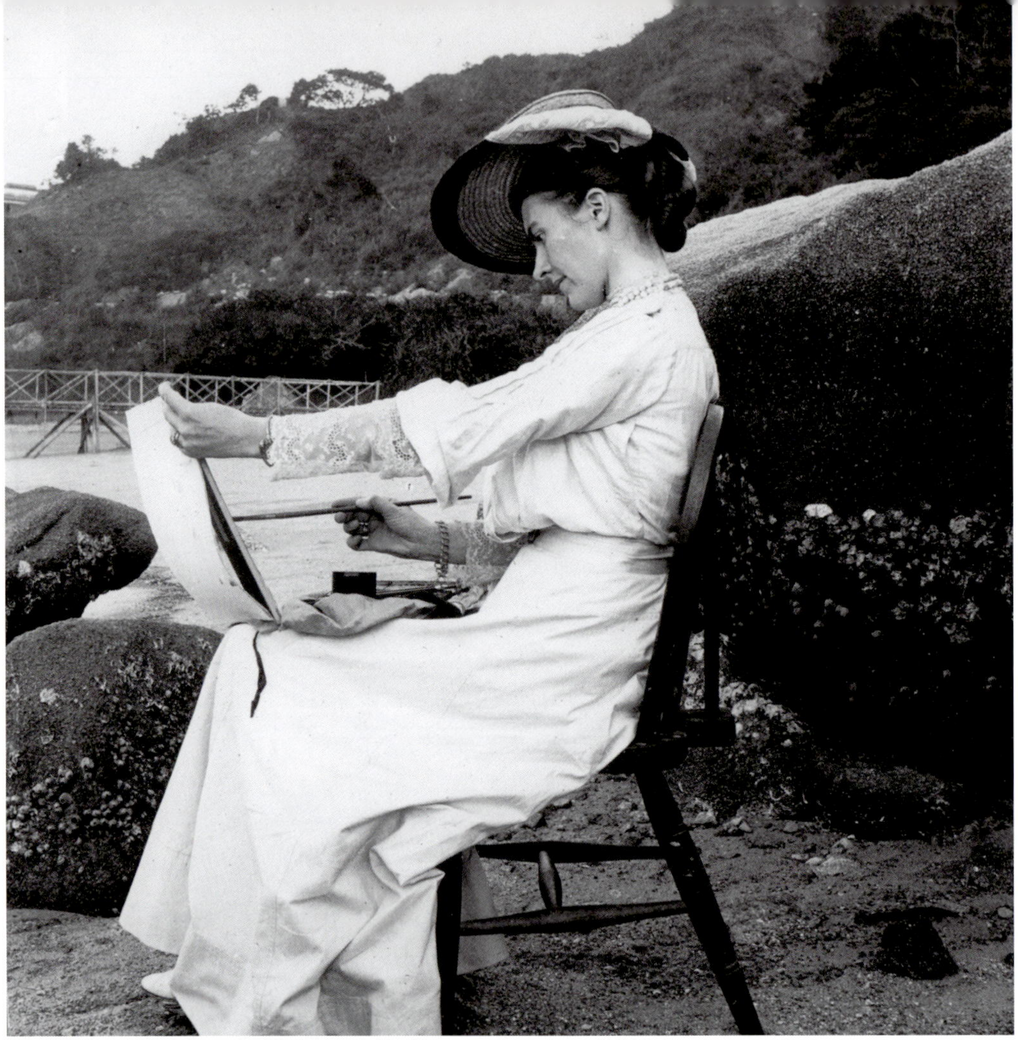

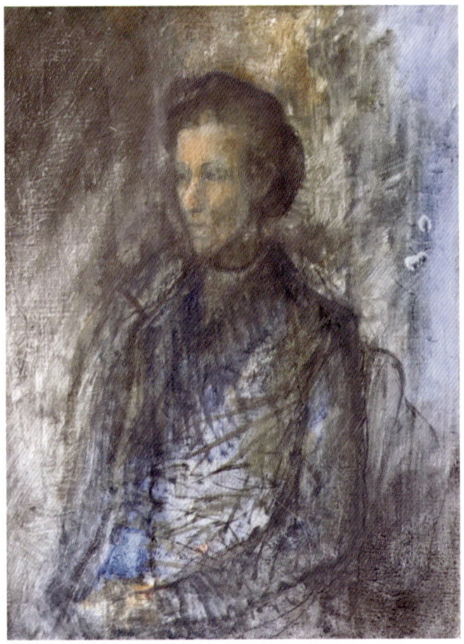

Portrait of Christian Lewis by Raphael Maklouf

colour; Auerbach, who was an incredible force of energy; when he was teaching the whole studio was covered with charcoal and paint. Euan Uglow, Michael Salaman, Charles Howard, Kitaj – they all taught there. It was in this environment that I met Raphael. From the start I was convinced that he was the man I would marry.' [3]

The two of them could hardly have come from more different backgrounds, although unlike Raphael's parents when they first met, they could at least speak each other's language. Marillyn's mother, Christian Robertson, came from a long line of Scots; her mother, a MacFarlan, was born in India, where her father, Lieut-General David MacFarlan CB, was in the Bengal Artillery and served through the Indian Mutiny and on the North-West frontier during the Afghan war. Marillyn's Welsh father, Gwilym Lewis, was, by the time he met his wife, already a decorated pilot from the First World War.

Gwilym Hugh Lewis, DFC, was a very strong character. Born in 1897, one of three brothers and three sisters, he was educated at Marlborough College, but ran away from

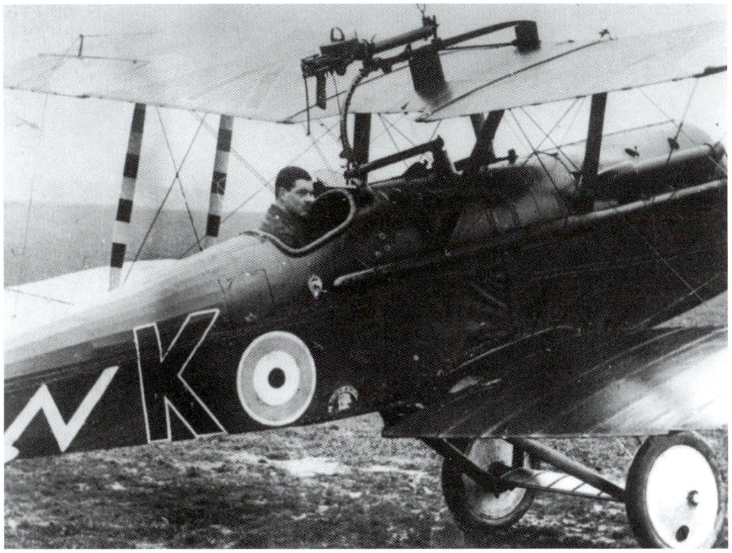

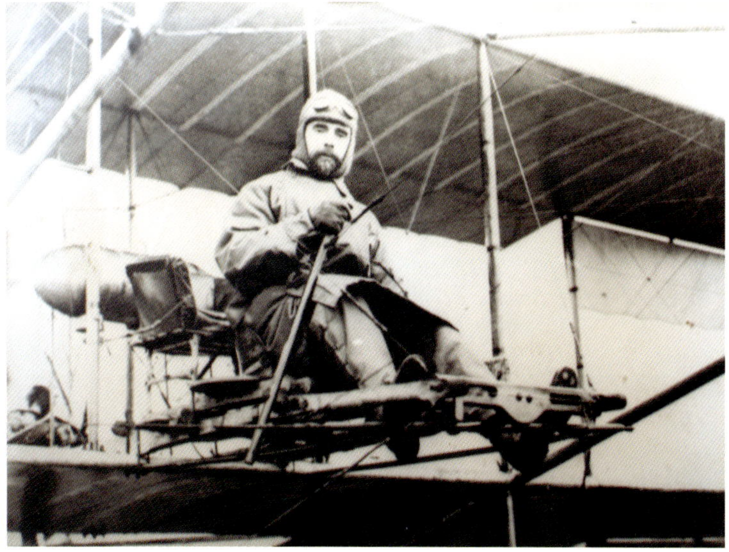

school to join the newly-formed Royal Flying Corps. He got his 'wings' on 23 April 1916 and served in France as the youngest member of 32 Squadron. His book *Wings over the Somme* (published in 1976), a collection of letters written to his family during his time behind the Front Lines in France, gives a vivid account of his day-by-day activities. In a letter from Léalvillers written on 29 October 1916 he exclaims 'I thought I had seen some pretty magnificent sights in my life, but I don't think I have ever seen anything like this. The whole country is a mere bog; for real genuine high-class mud I doubt if our variety can be beaten. We live in tents and most of us have tent boards, so of course we ought not to grumble. It is a mere detail that everything is covered in a thick film of moisture; after all I have a perfectly good wick lamp to dry my socks by…' [4]

Above left: Marillyn's father Gwilym Lewis in his plane 'The Artful Dodger'

Above right: Hugh Lewis learning to fly, 1915

Below: Hugh and Gwilym Lewis

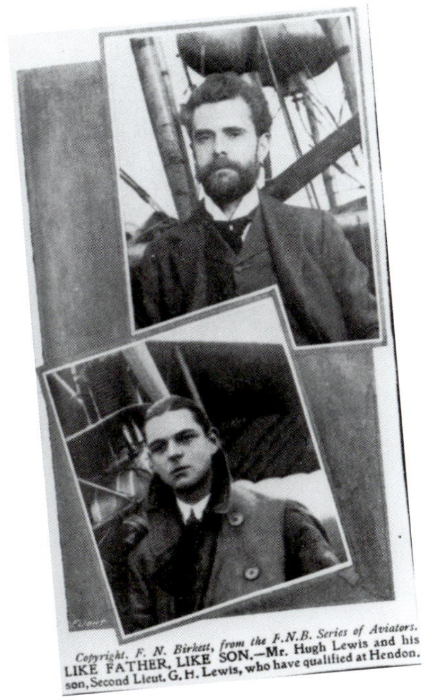

After a spell training new pilots at the Central Flying School in Upavon, Lewis was back at the Front with 40 Squadron, either on reconnaissance or engaging with the enemy whenever visibility allowed. In a letter of 24 April 1918 he noted the death of the infamous Red Baron (Rittmeister Manfred Freiherr von Richthofen, Germany's 'Ace of Aces', credited with eighty victories): 'We are all quite bucked that Richthofen is under the soil. Shot down by a Camel while attacking an RE8. Never admired him very much as he was such a boaster. I don't think the Huns were very fond of him either.' [5]

By July 1918 two pilots – Gwilym Lewis and Captain George Edward McElvoy, MC, DFC, the leading Irish fighter pilot – had accounted for around sixty enemy aircraft between them. Lewis wrote 'My weak little mad self is at last satisfied, and I have got the DFC. I therefore see no reason for staying in this dangerous country any longer, and have applied to go home.' But he left 40 Squadron with mixed feelings. 'This is a great squadron, and I am awfully sorry to leave. I had the happiest time of my life out here. I am awfully pleased that I had the luck not to lose a single fellow while I have been here, though two went down while I was on leave.' [6] His brother, Edmund Llewellyn Lewis, who had trained with him at the Central Flying School in 1916, had been killed in aerial combat over the German Lines on December 26th 1916, after a single-handed fight with five enemy machines when, 'after the scrap broke up, two machines went down.' Edmund, twenty-one years old, was gazetted Lieutenant the day after his death.

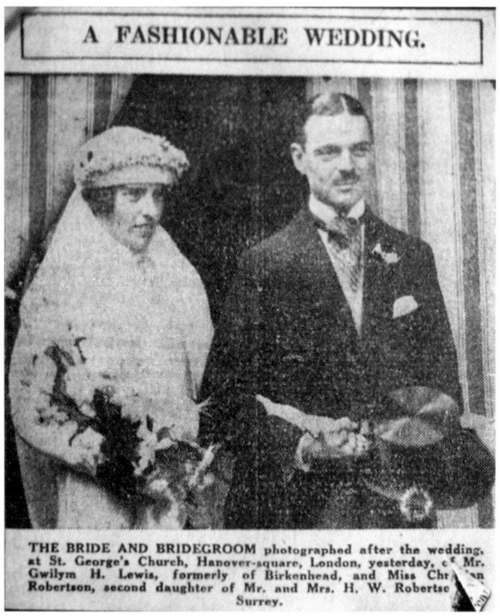
A FASHIONABLE WEDDING.

THE BRIDE AND BRIDEGROOM photographed after the wedding, at St. George's Church, Hanover-square, London, yesterday, c[illegible] Mr. Gwilym H. Lewis, formerly of Birkenhead, and Miss Chr[illegible]an Robertson, second daughter of Mr. and Mrs. H. W. Robertso[illegible] Surrey.

Christian and Gwilym Lewis on their wedding day

After the Armistice Gwilym Lewis returned to the Central Flying School with the prescient resolve to continue 'our training with our usual efficient style, everyone feeling grimly determined not to be found unprepared for the next war.' After being demobbed in January 1919 he joined Lloyds Brokers where he worked in Non-marine Insurance, and in 1925 he married Christian Robertson whom he declared to be 'as Scotch as I am Welsh'. In 1938, with war again looming, he was asked to join the Joint Service as one of the Air Force Officers, meeting with the Joint Planning Staffs in the Central War Rooms. He was made a Wing Commander in the RAF Volunteer Reserve.

Marillyn was the youngest of Gwilym and Christian Lewis's four children. She was born in Wales, where her mother was living in the family summer house in Rhosneigr with her three-year old son to escape the London bombing. Because he worked in the Cabinet Offices her father had remained at their house in St John's Wood in London, but her elder sister Olivia had been sent to Canada. An older brother had earlier died of meningitis. After the war was over Marillyn's education began. Her schooling turned out to be almost as erratic as Raphael's. At age six she was sent to a farm school, Odam Hill, near Barnstaple in Devon. For her first term she was taken there by her mother, but on other occasions she made the journey from London alone, in the care of the guard. The school was run by Reinhold Alfred Falkner, a German who had taught with the educator Kurt Hahn. The pupils addressed him as Herr. There were prisoners of war working on a nearby farm, and Marillyn remembers seeing an escapee caught and bundled into a sack. She was happy at the school. 'There were lots of animals, cows and horses and a huge fluffy sheep dog called Ben. The children helped to care for the animals and also took part in building projects. Lessons were a bit random, but it was a very child friendly place.'

Brought back to London to attend a small day school, Marillyn was then sent to a ballet school because her father thought she might succeed as a ballerina. As she recalled, 'I was there for a year but I was as wide as I was tall, not the right shape for a ballerina. It was all strictly ballet after lessons in the morning. My mother took me away because she didn't like the Art mistress who painted gloomy pictures. I was then sent to another boarding school in Hertfordshire. At that school I was naughty. There were an awful lot of bad marks you could collect, and I seemed to get most of them. My parents did see that something was not quite right. I was at home for a bit with a governess, but because my brother was at Bryanston and the headmaster, Thorold Coade, was a friend of my parents, they sent me to Bryanston's sister school, Cranborne Chase (known as Crichel, after the names of two small villages nearby). I really liked Crichel. It was a beautiful house with lovely surroundings, and it was run completely differently from my previous school. We were given responsibility for ourselves and our work was arranged on an assignment system.' [7]

Marillyn left Crichel after three years, having done her A-levels. She wanted to go to university but had not done Latin, then a pre-requisite for university entrance. 'So I did O-level Latin at home with a wonderful teacher. He had been a master at Winchester and he knew exactly what I had to learn for the O-level. It was hard work but I did it in three months. Then I went to France to a sort of Finishing School. 'Madame' was tiresome, but my lot was improved when my sister sent one of her boyfriends to take me out. Madame was impressed because he was a Count and clicked his heels nicely when he kissed her hand. That summer was spent with my brother-in-law's family in the South of France, and travelling to Florence with my sister and her husband. There I discovered the wonder of Florentine painting, Masaccio in particular. That autumn I sailed from Holyhead to Dun Leorie to spend a year reading Spanish and English at Trinity College Dublin. Although Dublin was a wonderful city I wasn't happy at Trinity. [7]

At Camberwell Marillyn did her NDD in the Painting Schools, but Raphael, who was then teaching part-time in the Sculpture School, occasionally came into the Painting Schools. As Michael Snowden and many friends observed with interest, after meeting Marillyn Raphael started to go there much more often.

In 1967 Raphael left his two part-time teaching jobs at Camberwell and Heatherley's Art School and went back to Safed, now in Israel, to see if he could work there. He still had cousins in Israel, and his friend Shia Yariv, who was already running a successful art gallery in Tel Aviv, was an important point of contact. In Safed Raphael found lodgings in a house near his grandmother Malka's old house, and there Marillyn joined him. It was just after the Six Day War, and Jerusalem was barricaded and spookily empty of people. Marillyn was searching for a wonderful Arab horse to buy, but any promise of the perfect steed always turned out to be a bag of bones. It soon became clear to both that they could not live permanently in Israel. But, despite the conditions, it was a romantic time for them, and it was there that they finally decided to get married.

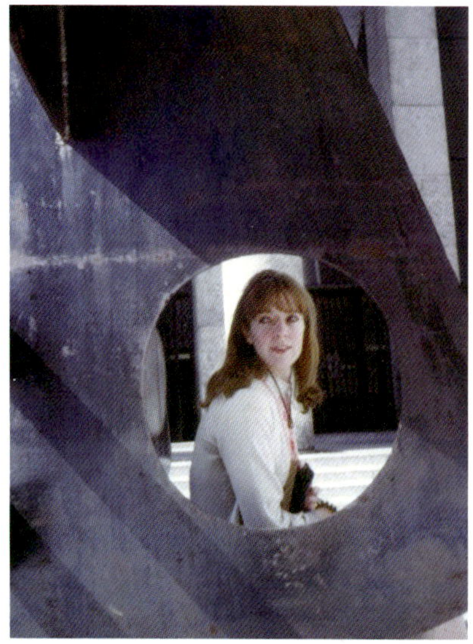

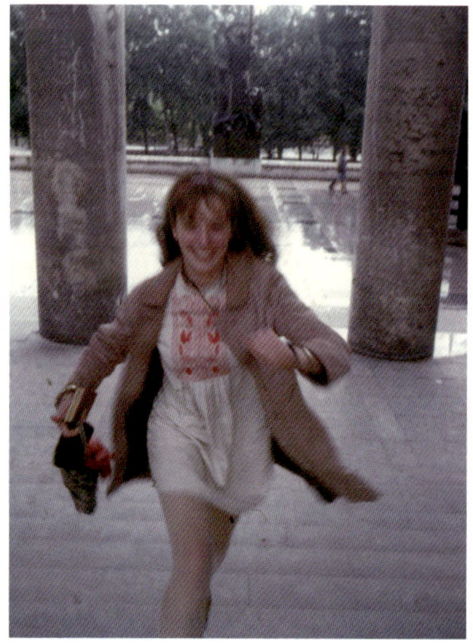

Camberwell days

Right: Terracotta Garden
Head of Marillyn
Far right: Terracotta Garden
Head of Christina Gascoigne
Photos by Kirsten Scully

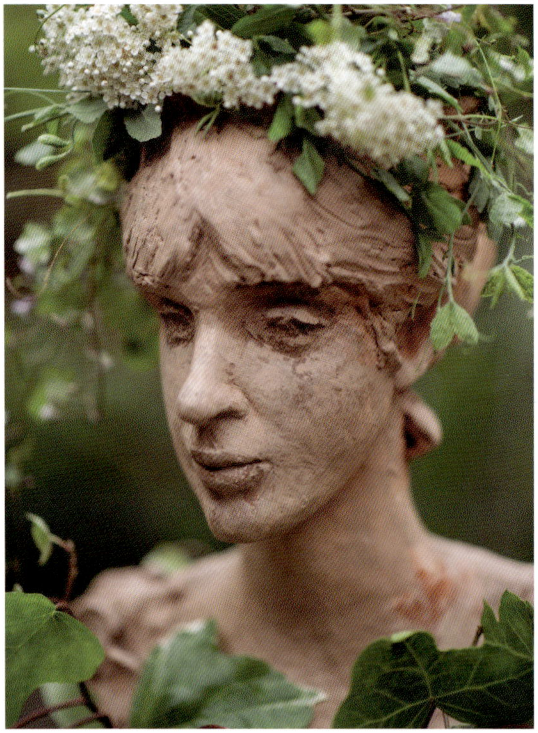

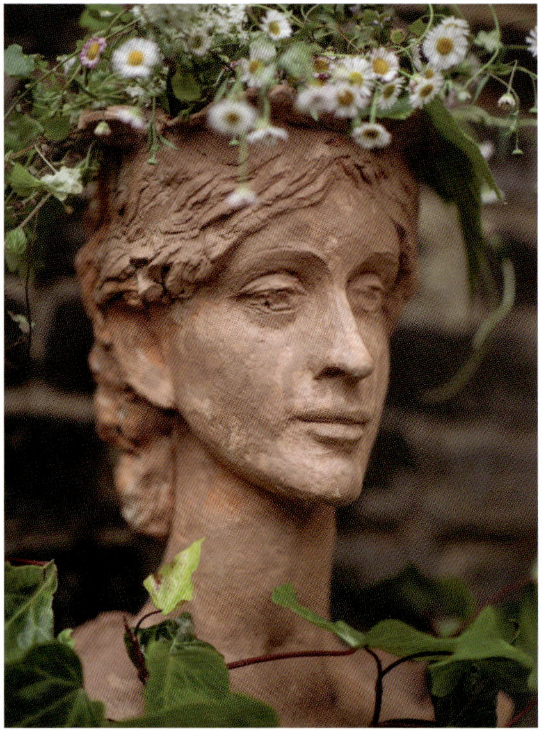

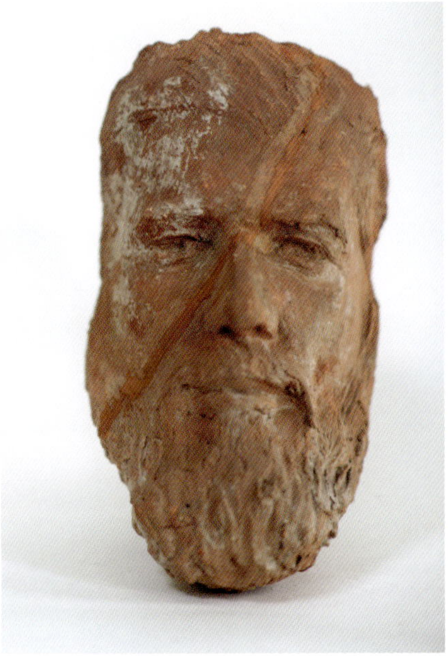

Terracotta portrait of Sandy MacTaggart
Photo by Kirsten Scully

Once the decision was made and Marillyn's parents were convinced that their daughter had made up her mind, they stood by her loyally. For obvious religious reasons they could not get married in Israel, so at first they thought of holding their wedding in Cyprus. Gwilym Lewis objected, saying 'be reasonable – you can't expect all of us to travel to Cyprus'. Marillyn then expressed a wish to be married by a vicar friend in a field, but that idea was shot down by Gwilym, who persisted in saying 'Claridges is very nice'. Finally she said that her dream was to be married in the Norman Chapel in the Tower of London, because the tutor who taught her Architectural Drawing at Camberwell had once taken her to see it. This idea was approved. As Raphael recounted. 'We went to have a look and were told that we couldn't get married there. It was a Chapel Royal. However, there is a chapel in the Tower called St Peter's ad Vincula so we went there. In order to get married there we had to have permission from the Chaplain. We also had to have some contact with the Tower. Marillyn's brother had a connection. We made an appointment and went with her parents to talk to the Queen's Chaplain. When we walked in the door the chaplain said "Hello Raphael". He turned out to be the Reverend John Nicholls, the vicar from St Giles in Camberwell, for whom I had made the doors and the Saint Christopher for St Giles church. He had since become the Queen's Chaplain. He led me to another room and really took the wind out of my sails by asking "Are you marrying Marillyn for the right reasons?" I couldn't think what he was talking about, but I discovered that he thought I was a Muslim and was marrying to take Marillyn out of her own religion. I said "I'm not a Muslim but I'm not a Christian either. I'm afraid I am not religious." Nichols said he would marry us on one other condition. He said "Do you remember that piece of sculpture you did for me? I want you to produce a bronze bust of Sir Thomas More for the crypt here where Sir Thomas More is buried. So I produced this lifesize bust for him. One of the things about being uneducated and not going through the system is that you don't know there are things you shouldn't do. I knew Holbein had done a lovely drawing of More, so I sought permission from the Royal Collection to see it and I ended up going to Windsor Castle and sitting in a room with a folder of the Queen's drawings – Holbein, Michelangelo, Leonardo and my namesake, Raphael. I touched every single drawing. I got a copy of the Holbein Thomas More, and then when I stayed with friends in Herefordshire I saw this farmer walking along and thought he looked just like Holbein's portrait of Thomas More. Because my friends had clay and an armature I got the farmer to stand for me and quickly made a head.' [8]

Fulfilling the Chaplain's condition for the wedding had further unexpected consequences. As Raphael remembered, 'the sculpture had to be consecrated and because More was a Catholic someone called Cardinal Heenan came, and because it was on crown land the Bishop of London had to be there. It became an important event and was in all the papers. I thought that all this publicity was wonderful and would lead to lots of ecclesiastical work. However, for a long time nothing happened.' [9]

A photograph of Raphael's bust appeared in the *Daily Telegraph* with the caption: 'The Rev John G Nichols, Chaplain to the Tower of London, admiring Raphael Maklouf's bust of Sir Thomas More yesterday in the crypt of the Chapel Royal of St Peter, part of which is to become a shrine to the saint. Dr Stopford, Bishop of London, will dedicate the bust at a service on April 26 when the address will be given by Cardinal Heenan, Roman Catholic Archbishop of Westminster.' [10] Raphael's bust, illustrated in Pitkins Pictorial booklet, still presides over the tomb which bears the inscription 'THOMAS MORE, Knight, Scholar, Writer, Statesman, Lord Chancellor of England 1529-32, Beheaded on Tower Hill, buried in this chapel 1535. Canonised by Pope Pius XI 1935.'

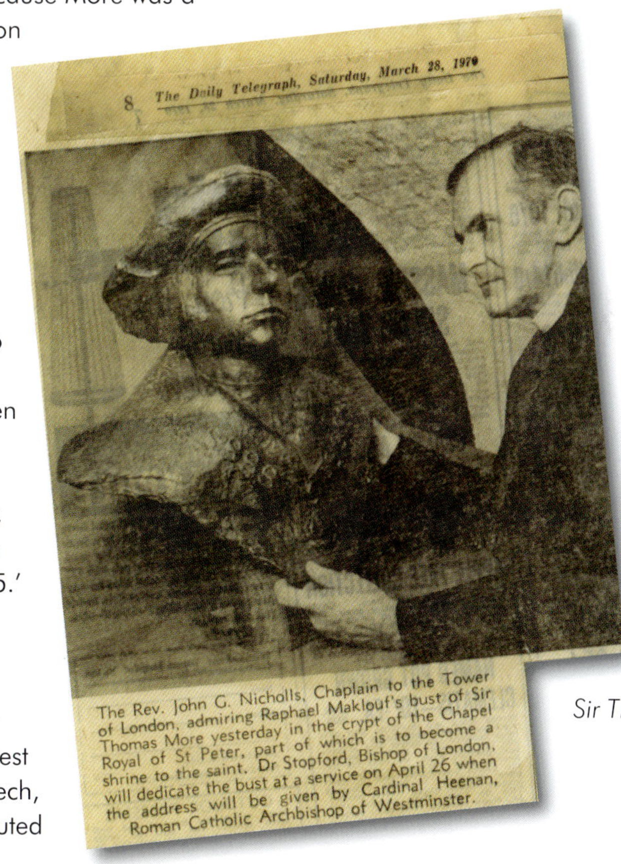
8 The Daily Telegraph, Saturday, March 28, 1970

The Rev. John G. Nicholls, Chaplain to the Tower of London, admiring Raphael Maklouf's bust of Sir Thomas More yesterday in the crypt of the Chapel Royal of St Peter, part of which is to become a shrine to the saint. Dr Stopford, Bishop of London, will dedicate the bust at a service on April 26 when the address will be given by Cardinal Heenan, Roman Catholic Archbishop of Westminster.

Sir Thomas More

In October 1968 Raphael and Marillyn got married in St Peter's ad Vincula, with the wedding reception at Claridges. As Raphael remembered, 'I had never been to a marriage before, so I didn't know what to expect. All my artist friends came. My parents were there. My Best Man was Marillyn's sister's husband. Her uncle gave an incredible speech, but no one had told me that there had to be a response. Everyone shouted

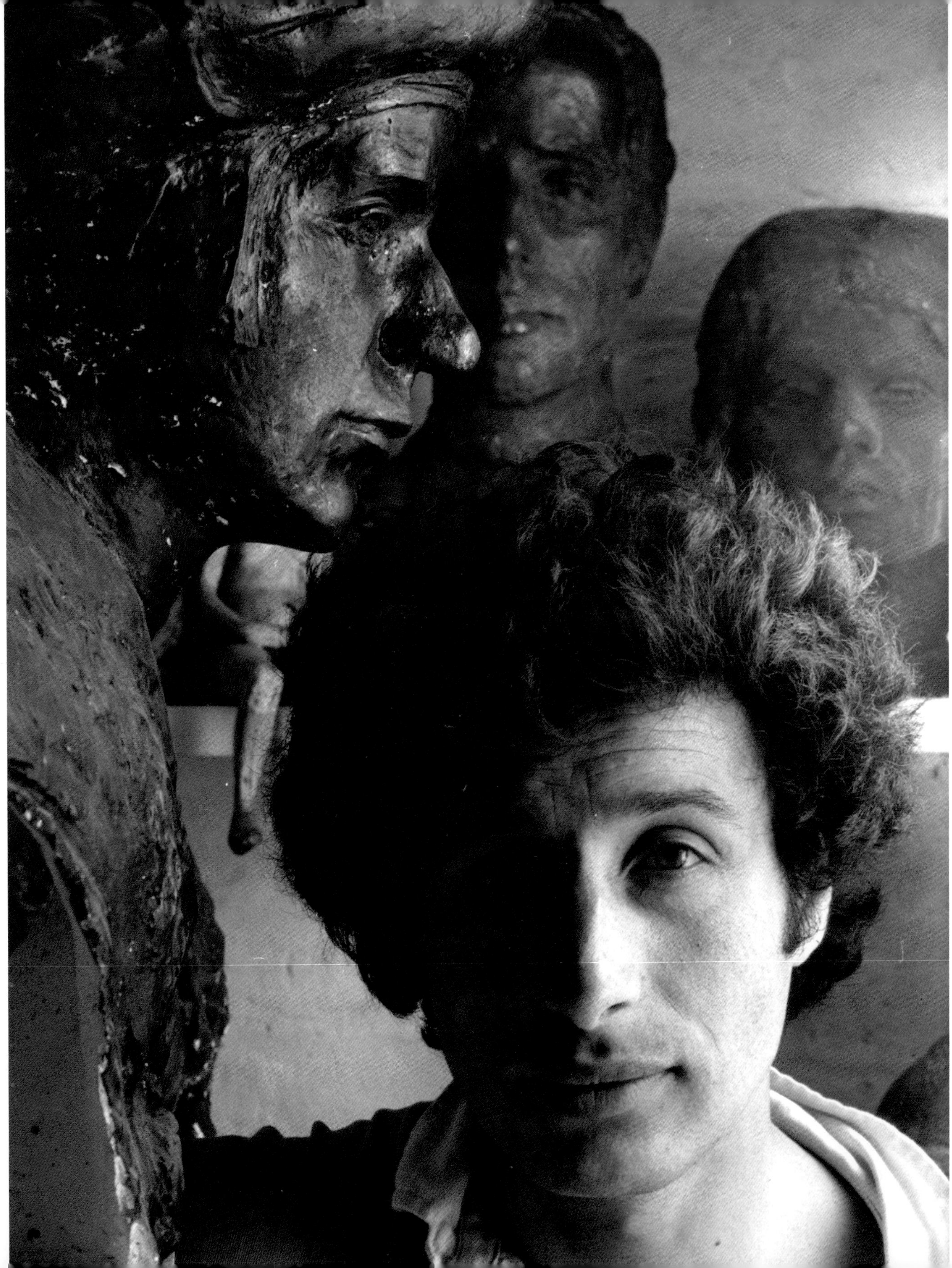

"Speech Speech!" All I managed to say was "I am NEVER going through this again!" at which there was a huge cheer. I don't drink so I wasn't drunk enough to cope. For our honeymoon, Marillyn's aunt had suggested going to Scotland. She organised all the places for us to visit. Because it was October it was obvious that everyone was stag hunting and sometimes we were the only people around. It was wonderful, with wonderful rainbows everywhere.' [11]

Family life in their house in Richmond suited Raphael, although he was still teaching part-time at Birmingham Art School. The children, David born in 1971, Laetitia born in 1973, and Edmund born in 1974, added a new dimension. Raphael proved a very natural father. He loved babies, and frequently picked them up to enjoy the solid feel of them. His elder son David, now a psychotherapist, gives a vivid insight into his father's work and character. 'The interesting thing about his sculpture is that it is very tactile – that's the distinction, touch. He minds about the feel of things, hates anything scratchy. He was a very 'huggy' father and played with us children; there was lots of rough and tumble, no standoffishness. He was not so much interested in our academic achievements, but wanted us to be 'capable'. Because we lived by the river he wanted us to be capable swimmers. We had wonderful summer holidays at Marillyn's parents' summer house in Anglesey, with endless games of Frisbee, cricket, and croquet. Raphael was the instigator of all the games, setting out the stones to make pitches.' [12]

Raphael became an integral part of the children's daily life, taking them to nursery school and driving them around on sculpture forays with the dog Oscar in the car. As David testified, throughout his life Raphael has invariably remained a happy extrovert, self-reliant, without hang-ups or any concept of nationalism or class. 'He is direct, never afraid to ask questions. He does look foreign, and I have seen some people taken aback by his un-English approach, but they are soon engaged. He's not interested in high status. I can think of many illustrations of his kindness and open attitude. I particularly remember an occasion at my brother's house at Eton when Camilla Parker-Bowles came in. There was a lot of media interest in her then, and in that very English way people stayed away from her. My father saw that no-one was talking to her and went up and engaged her in conversation. On another occasion at the Chelsea Arts Club he saw a wobbly old man struggling to get up and went to help him. He also took the trouble to telephone my dying godfather. These are all situations where many people would feel embarrassed in case it created a scene, social or emotional. He doesn't feel the awkwardness.' [13]

Looking back, David remembered one particular incident when he was at his prep school in Sussex. 'After one long weekend exeat I arrived at school without my overnight case. My adult self cannot understand why this article absolutely had to be with me, apparently as vital as the Prime Minister's code for the nuclear deterrent. Anyway, it did. So Raphael

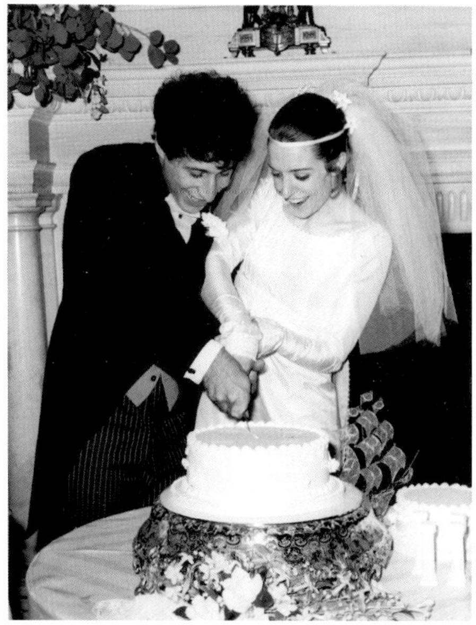

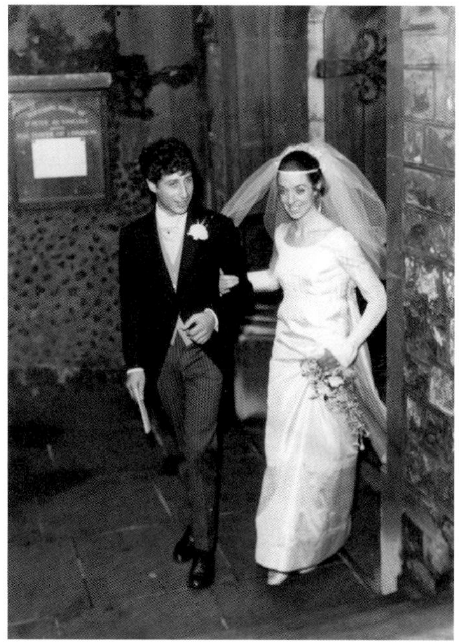

Raphael and Marillyn on their wedding day

Opposite: Raphael with bronze of Sir Thomas More

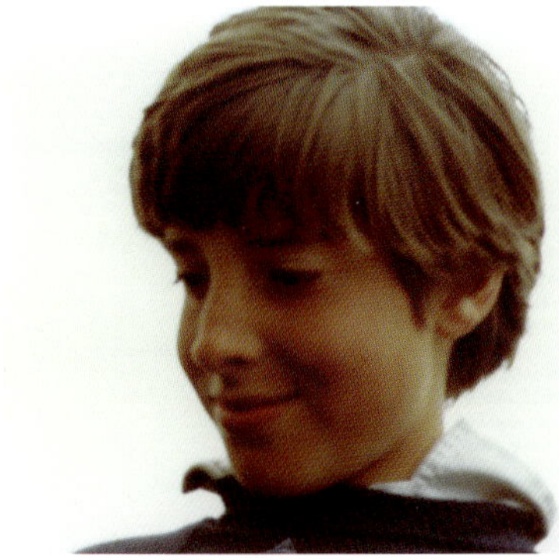

David

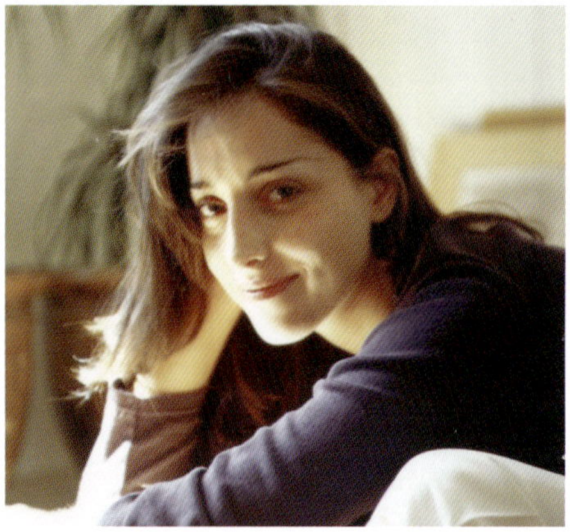

Laetitia

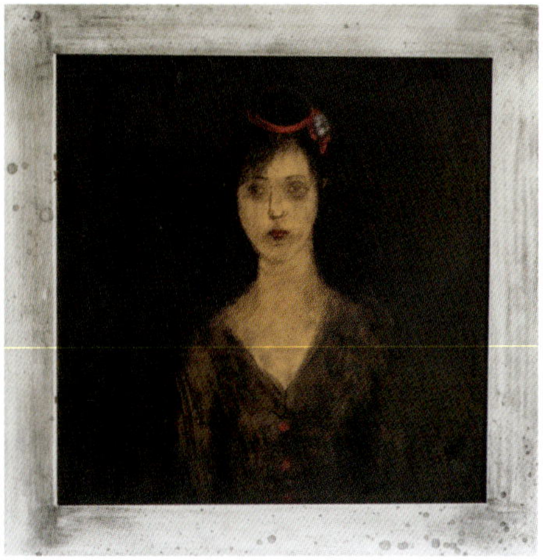

Painting of Laetitia
Photo by Kirsten Scully

went all the way back to Richmond and then back to Sussex that same evening, arriving late after the pupils had gone to bed. The Headmaster invited him to supper – he was extremely fond of Raphael. However, he was most definitely not fond of me! He saw me as a child whose mission was to subvert his school and its structures. He was probably right, and it enraged him. Next morning I was summoned to the Headmaster's study. A furious man awaited me, the embodiment of 'apoplectic'. "How dare you wind your father up like that! Your father loves you very much and that means you can wind him round your little finger. How dare you do that!" It transpired that Raphael had been arguing for my wish to be exempt from games. His mission has always been for his children to be happy and he knew that would have made my schooldays happier, so he pushed for that. I am now grateful for that telling-off because it shows me once again what a supportive father I have.' [14]

Laetitita recalled that whenever her father dropped her off at boarding school, either after a weekend exeat or the holidays, he would call out loudly from the car "Don't you dare work too hard!". Her main memory as a teenager was Raphael's protectiveness. 'He insisted on coming to get me from whatever nightclub I was dancing at (usually somewhere in Brixton) at two or three in the morning. Back then I found it all massively embarrassing, but now I'm hugely grateful and fond of him for doing so.' [15]

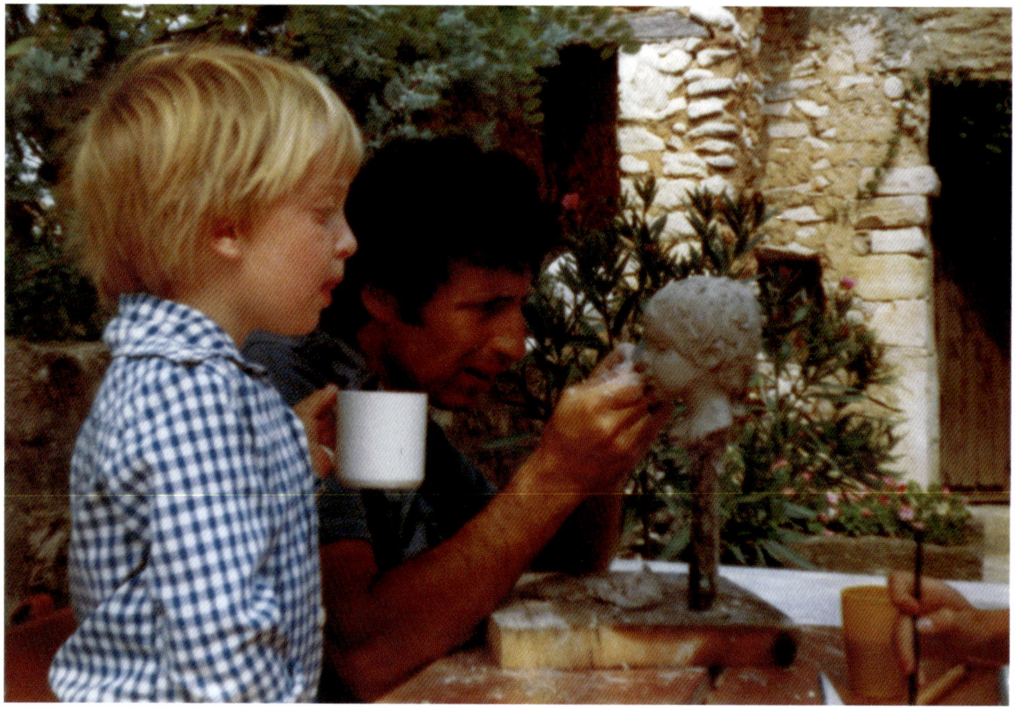

Modelling Edmund

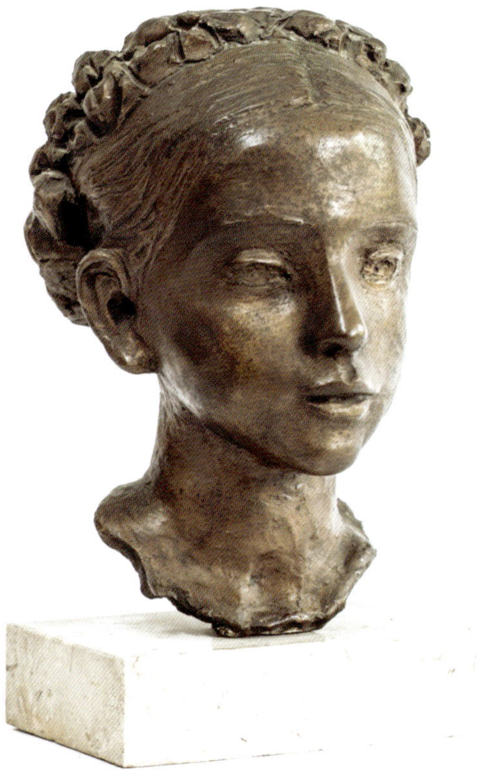

Bronze head of Laetitia
Photo by Kirsten Scully

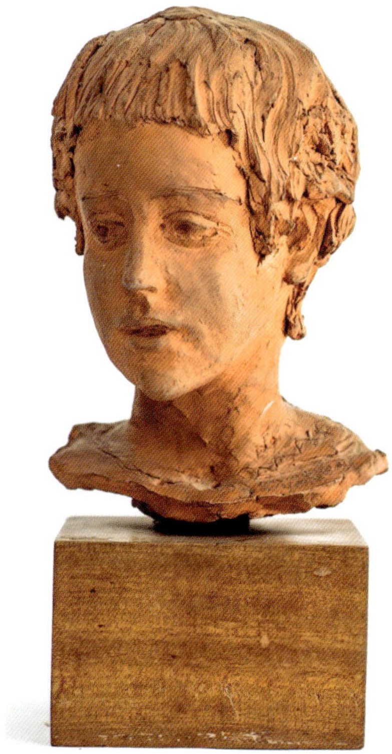

Teracotta of David
Photo by Kirsten Scully

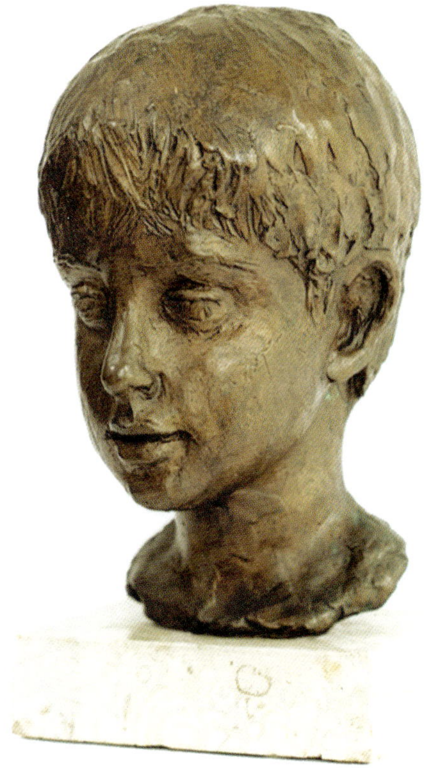

Bronze head of Edmund
Photo by Kirsten Scully

Raphael in his Richmond studio

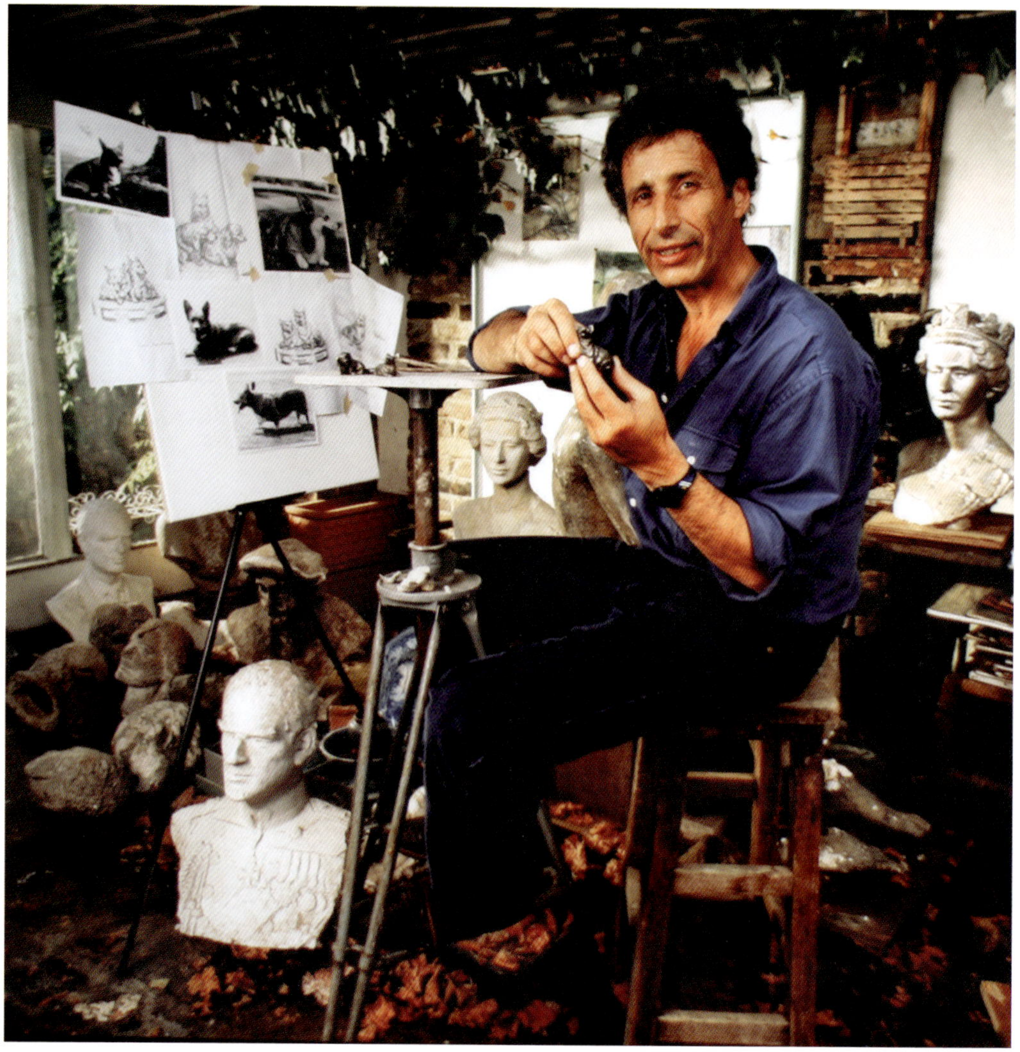

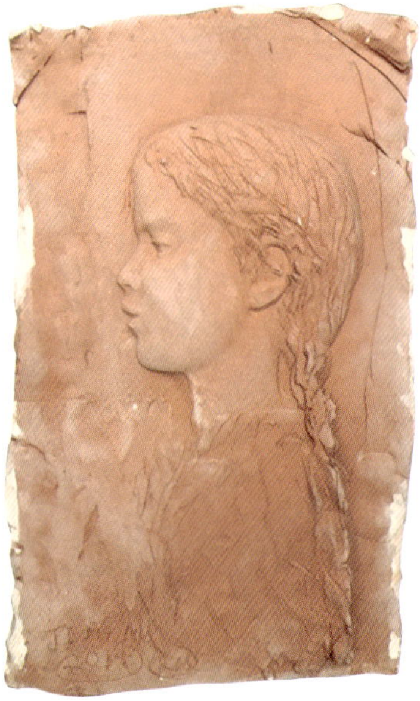

Terracotta bas-relief of Jemima age 5

Opposite: Left to right: David, Laetitia, Marillyn, Edmund. Portrait by Raphael Maklouf

Over the years Marillyn's parents became extremely fond of their son-in-law. Gwilym's strong sense of family loyalty now fully encompassed Raphael, and in 1983 he was moved to express his admiration for him in a letter: 'In the family grouping, which at all times is a thrill to me, you take a unique place. For me this grouping started, more or less, when that great Welsh Evangelist preacher – Reverend John Lewis – opened his family umbrella at Birmingham. From under that umbrella has developed a fantastic group... It is under this umbrella that you find yourself, making a unique contribution, quite unlike anything before, with a fantastic wife... and a very beautiful family.' [16]

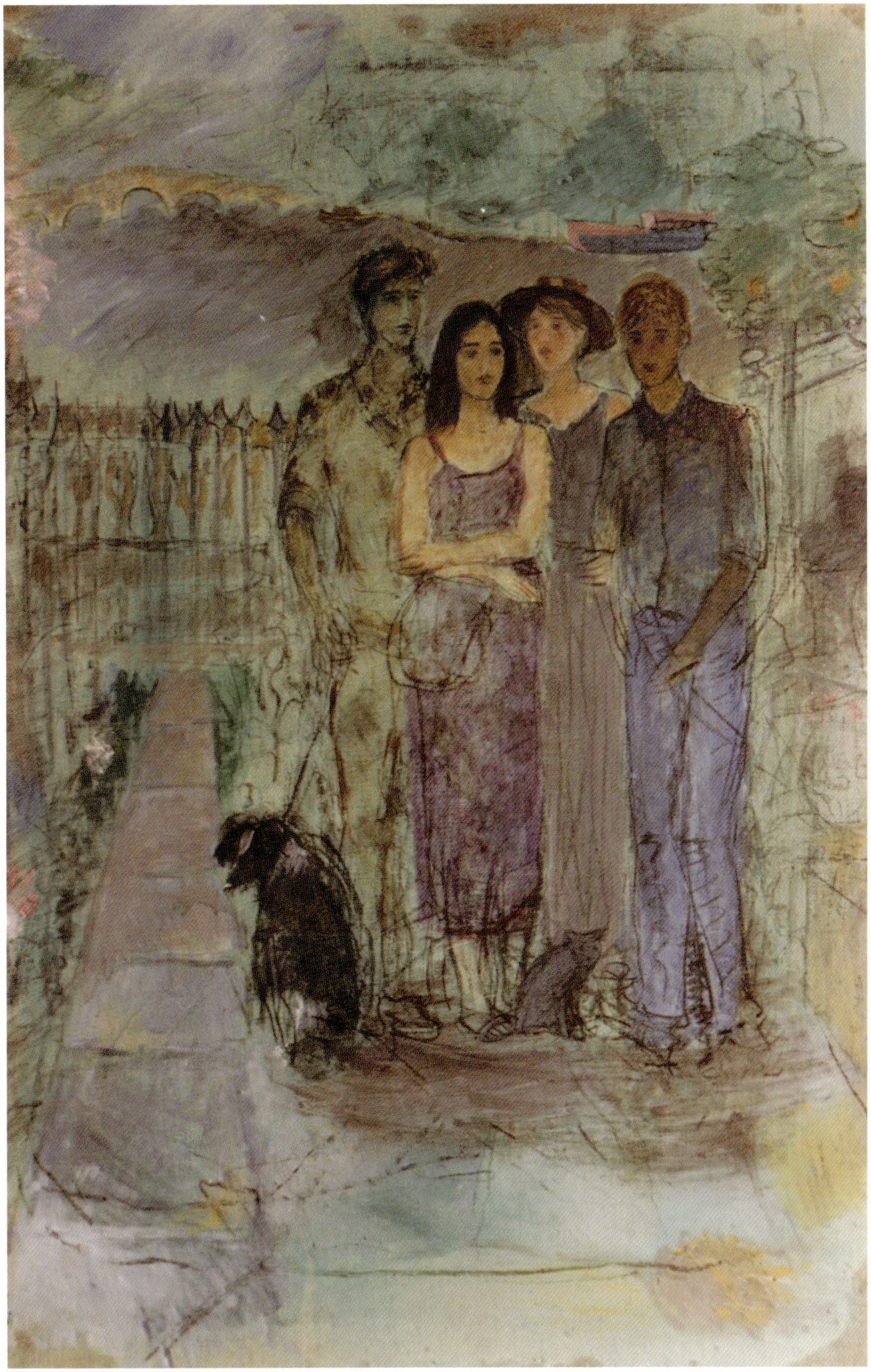

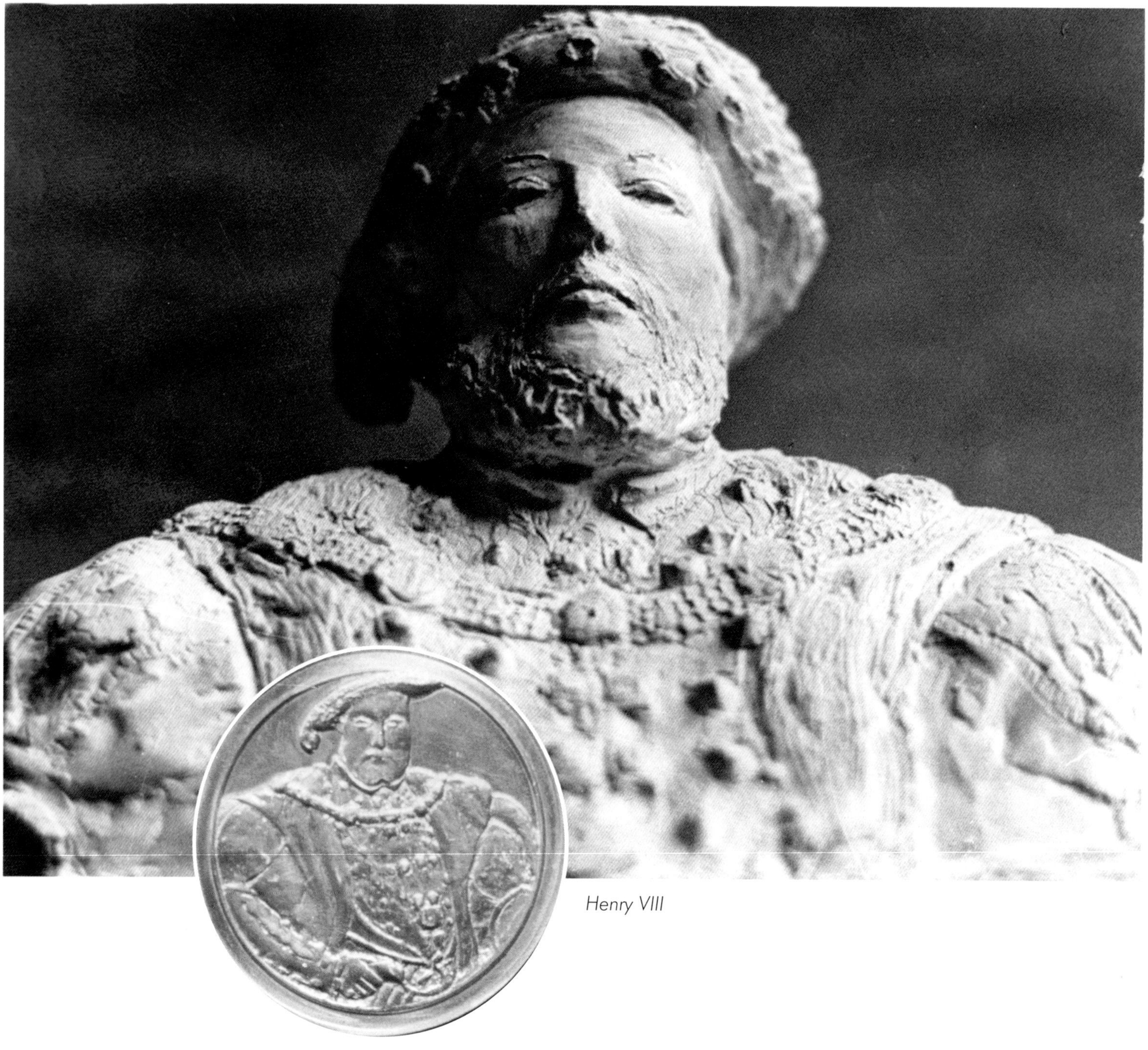

Henry VIII

Chapter 6
Tower Mint

WITH A GROWING family at home, Raphael was reluctant to spend teaching days away. Despite his hopes that the publicity surrounding his Thomas More portrait might bring more commissions nearer home, it was a long time before this happened. Then one day out of the blue the telephone rang. As Raphael recounted, 'a man named Brian Bayliss said "I gather you are the author of the Thomas More sculpture. Would you mind if we reproduced it as postcards?". Later he asked "Do you think you could make little maquettes of the bust? I think people would like to buy them." When I told him that the maquettes would have to be in bronze because the original was bronze, he asked me to find out how much it would cost to make some small bronzes that would sell for under £7. I was still teaching every Monday at Birmingham School of Art, so during my lunch hour I went to Birmingham's jewellery quarter where they do casting, to try and find a bronze caster. It turned out that bronze busts would be too expensive, so Bayliss asked "what about plastic?". I didn't want any of that, so I said no. Then he said, "if you insist on bronze, what about a bas relief bronze medal?". I found a guy who could stamp bronze medals but when he asked how many I wanted, I asked for ten. He told me to get lost because he wasn't going to do just ten. I now understand that it takes two hours to set up for striking and it's not worth doing in small numbers. He agreed to do a minimum of a hundred in brass. I decided to take a chance on it but I didn't tell Brian. I had the medals made and brought them all down from Birmingham on the train, and then went to Clerkenwell where there were lots of jewellers who sold presentation cases. I put the medals in cases and in my minivan I delivered the requested ten to the souvenir shop in the Tower of London. As soon as I got home Marillyn said that Brian Bayliss had telephoned to say that they had all gone, and asked if they could have ten more. I thought, this is ridiculous – I can't keep popping over to the Tower, so I took the other ninety and asked the guy in the storeroom if I could leave them there. The medals proved so successful that Brian Bayliss immediately asked if I could create a Henry VIII medal for Hampton Court Palace. The hugely successful television series on Henry VIII was running at that time. So there I was, still going to teach in Birmingham, still doing my own original work, and then being asked to do other medallions – for Caernavon Castle, Holyrood House etc – and I had hardly any time to spare. [1]

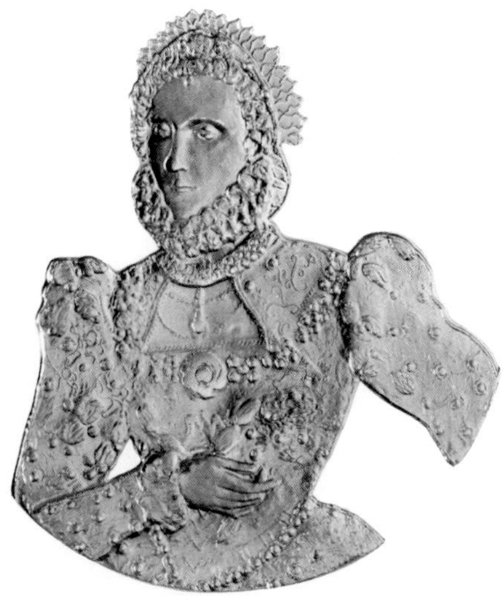

Queen Elizabeth I

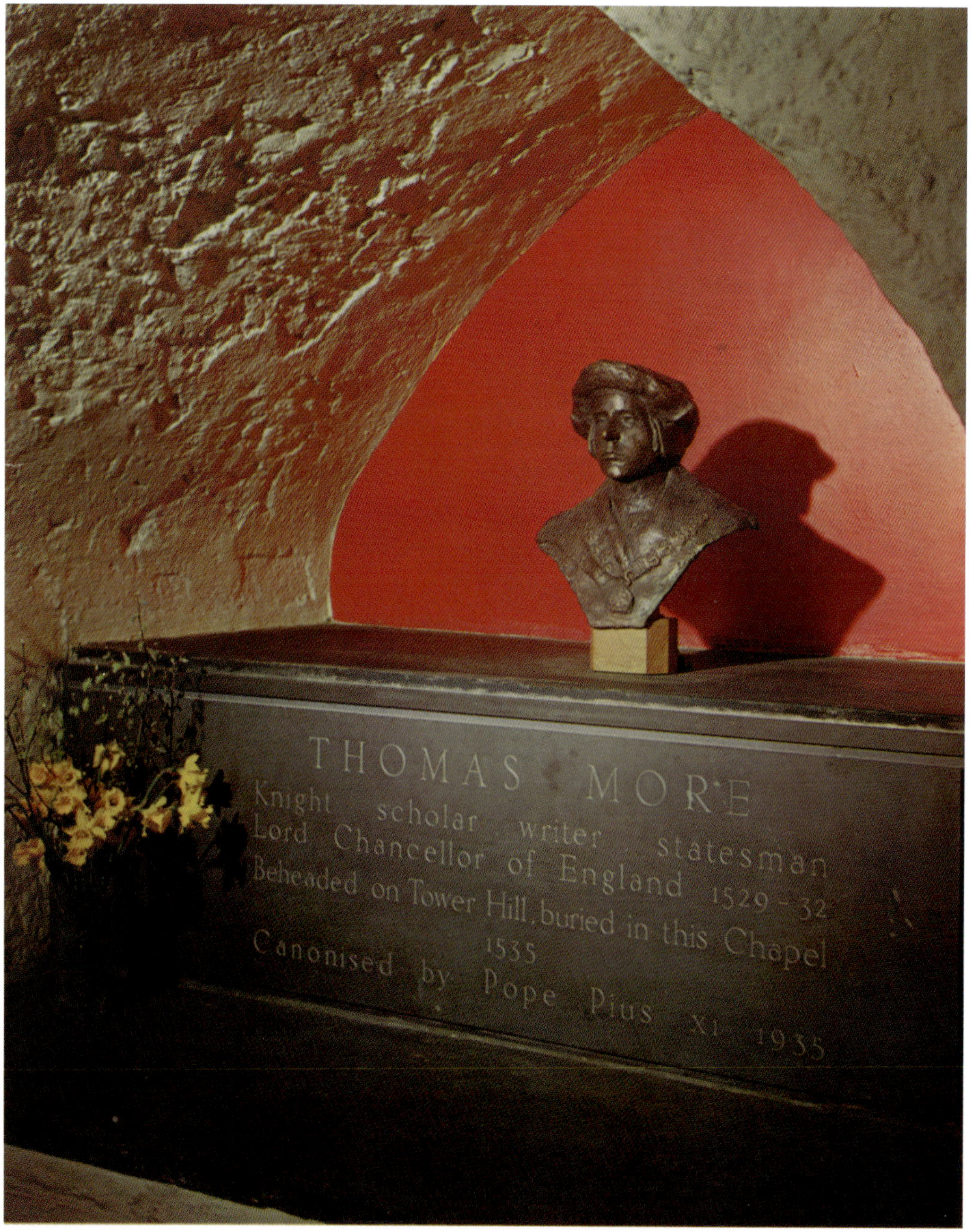

Bronze bust of Sir Thomas More. The Crypt of St Peter ad Vincula

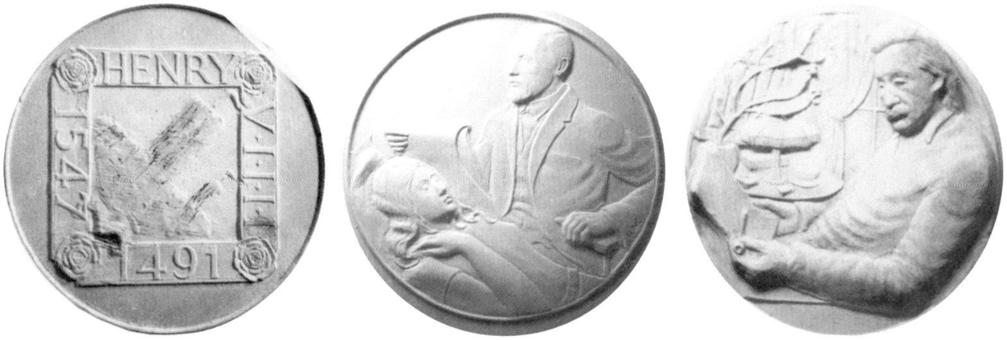

Early medals by Raphael Maklouf

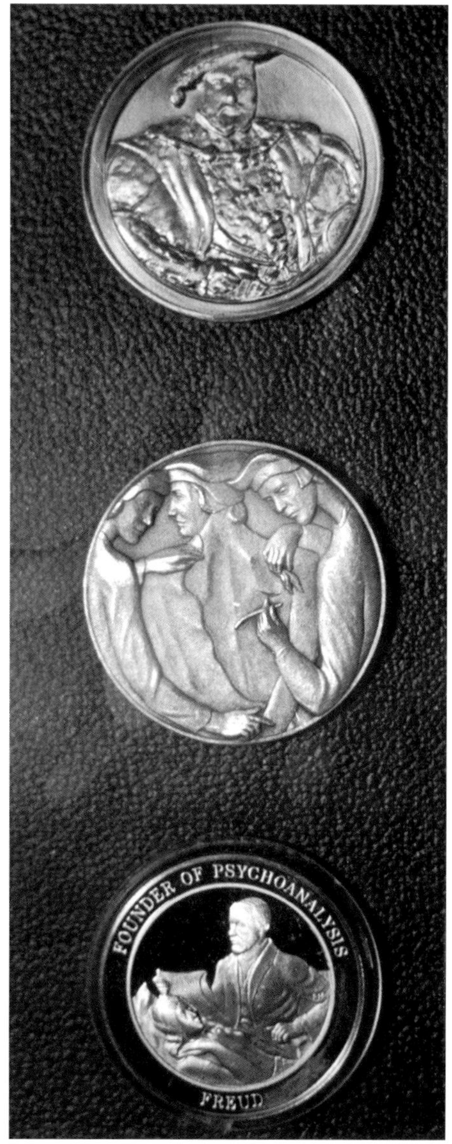

Raphael's life now began to take a completely new direction. His minting operation was started by pure chance, triggered by his bust of Thomas More, and it continued in a rather haphazard way. Those early years remain vividly fresh in his memory. 'I was getting my medals made with Roger Hazeldene at York Stampings, but when he decided to expand the business, he overreached himself and went into receivership. I then applied to the successful Birmingham Mint, but they were not interested in my small numbers. I had to find someone else to make my medals so I went to the Royal Mint at Tower Hill. When I asked if they would do some minting for me, they said "no way – decimalisation is taking all our time". I didn't even realise that the Royal Mint had moved to South Wales because of decimalisation.' [2]

The Royal Mint in its 1880s buildings adjacent to the Tower of London had reached full capacity ahead of decimalisation in 1971, with the need to strike hundreds of millions of new decimal coins without neglecting its overseas customers. From 1967 it had been gradually moving to its new premises in Llantrisant, near Cardiff, and the last coin was struck in London in 1975. South Wales was chosen for the new site because the coal mines were shutting down and a new heavy industry providing jobs for the miners was needed there. As Raphael recalled, 'because they were moving to a greenfield site they wanted all new machinery, everything new. However, the vestiges of the Mint were still at the Tower. The antiquated machinery was being sold as scrap, disabled so as not to be used for the wrong reasons. I happened to arrive just after the move, when there were two old-timers, Ron Langdon and Charlie Miskin, who had the task of disabling the redundant machinery. Then one of the Mint's engravers, Bob Elderton, suggested that I should set up my own mint. The idea had never occurred to me. Ron and Charlie were still there because they had worked at the Royal Mint in London all their lives, and they didn't want to move to Wales. Their parents had worked at Woolwich Arsenal. I asked them if they would consider *not* disabling one of the presses – I would buy it. I was living in Richmond and I had to go to the Scrap Auction in the newly built Tower Hotel. There were lots of scrap merchants there, all smoking. I had flu and a high temperature. In fact I was almost delirious. I sat between Ron and Charlie and asked them to give me a

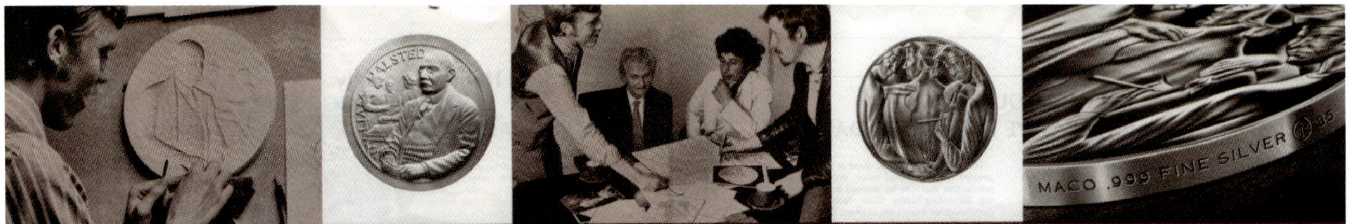

THE MEDALLIC TRIBUTE TO SURGICAL HISTORY

commemorates the 36 most significant contributions to surgery

Thirty-six fine art medals struck expressly to your order... limited first edition...subscription rolls close October 31, 1971

"The quality of the research and historical resources which have been used in acquiring and assimilating the historical facts and biographical details are, indeed, quite substantial."

Robert M. Bartlow, Ph.D.
Manager, Historical Research
Medical Heritage Society

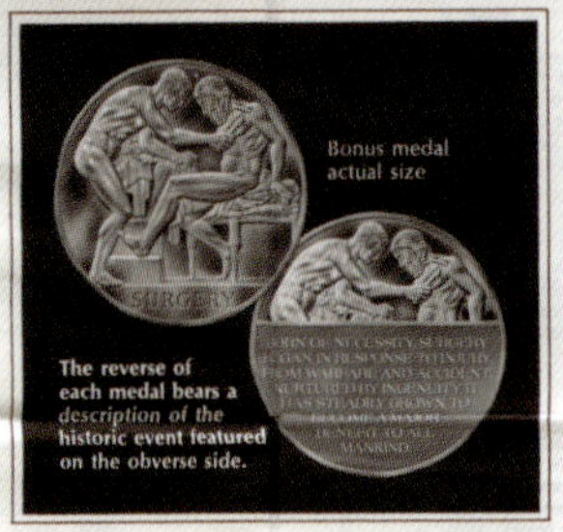

The reverse of each medal bears a *description of the* historic event featured on the obverse side.

The worldwide scope of surgery is sculpted here in the most artistic detail ...the remote past linked to the exciting present. Thirty-six of the most significant surgical achievements have been developed into privately-minted, limited first edition sets. Available by advance subscription only.

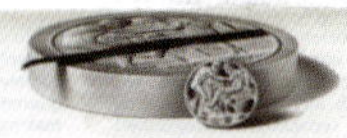

Typical of the many milestones considered by the advisory board were the famous papyri on ancient Egyptian surgery (1600 B.C.) discovered by Edwin Smith.

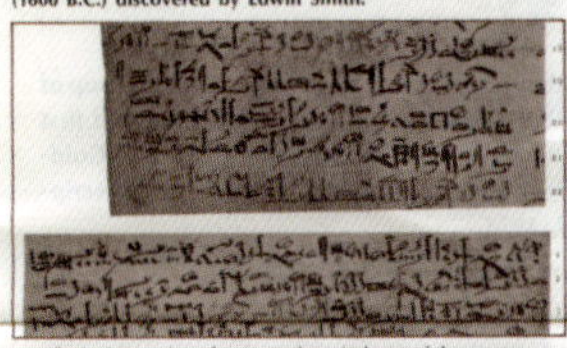

Beginning portion of one actual surgical case of the papyrus entitled *"Instructions Concerning a Wound in his Throat."*

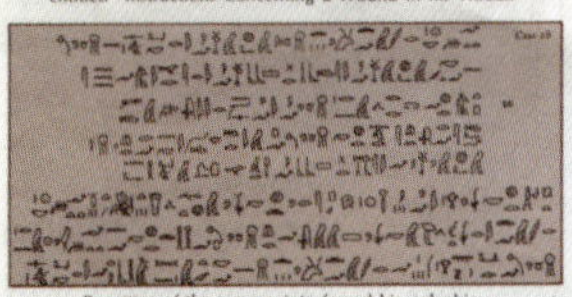

Rewriting of the papyrus into formal hieroglyphics.

Translation of Surgical Case Number Twenty-Eight of the Seventeenth Century B.C. Edwin Smith Egyptian Surgical Papyrus

18. Instructions concerning a wound in his throat. If thou examinest a man
19. Having a gaping wound in his throat, piercing through to his gullet, if he drinks water he chokes
20. It comes out of the mouth of his wound, it is greatly inflamed, so that he
21. Develops fever from it, thou shouldst draw together that wound with stitching. Thou shouldst say concerning him: "One having a wound in his
22. Throat, piercing through to his gullet. An ailment with which I will contend."

1. Thou shouldst bind it with fresh meat the first day. Thou shouldst treat it afterward with grease, honey and lint every day,
2. Until he recovers. If, however, thou findest him continuing to have fever from that wound, thou shouldst apply for him dry lint in the mouth of his wound
3. And moor him at his mooring stakes until he recovers.

A special wall-hanging depicting a section of this ancient Egyptian papyrus with its accompanying hieroglyphic version, and translation into English, is available as a bonus. This is the oldest known scientific document in the world...and it deals with surgery. If your application is postmarked by 10 days prior to closing (Oct. 21), we will send you this unusual 15" x 36" hanging with your subscription acknowledgement.

For the first time in history, man pays medallic tribute to the origins of surgical knowledge

The number of landmarks and persons to be observed and considered in a comprehensive review of surgical history is large. Thus the journey is long and arduous if the most significant contributions are to be selected . . .

Our advisory board's considerations span 5,000 years . . . going back to Babylon—where Hammurabi decrees the exact fees a surgeon was to receive for ophthalmology and other practices . . . through Sumeria, where a high order of surgery was practiced by the *Asu*.

They reviewed Egyptian surgical treatments such as trepanning with religious permission . . . and before that, into the ancient East Indian Sacred Books on surgery used in the first hospitals, the "Houses of Benevolence."

In Egypt and Mesopotamia, there are documents carved in stone or written on papyrus, describing surgical practice dating back to 3,000 B.C. Archaeologists have also discovered skeletal remains and artifacts that give us a picture of surgical practice in very ancient times.

The anatomical conclusions of Galen, the genius who compiled centuries of observations at the twilight of the Golden Age were observed.

In their search for surgical landmarks, our advisors encountered Nestorius' contributions: Mohammedan translations that kept alive the knowledge of Greek surgery during the European Dark Ages. They scouted Italy—the innovations of Roger of Salerno and Roland of Perma. And then, in France, they observed the numerous contributions of Guy de Chauliac and his writings on the practice of surgery.

The board revisited the conquering of pain through anesthesia's discovery, one of the greatest adjuvants to surgery. Their studies reviewed procedures at which veteran surgeons once stood aghast. They examined breakthroughs in ancient and new techniques . . . early transplants . . . sutures . . . ligatures . . . dressings . . . fractures . . . incisions . . . cryosurgery. More was seen achieved as surgical knowledge kept increasing the pace of progress, year after year.

And from all this and more . . . 36 of the highest points in surgical history are to be preserved for all time in this unique medallic tribute.

Interpreted Internationally by a Select Assemblage of Famous Medallic Sculptors

From Great Britain . . . Italy . . . France . . . Germany . . . the United States and other countries . . . some of the world's most gifted medallic sculptors are being gathered. The talented hands of these recognized artists are creating individual interpretations of the 36 highlights of surgical history. These fine art sculptures will then be struck in 24K Gold-over-Fine Silver, All Fine Silver, and Solid Bronze, by Medallic Art Company of New York—the leading producer of high relief medallic sculpture in the United States. And to further assure the greatest quality of workmanship, the Medical Heritage Society has enlisted the consulting services of Walter Newman, M.V.O., Chief Engraver of the Royal Mint in London.

High Relief Sculpturing: The Technique of Emphasized Realism in Art Medals—plus Touchable, Toned Finish

The Medallic Tribute To Surgical History will be minted in high relief — creating a dramatic three-dimensional effect. To add still further depth, each medal's surface will be toned to produce a rich patina . . . and finished to allow it to be handled without concern about fingerprinting or tarnishing the surface. Even after years of display and admiration, these fine art medals will look as attractive as the day they were minted for you.

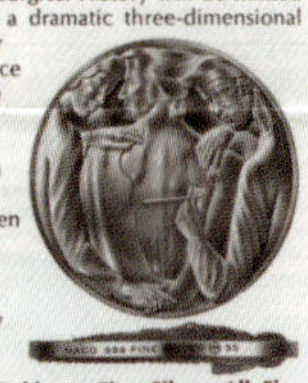

Choose from 24 Karat Gold-over-Fine Silver, All Fine Silver, or Solid bronze . . . A Valuable Collection for Anyone With An Interest in Surgery or Rare Fine Art Medals

A Special Note About Precious Metals:

The 24 Karat Gold layer (a heavy jeweler's electroplate) over Fine Silver is the finest quality gold possible in minting. Fine Silver is .999 pure (99.9%) silver—actually a finer grade than Sterling Silver which is .925 pure. Bronze used in our fine art medals must meet strict standards to assure perfect minting. The three editions assure a collector's set for virtually every level of interest or investment. One fine art medal will be struck each month, for a total of 36 months. Each medal will be 44 mm (1¾") in diameter; substantially larger and thicker than a silver dollar.

Every Medal Hallmarked To Show Its Origin . . . and the 24K Gold-over-Fine Silver and Fine Silver Sets Are Individually Registered For You

Hallmarked medals are edge-marked to identify the issuing mint and metal in which the medal is struck—a mark of authenticity of origin and quality of metal. Edge-numbering is a personalized mark of value: a set's subscription number is individually registered on the edge of every medal in the 24K Gold-over-Fine Silver and All Fine Silver sets.

Absolutely Limited Number of Sets

The total number of sets to be minted in this edition will be restricted to exactly the number of subscription applications postmarked on or before October 31, 1971, plus 10 sets for presentations to museums and historians. No additional sets will be struck in these metals, size and finishes again for the United States. After minting, all dies are destroyed. (Because of scheduling differences, international announcement dates may not coincide with the exact dates of this offer.) And to further increase the collection's rarity and inherent value, this offer will be made *exclusively* to those associated with the health professions and to known collectors.

This Unique Fine Art Collection's Potential Value Presaged by Established Appreciation of Previous Medical Heritage Society Collections

The continuing demand for earlier series issued by the Medical Heritage Society points to important collector potential. Add to that the historical authenticity, exquisite artistry and the assured rarity of a limited edition, combined with the long-term trend of increasing values in precious metals . . . and you have a good basis for assessing the potential value of this unique series of fine art medals.

Distinctive fine art medals display chest

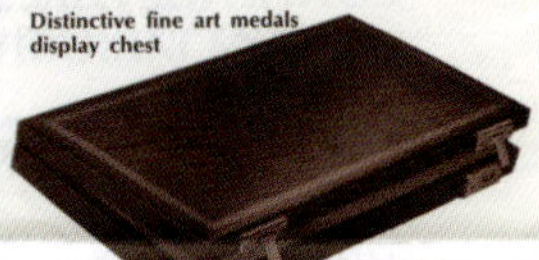

Included with each subscription at no extra charge—this custom crafted chest that both displays and protects your Medallic Tribute To Surgical History. Historical reference literature accompanies each medal you receive.

PRICE PROTECTION GUARANTEE

Regardless of how much the price of precious metals may *increase* during the term of subscription, the Medical Heritage Society guarantees that your subscription price will remain the same throughout the entire series.

Subscribe now...before deadline on October 31, 1971. See unique bonus medal on preceding page.

nudge when my machine came up for sale. I was so feverish that I bid for it twice, and I remember the auctioneer saying "Sir, don't outbid yourself"! That's where I got my first press – a Heaton press, built in the nineteenth century in Birmingham, designed for making round pennies. We had to collect the press within a few days, and luckily a friend who had a factory not far away agreed to store it for me.' [3]

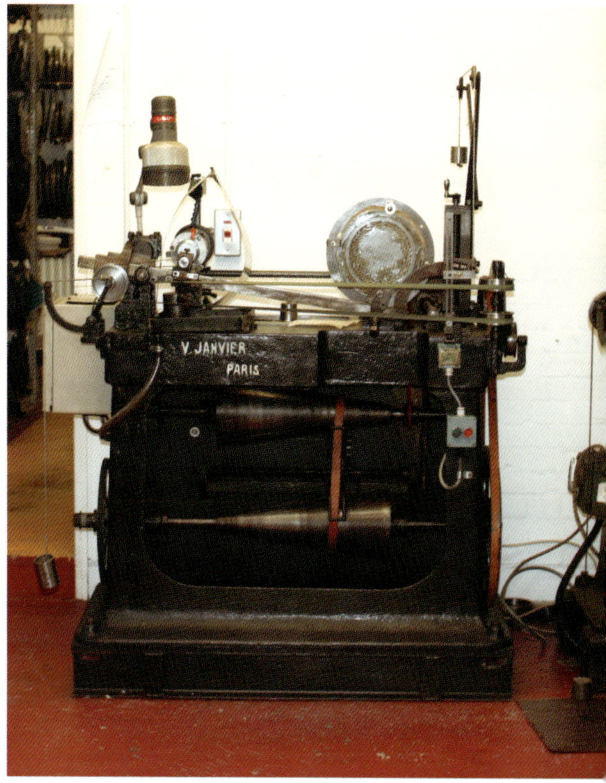

Die cutting reducing machine

Raphael, now the proud possessor of one antique press, set about organising his Mint. His first task was to find premises in which to work. He bought the freehold of a small sweet shop in Royal Mint Street, the idea being to demonstrate medals being minted to visitors to the Tower of London. But because he could not get planning permission for light industrial work there, he was obliged to look for other premises. In the Evening Standard he saw an advertisement for an old flour mill in Greenwich High Road. Because Ron and Charlie lived nearby, he decided to rent this. Mumford's Flour Mill, belonging to a Mr Eliot, consisted of a smallish room backing onto a creek, a dungeon-like basement, and an outside lavatory. He rented the place for a peppercorn rent of £15 per week, the deal being that he was responsible for all maintenance and improvements. As he recalled, 'it took about three months to move the machine in there and to get Ron and Charlie on side'.

With the premises partially tidied up and the machine in situ, Raphael set up his new company. Ron was appointed Foreman and Charlie was the Press Operator. The three of them made an odd team. Charlie, who had been a press operator all his life, could not read or write. He had only two teeth, between which he would stick his hand-rolled cigarettes. While Raphael drove an old minivan, Ron, vain enough to sport a comb-over, drove an Austin Princess of which he was inordinately proud. Raphael had had no business education or experience, and in order to start a brand new company he was forced to improvise, as he remembers in minute detail. 'This is the way I worked it out. I worked out how much the rent cost, how much I would have to pay Ron and Charlie, and how many medals we would have to make to cover it. In those days there was no VAT. I was still doing a day a week teaching in Birmingham so I didn't include a salary for myself. I had all the dies from York Stampings which I took down to London after I had them re-cut in Birmingham to fit our own press. I suggested to Ron and Charlie that instead of wages we should each have a third of the company. They said they would have to talk it over with the Missus and they would let me know on Monday. Monday came and they both said they would like to work for the company, but they would rather have their wages paid for a year; then, if the business looked like working out, they would take a third share. I said "you can't do that. If it works I wouldn't have to ask you to share the cost. Please reconsider." Neither would change his mind so I agreed to pay their wages, which proved quite a struggle.'

Opposite: In the small photograph, centre top: Barry Stanton, Alan Wallace, Deputy of the Royal Mint, with Raphael

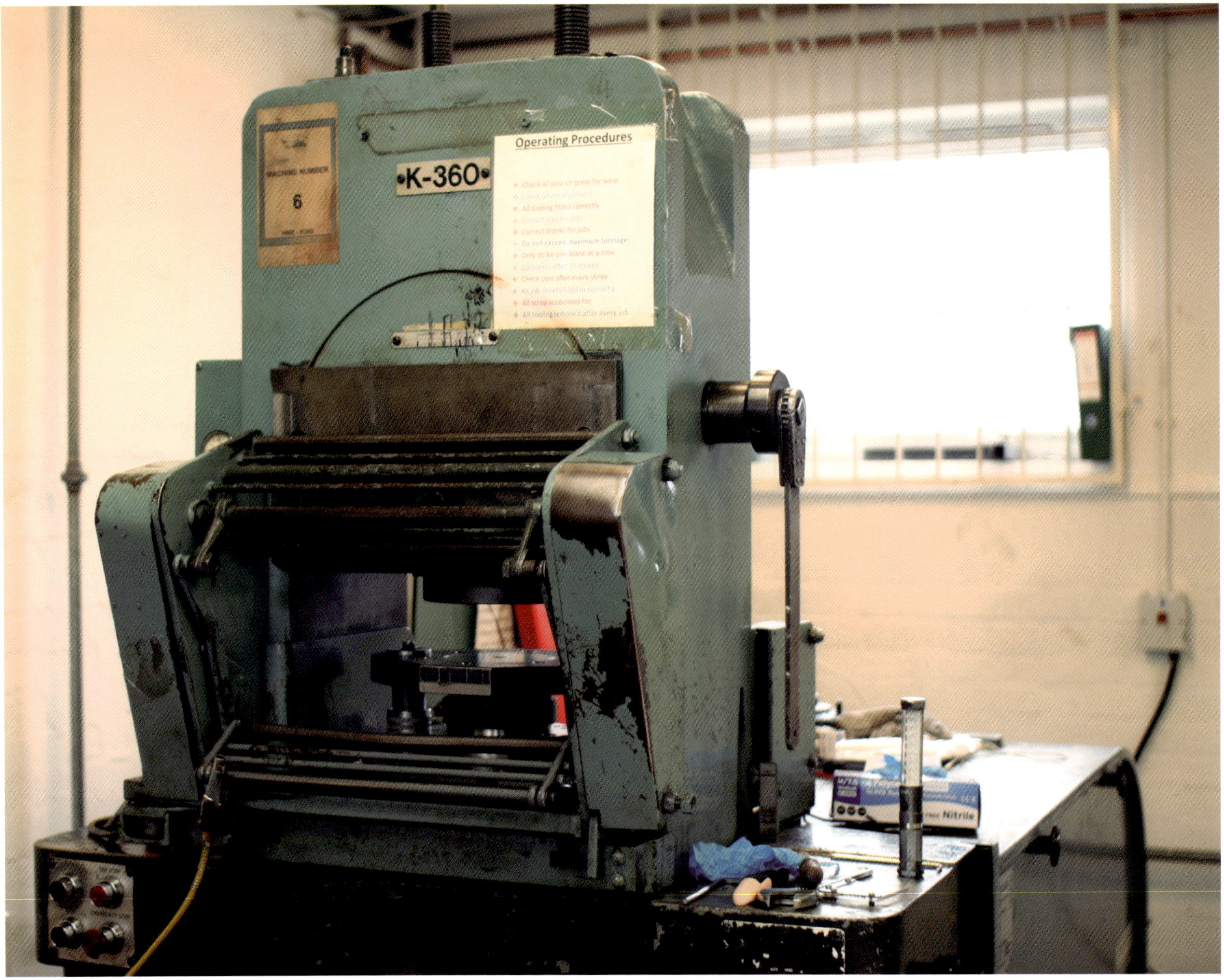

Raphael's first 'new' HME 360 ton press, purchased 1970

'Orders started to come in and after six months it was obvious that we were succeeding. Ron then came to me and said "Because I have helped you to succeed I want you to pay me more because a new model Rover car has just come out and I want to have it. If you don't agree, I shall leave. And for my help setting up you owe me at least £250." I was upset and said "Charlie is not asking for anything, You.ve got an Austin Princess and I am driving an old minivan. But I owe you more than that. I will give you £300. Now go!" When I told Charlie that Ron was leaving I asked him if he also wanted to leave. He said no, he wanted to stay, so I told him that he would have to be the Manager and train somebody else to operate the press. Charlie turned out to be an amazing manager, and without him the business would not have worked. He knew a fantastic amount. He recounted that as a young press operator he had an idea to improve on the way a press would work. He explained his idea to his supervisor who told him not to be impertinent and get on with his work. He never suggested anything again. We then took on Nicky Nikolaides, a Greek Cypriot who had been a die-cutter at Franklin Mint, the private mint founded by Joseph Segal in Pennsylvania in the 1960s. When Franklin Mint closed their English operation I bought one of their die-cutting machines and invited Nicky to come with it.' [4]

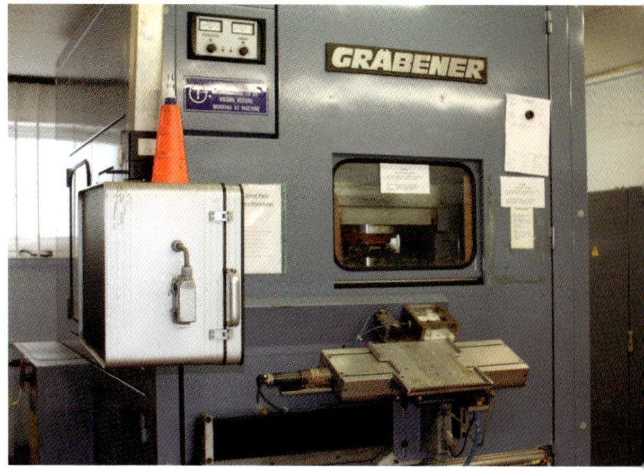

Grabener automatic coin minting press

Tower Mint Ltd was registered as a limited company on 13 September 1976. Soon Tower Mint was being asked to strike larger medals, and it needed a higher tonnage press. Raphael went to Birmingham press makers HME in search of the necessary machine. These presses, made to order, were enormously expensive, almost beyond the reach of his small company. However, Raphael went ahead and negotiated the purchase of a state-of-the-art new machine and put down a deposit on it. At the time there was a long queue for these machines, and on several occasions Raphael was offered substantial sums of money for ceding his place in the queue. He resisted, however, and, as luck would have it, one of Tower Mint's first orders using the new machine was for striking silver and gold ingots for the 1977 Silver Jubilee. The 'dog tag' ingots were very popular, and the new machine proved its worth within three months.

As the enterprise took off, other staff were appointed, either by word of mouth or in answer to advertisements. At the age of twenty-two Jane Poole, now a senior director, discovered Tower Mint through an advertisement in her local paper searching for a clerical assistant. At her initial interview she was thrilled to find the Mint in such old premises in Greenwich. 'You went into a courtyard and it didn't look like an office. As soon as I walked in the door I felt welcomed. There were Raphael and Charlie with three other guys, and Nicky, who was the die-cutter from the start. There were four packers, and other staff were gradually added. The work then was seasonal – Christmas and Easter, and the school holidays for souvenir medallions. There was a tough period when we were on a three-day week, but the company had by then become like a family, and we all pulled together to get through it. Everyone was very accommodating because we all wanted to stay with the company. It's a caring company, built on trust. We have a yearly office party. Raphael is very understanding and a very good mentor. He has been like a father figure to me.' [5]

When the whole process of making commemorative medals began to take over Raphael's life, Marilyn complained. When she asked 'What do people do with these medals?' Raphael replied that people probably looked at them once and then put them in a drawer and forgot about them. She grumbled 'That's so boring. I married an artist, not a business man. At least make something with an element of fun in it – something for children.' She brought along a bag of chocolate coins and said 'Why don't you make something like this?' Her idea was taken up with alacrity. Raphael telephoned twenty of his regular clients to see if they would also like chocolate coins with the same designs. All were very keen. The problem was finding somebody to make them. Through the Yellow Pages he contacted several companies, but none would make them. Marilyn's brother then put him in touch with someone in the chocolate world, who said 'you're a quarter of a century too late. Nobody in Britain has made them for twenty-five years. They are all made on the continent. You will have to look abroad.' Raphael found a German family firm who made a batch of chocolate coins for St Paul's cathedral, but their quality was so

Chocolate coins

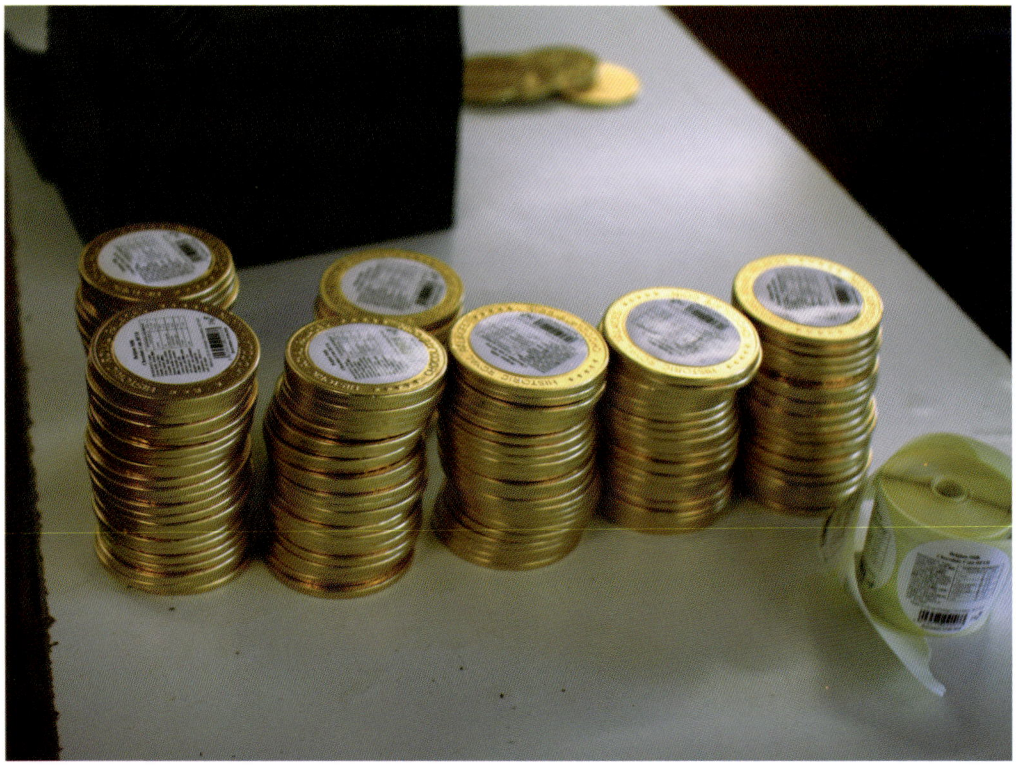

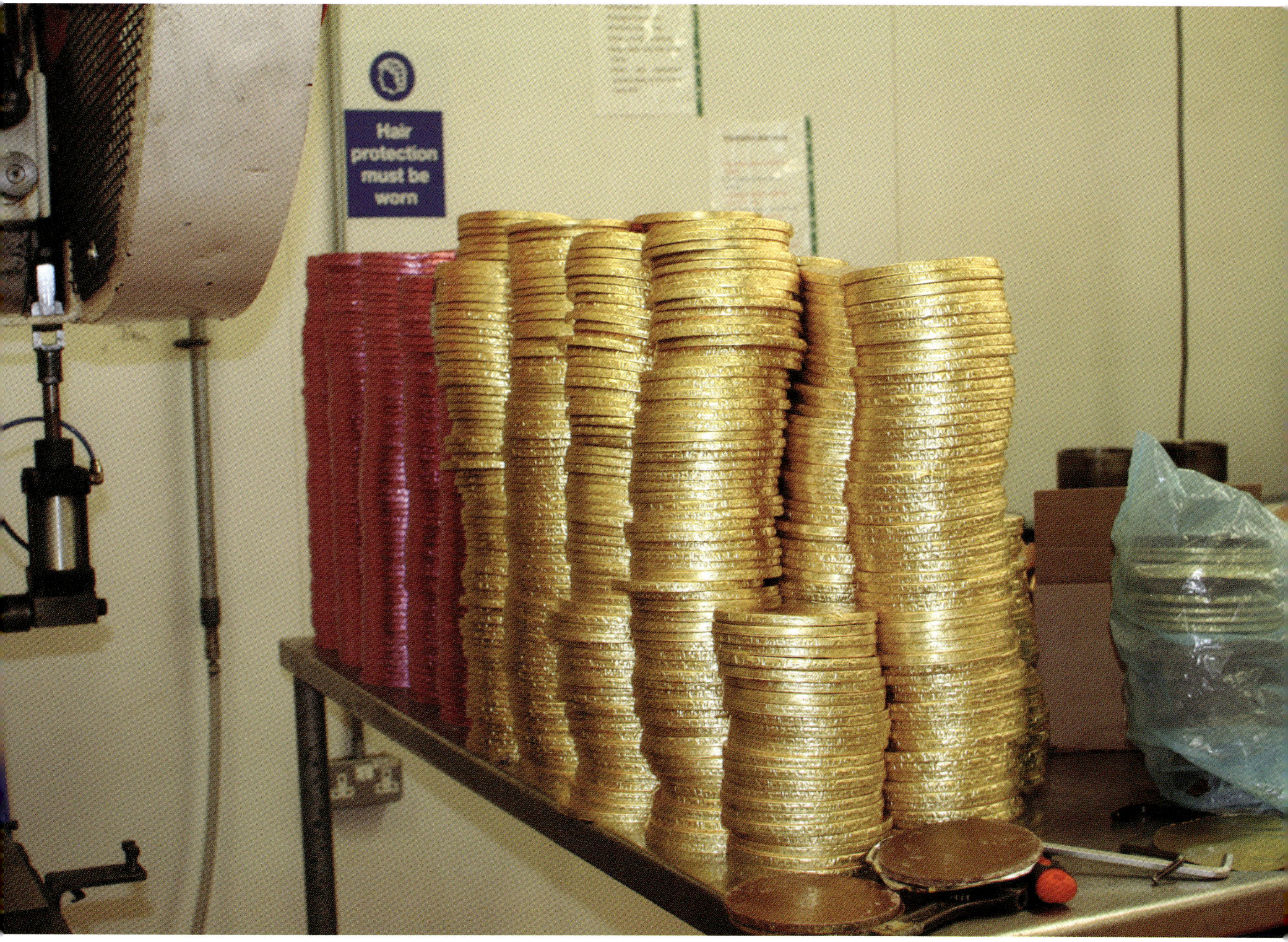

Foiled chocolates before embossing

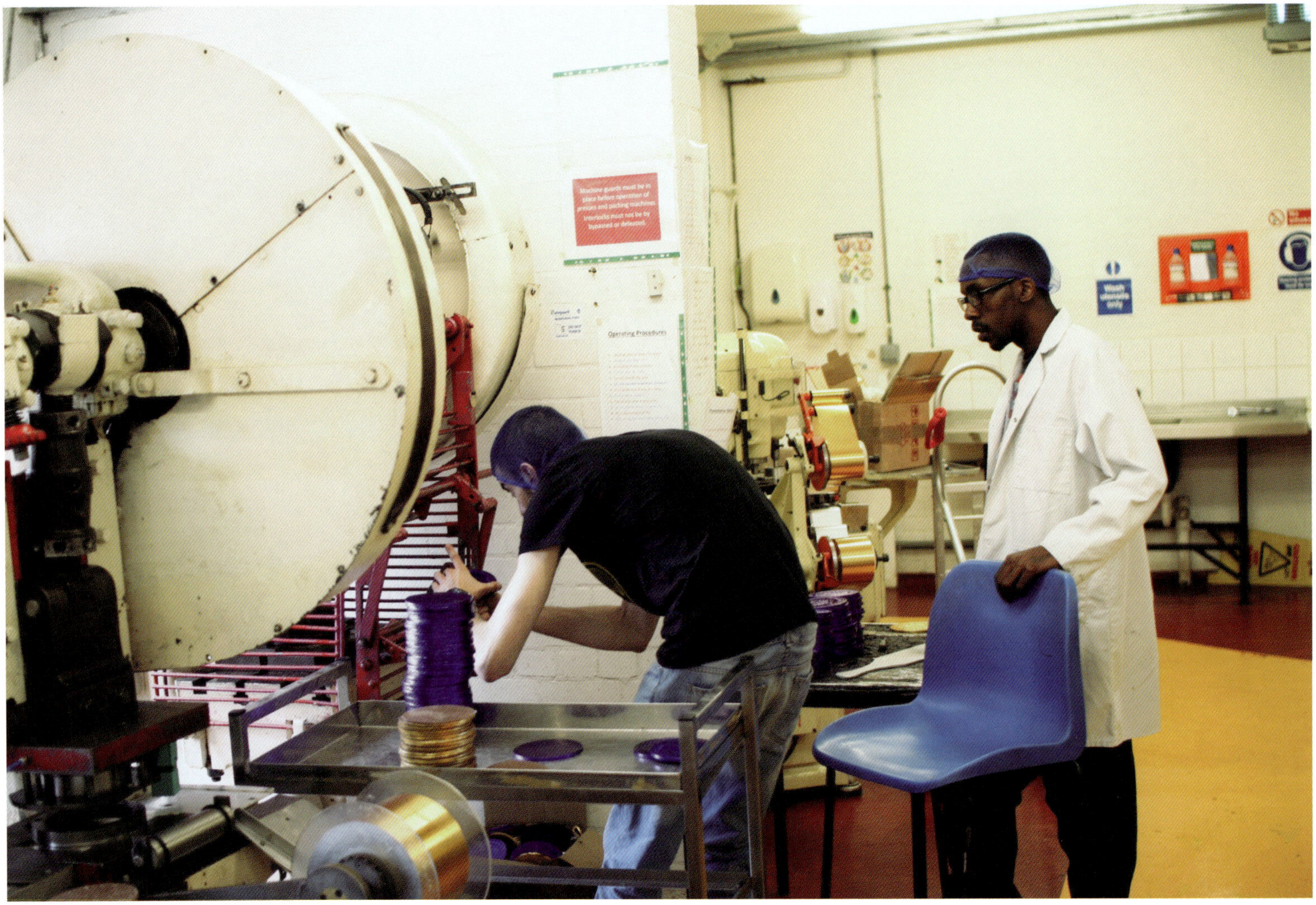

Chocolate foiling cutter press

poor that he decided that the only thing was to make them himself. In search of the necessary machine he went to the dedicated firm of machine makers, Dominici in Milan, but the huge cost of a new machine would have made the chocolate coins unduly expensive. Then hearing of a second-hand Dominici machine north of Milan, he fell in with some charming rogues who assured him they had just what he needed. They took him to their place in the countryside where a field like a graveyard was full of rusting machines, among them the second-hand Dominici machine he needed. He agreed to buy the machine if they could get it to work, and they asked for foil and chocolate blanks.

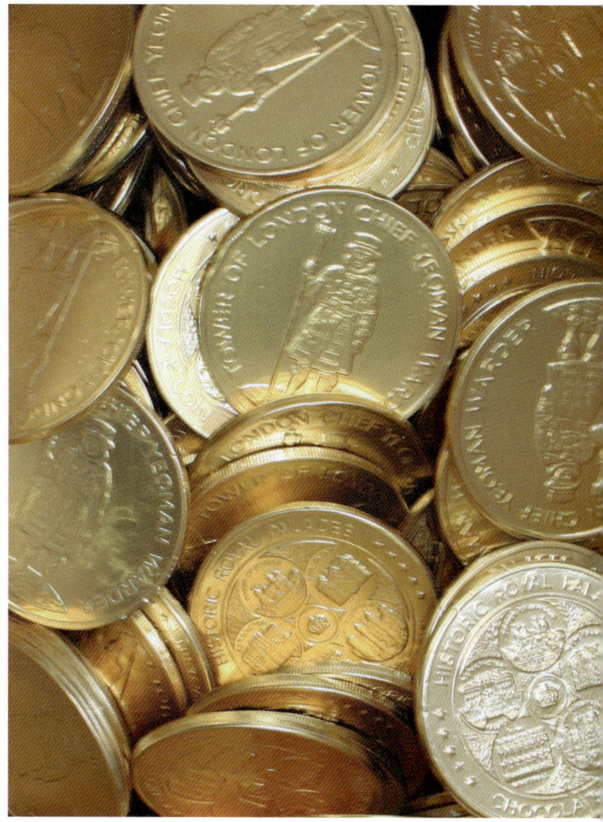

Chocolate coins

Meanwhile in Greenwich Raphael and Jane Poole had experimented with making chocolate blanks, as Jane recalled. 'Raphael said "let's try and make chocolate blanks to send to the people in Italy." I bought a block of chocolate and we went into the tiny kitchen to melt it down and see if we could make a chocolate coin. It was crazy with the two of us in the kitchen trying to mould it.' They discovered that they could indeed mould it. However, no news had come from Milan, where they had already sent foil and re-cut dies for the first chocolate coin orders. Raphael telephoned and was told to come the following week when the machine would be ready. When he arrived he found six people huddled over it, still trying to get it to work. The Italians deposited him in a restaurant in the backwoods and assured him that the machine would be working by the time he finished his lunch. Raphael waited and waited, then asked the Patrone to telephone because he needed to return to Milan to catch his plane. Unsurprisingly, the machine had failed to work. He finally he did a deal with the Italians to pay half price for the machine once it was shipped over to England. When he took it to be restored he was told that it was too old and worn to be worth spending money on. But, by coincidence, the restorers knew of another Dominici machine that was lying mothballed in Chile, designed for wrapping chewing gum. He bought that machine sight unseen and had it shipped over, and on it Tower Mint made their first batch of chocolate coins. Although they were late with the order, their clients were delighted with the results.

More orders started to come, for bespoke chocolate coins in different sizes. Raphael took his samples to the European Confectionery Show in Cologne. There he met two Belgians who knew of half a dozen Dominici machines belonging to a German company that was closing down and selling all its machinery at once. Raphael took a chance, and on the spot wrote an enormous cheque for all their machines. He appointed a new Managing Director, Rodney Sugden, who had come from the food industry, and was well placed to handle the new chocolate section of the minting business. Commemorative dies were re-cut to accommodate the soft material, and high quality chocolate blanks were bought in from Belgium. Foil in gold, silver and other metallic colours was used to wrap the blanks and die stamp them, embossing the image on both sides of the coin as well as on the chocolate inside. They were then bagged in gold string bags for sale at many different

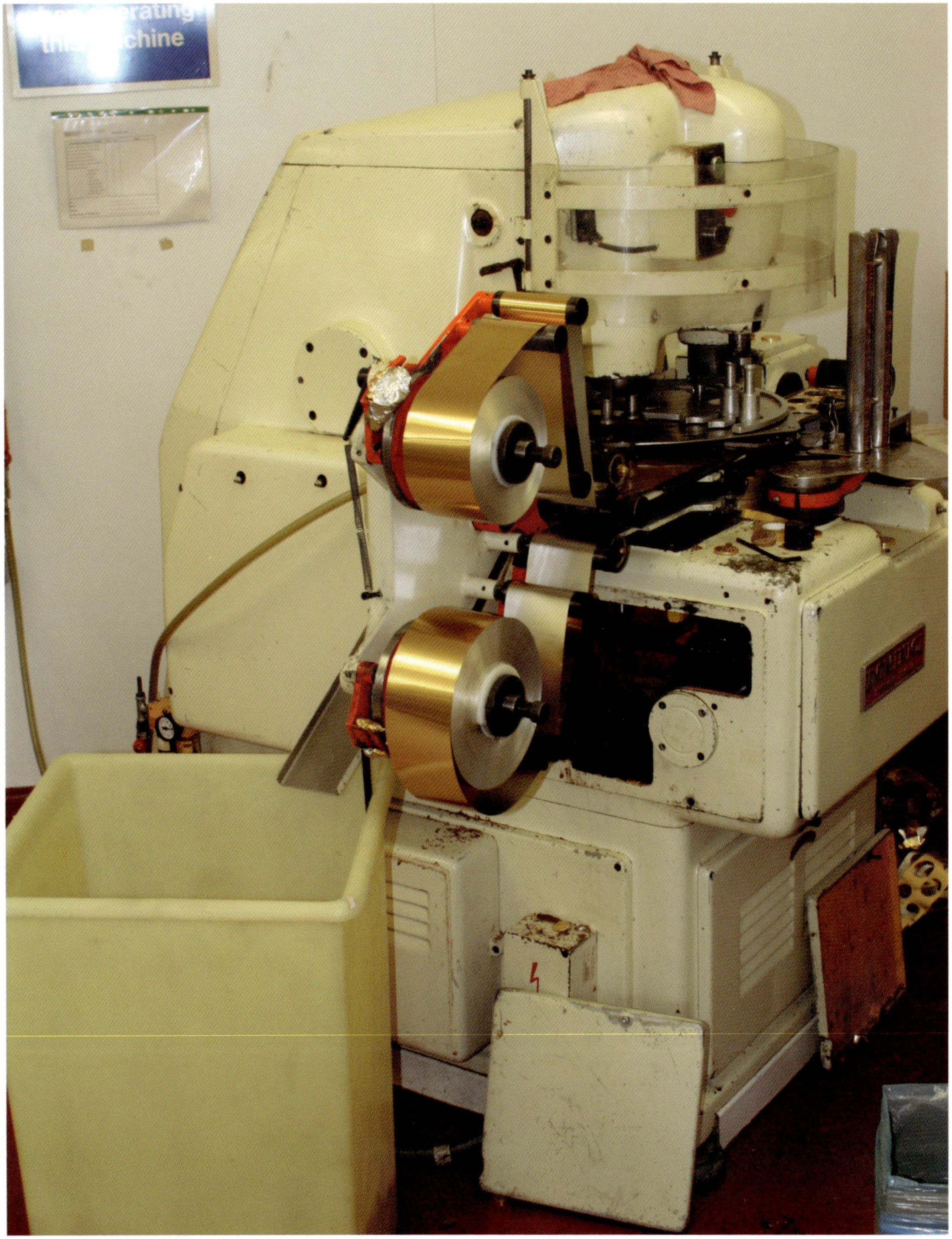

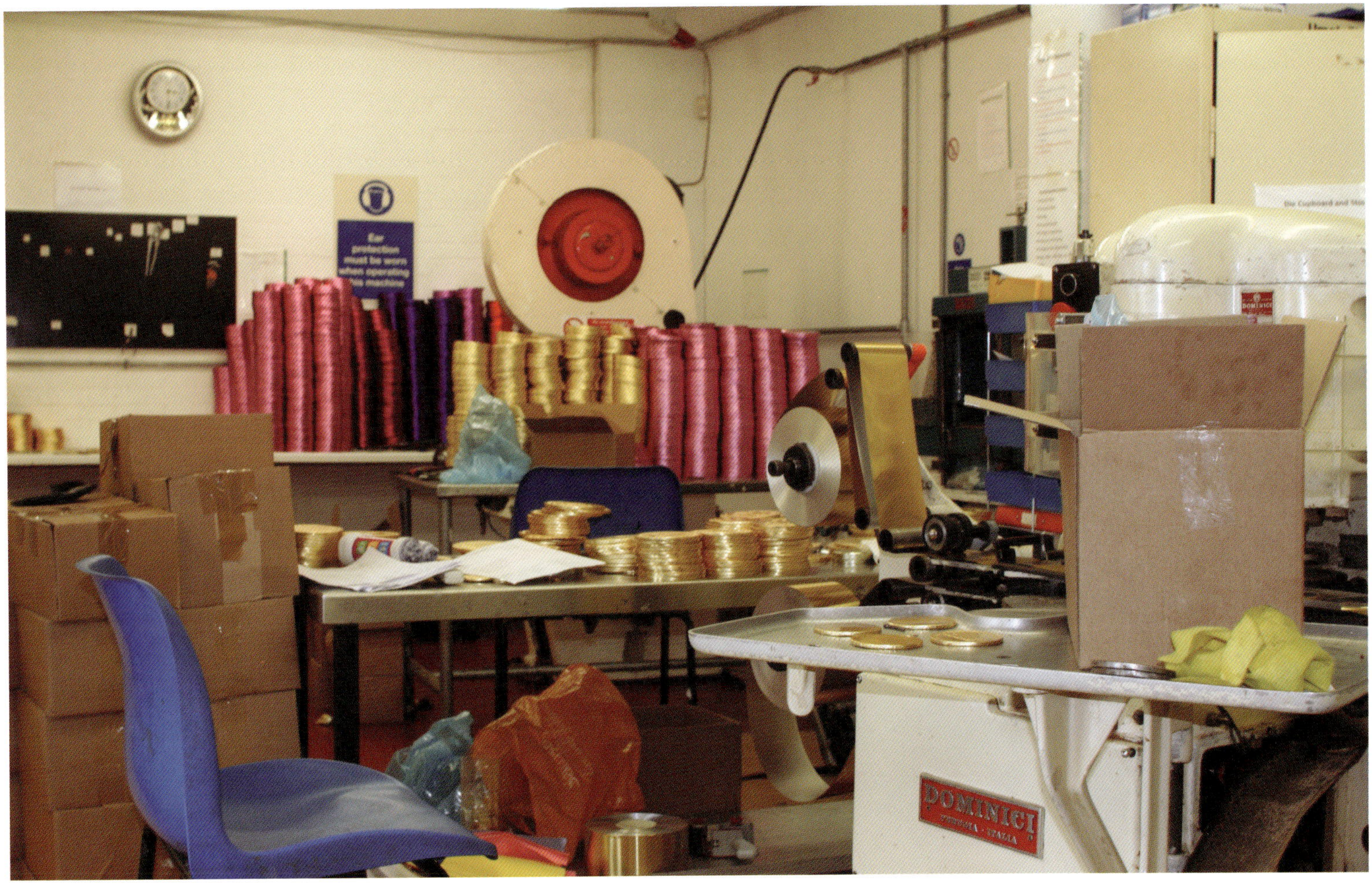

Foiled chocolate blanks before embossing

venues, among them Buckingham Palace, Windsor Castle and Harrods. Heritage Chocolates, a company launched within a company, was, as Jane Poole emphasised, an instant success, 'covering the time over the Christmas period when we are not so busy.'

After Tower Mint had operated for twenty-five years in Greenwich, the owner of the flour mill died and his wife decided to sell the building. Raphael was forced to look for new premises, and he found them near to his old stamping ground of Camberwell. Lambeth County Council were auctioning an industrial estate with twenty-one units built for craft workers in South East London. He was able to buy them cheaply because they were in a dreadful state. The windows were made of perspex and the outside walls were lined with asbestos. Considerable renovation was needed to make them fit for their new purpose.

Opposite: Dominici embossing press

Chocolate foil

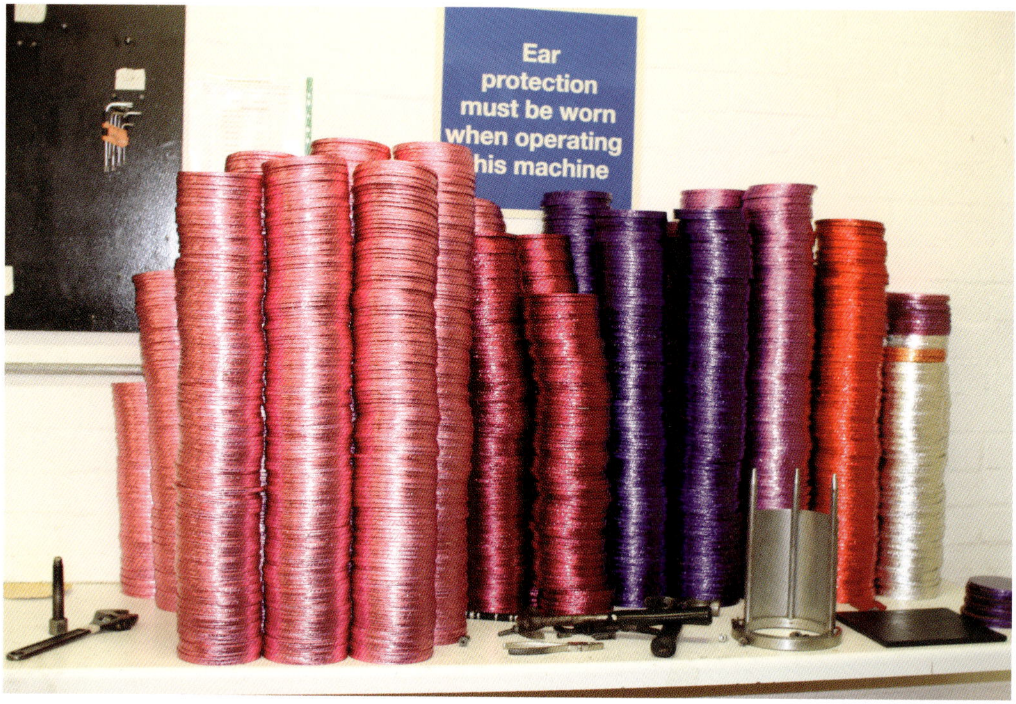

The move in 1999 from Greenwich to Camberwell was brilliantly handled by Rodney Sugden. As Jane Poole recalled, 'it was quite a big move for us. I lived in Greenwich and used to go home for lunch. Raphael came in one day and shocked us by saying "I have purchased this property in Camberwell." But despite the travelling involved a lot of the staff stayed on. I commute from Greenwich – it's a horrid commute, a tiring journey with the traffic – but I want to stay. It's exciting – every day is different at Tower Mint. There is always a project on the go.' [5]

After forty years Tower Mint is thriving, with a permanent staff of thirty. Besides the chocolate, hygienically separated from the medals and coins, it produces a huge array of medals for museums and tourist attractions, companies, schools, youth organisations, confirmation, communion, sports and social clubs, with novelty medals commemorating particular events such as The World War I Remembrance Medal or the medal to mark the birth of the Queen's Great-Grandson Prince George. Legal tender, including coinage for Gibraltar, Australia, Ghana, Hong Kong, Andorra and Tuvalu, is a staple of the business. After April 2017 this included the Isle of Man. As Jane Poole stressed, 'the pressure is on all the time. We have customers with marketing plans and we have to meet their deadlines.'

Opposite: Clockwise from top left:
Chocolate coins;
Chocolate coins;
Chocolate foil;
Chocolate room

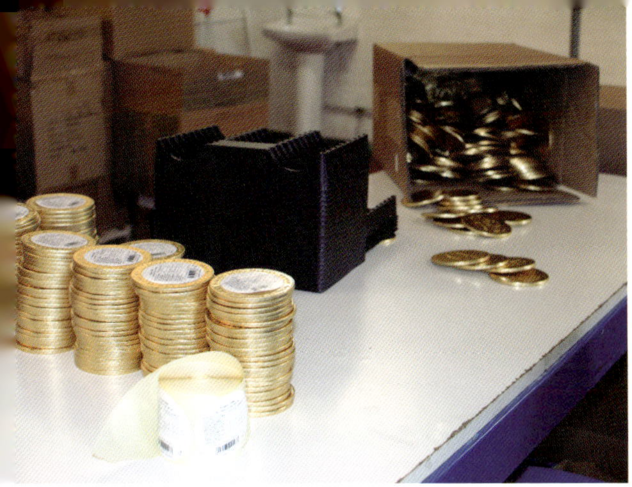

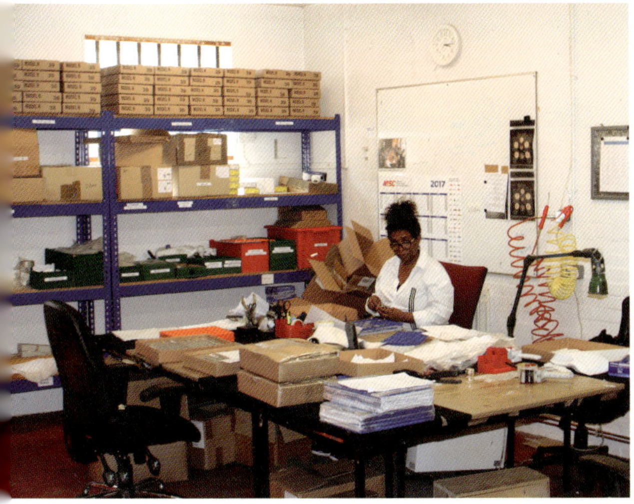

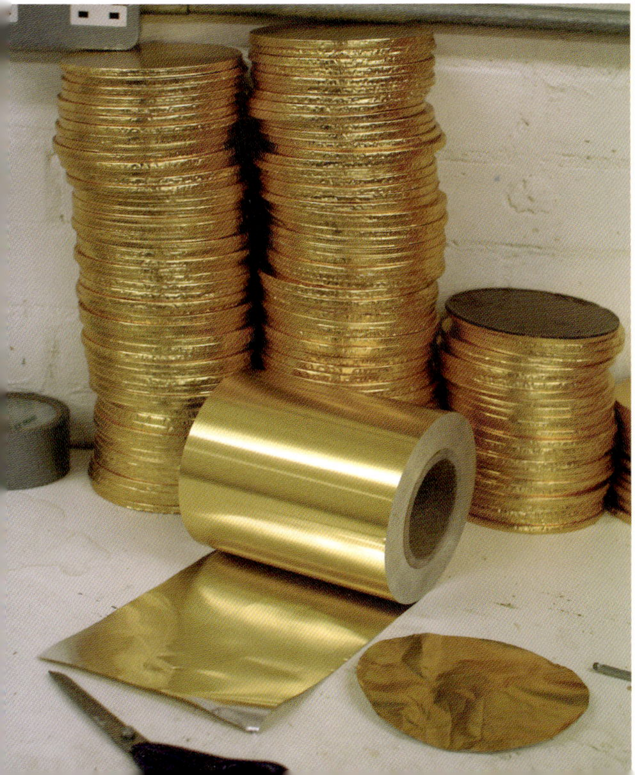

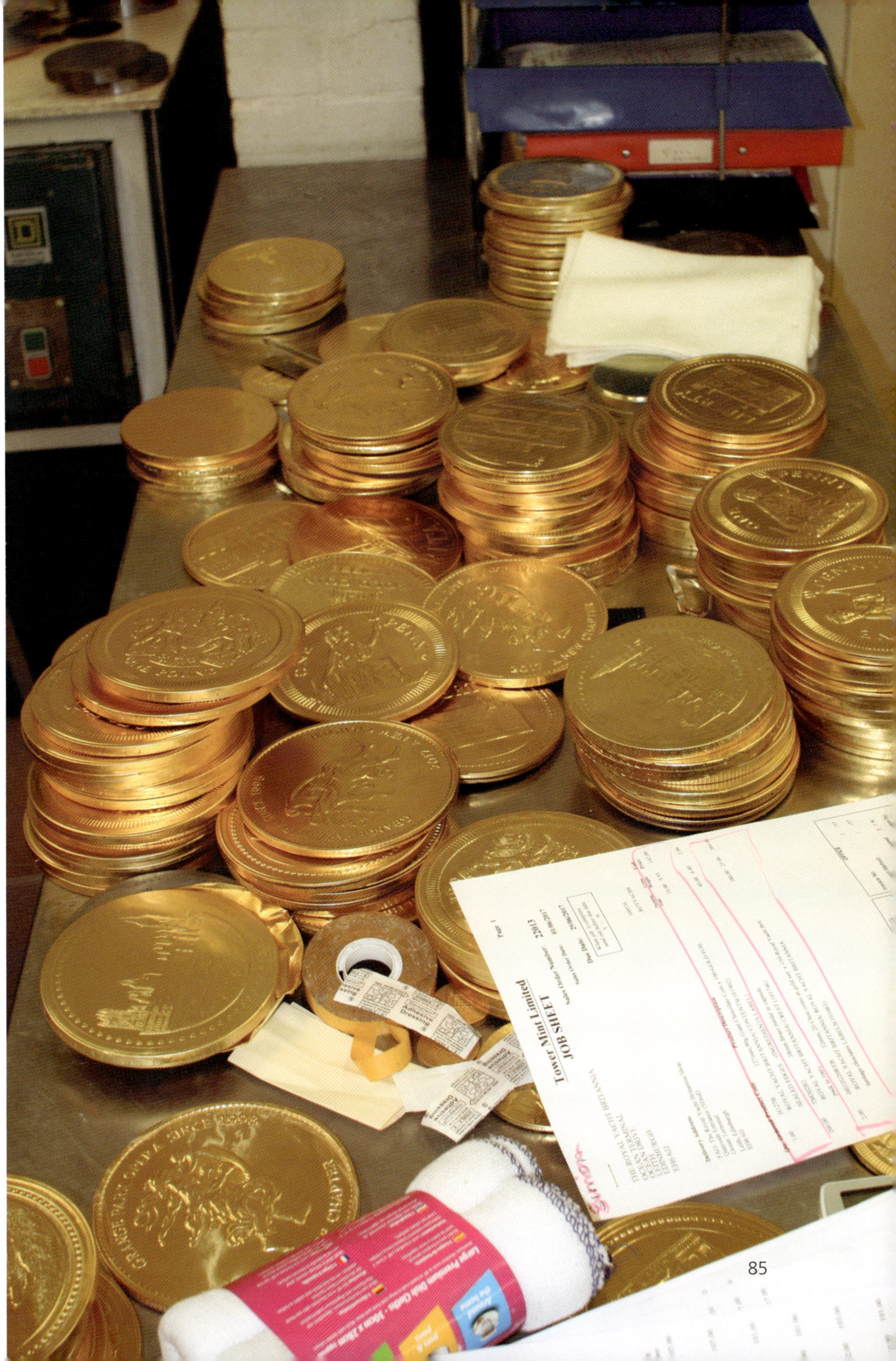
Tower Mint Limited
JOB SHEET

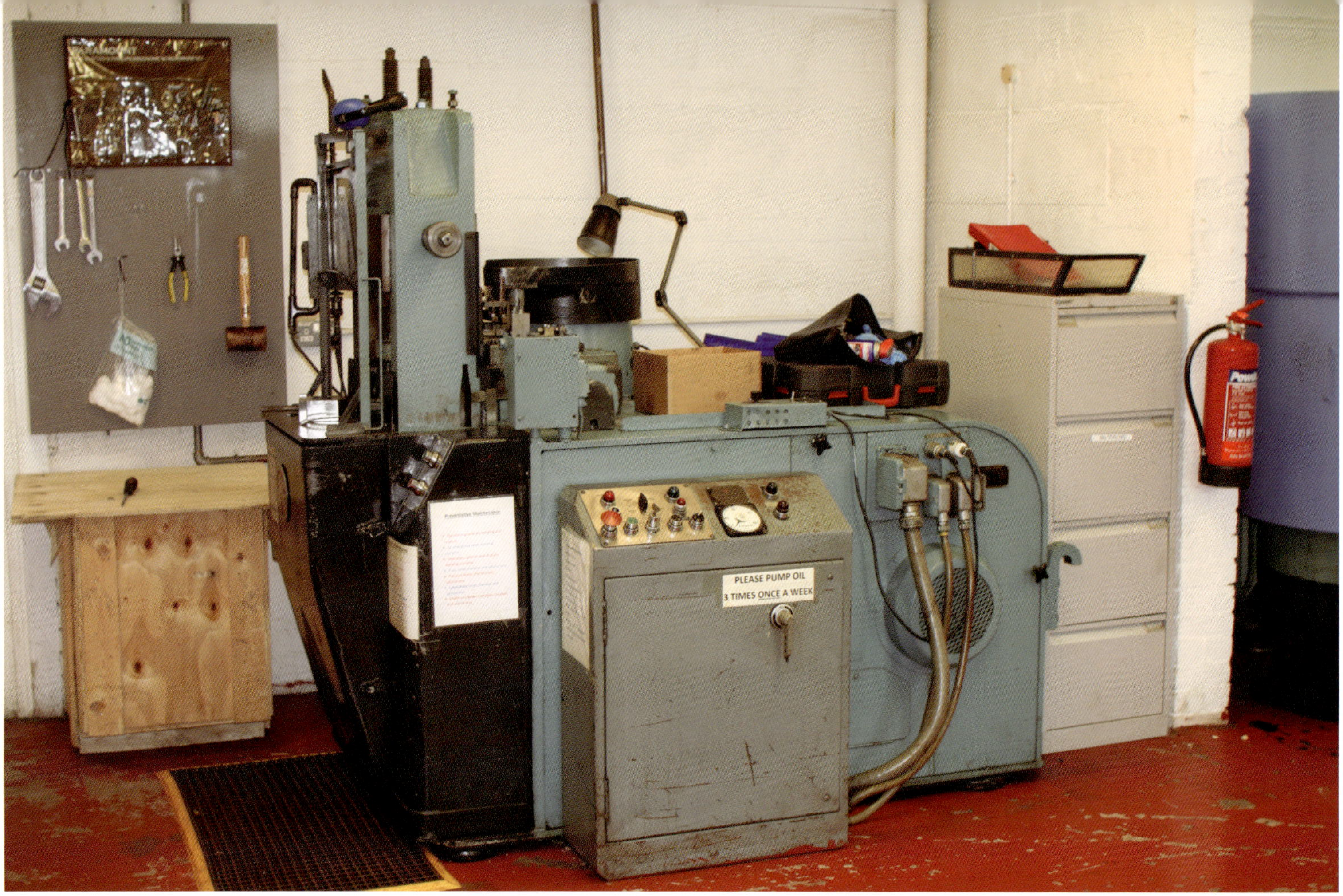

Above: The automatic press

Right: Blanks ready to insert into the automatic press

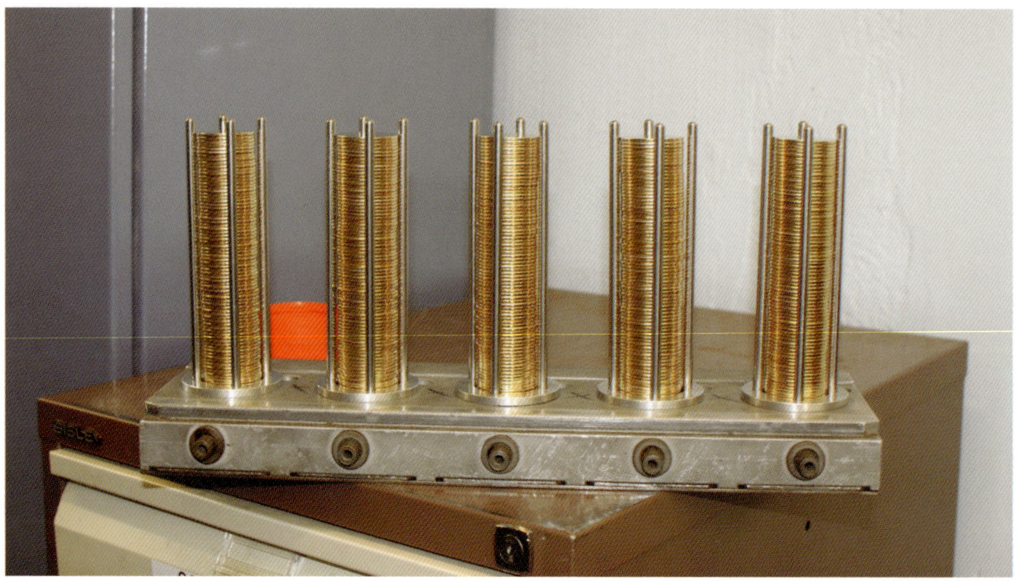

Recently Tower Mint has added another string to its bow by entering the field of Numismatics. This is a very active field, and Tower Mint now takes a stand at several of the international conferences. Collectors of coins from all over the world attend these annual conferences, of which the oldest and largest is hosted by the American Numismatic Association. The ANA was founded in 1891 to advance the knowledge of numismatics along educational, historical, and scientific lines, as well as to promote interest in coin collecting as a hobby. It has a world-wide membership of about 24,000, and in 1967 opened a purpose-built building to house its national headquarters in Colorado Springs.

Kay 360 1070s hand fed proof press

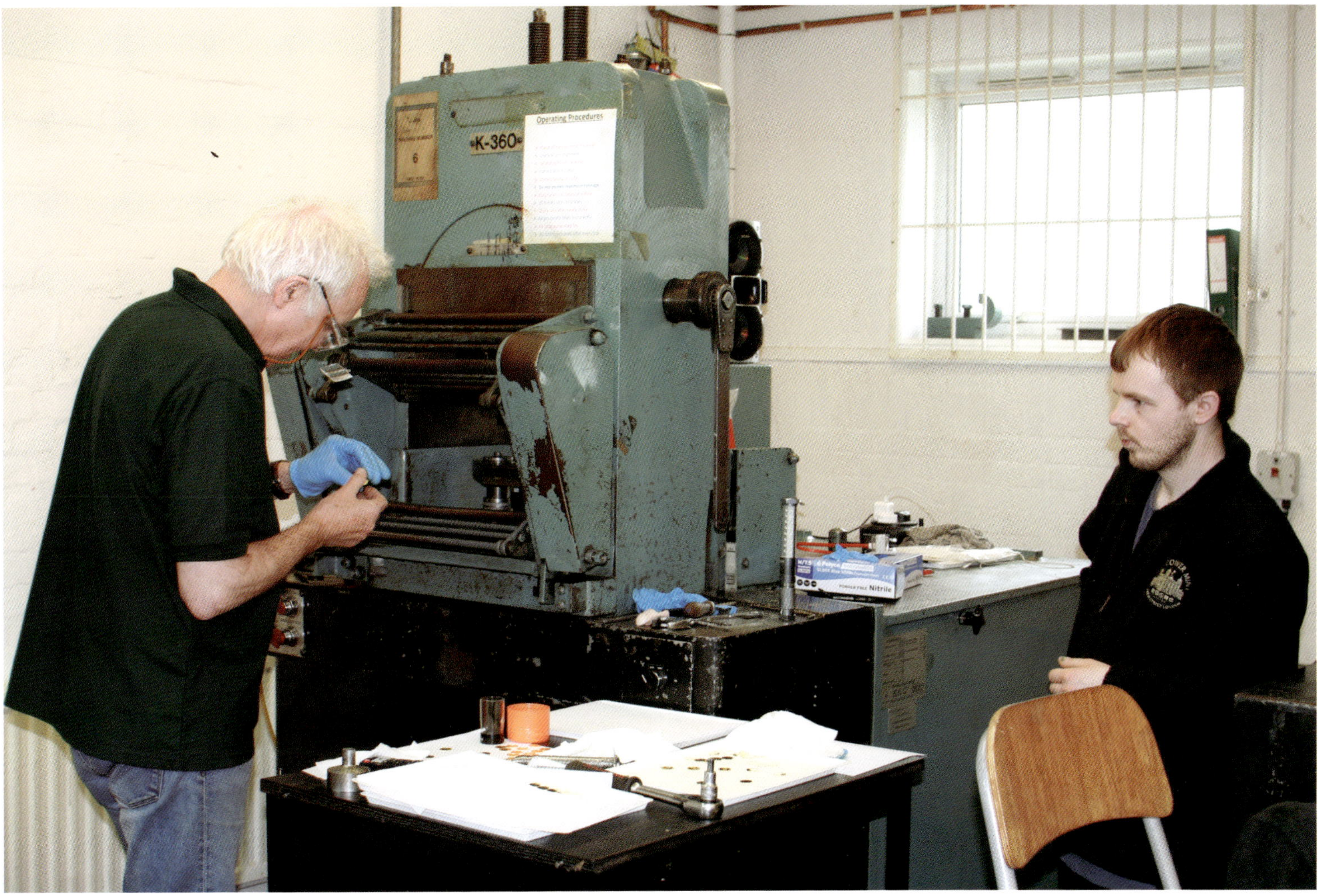

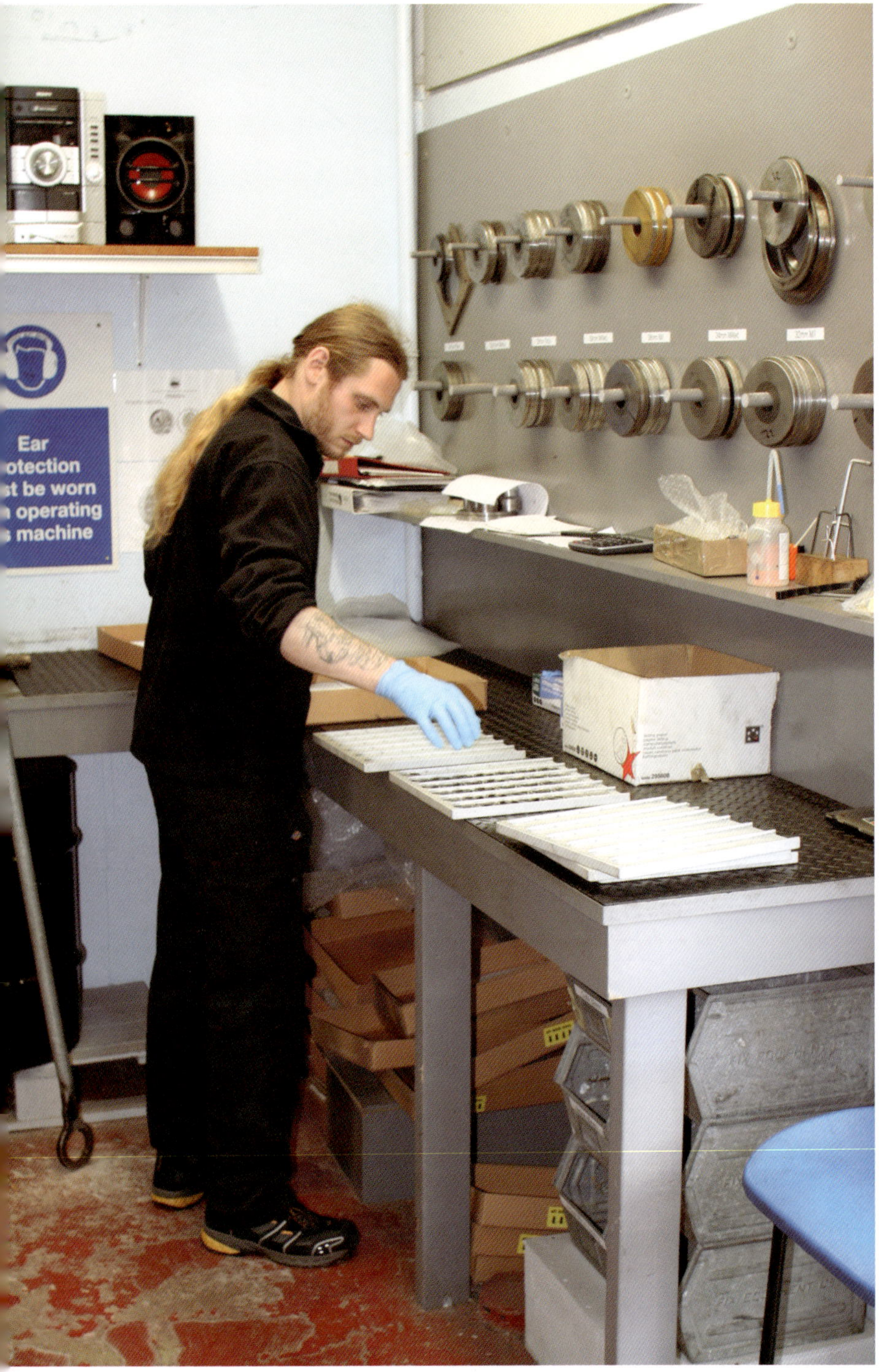
Ear
otection
st be worn
n operating
s machine

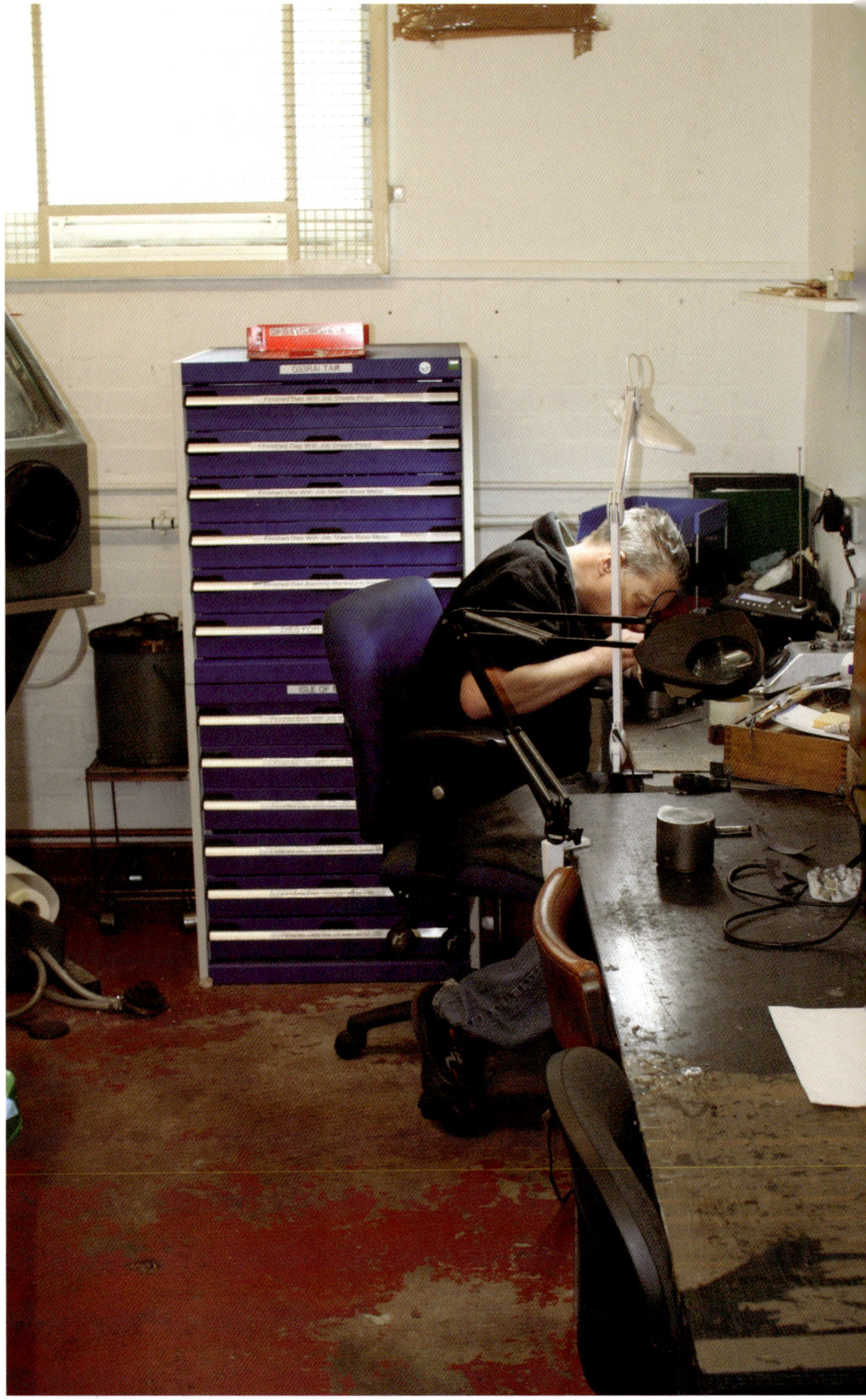

At the same time new links with the Samlerhuset Group have vastly increased Tower Mint's marketing ability. Samlerhuset, founded in 1994, is a Norwegian-owned mail order company with subsidiaries in sixteen countries, including the UK. It is part-owner of the Berlin coin fair and of the Norwegian Mint, producer of Nobel Prize medals as well as legal tender for Norway. Its key activity is the direct marketing of coins, medals, and other collectibles to national markets. Among its many activities, it was awarded contracts for the Fifa World Cup and the Olympic Games in Beijing and London.

With its core business in Britain and its expanding links overseas, Raphael's unexpected brainchild has become a major player in its field. In its forty years of existence Tower Mint has grown from a single off-the-cuff idea to its present dynamic enterprise.

Opposite left: Automatic press room, removing coins from press trays

Right: Die polishing

Lathe turning dies to size

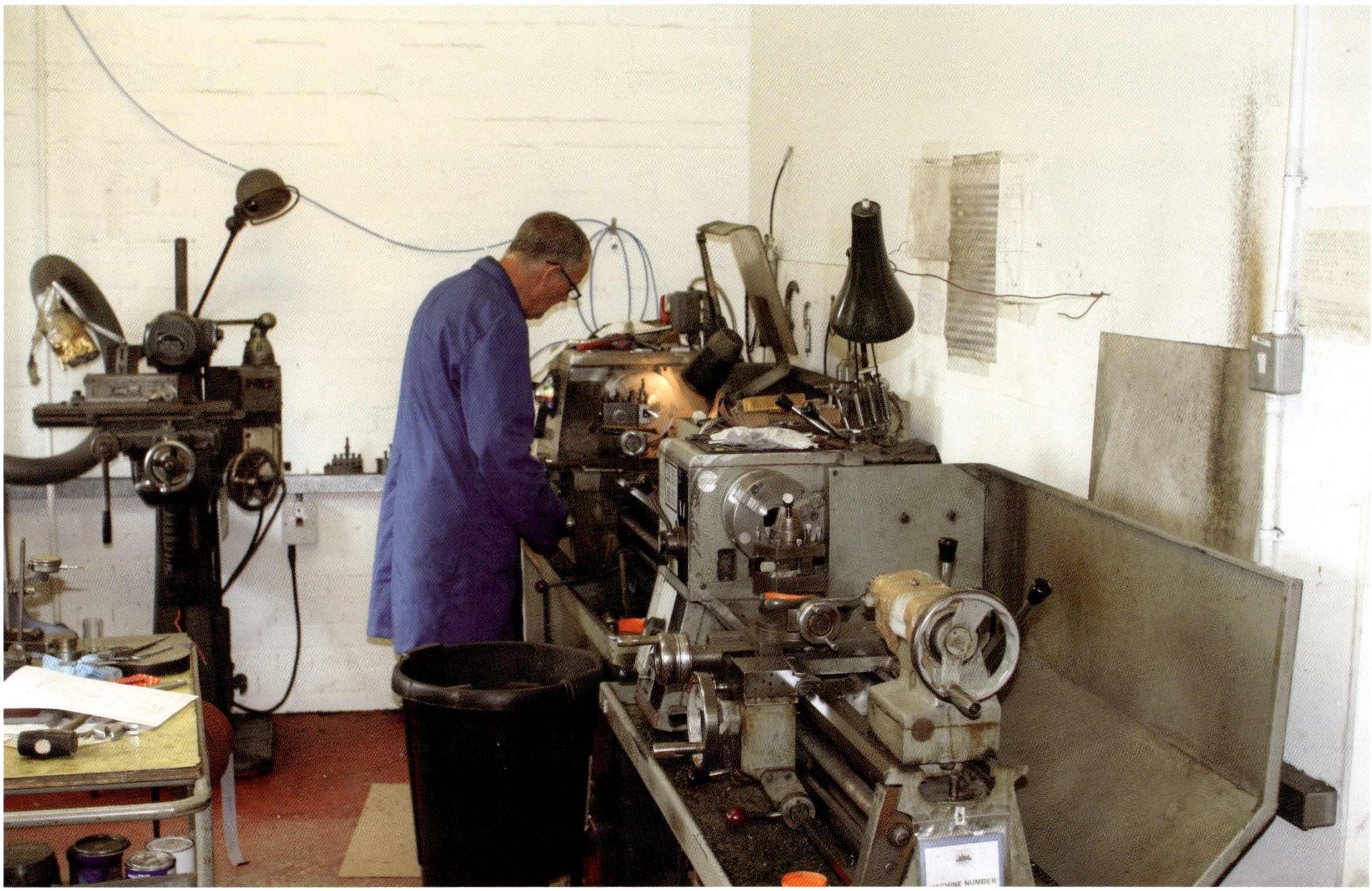

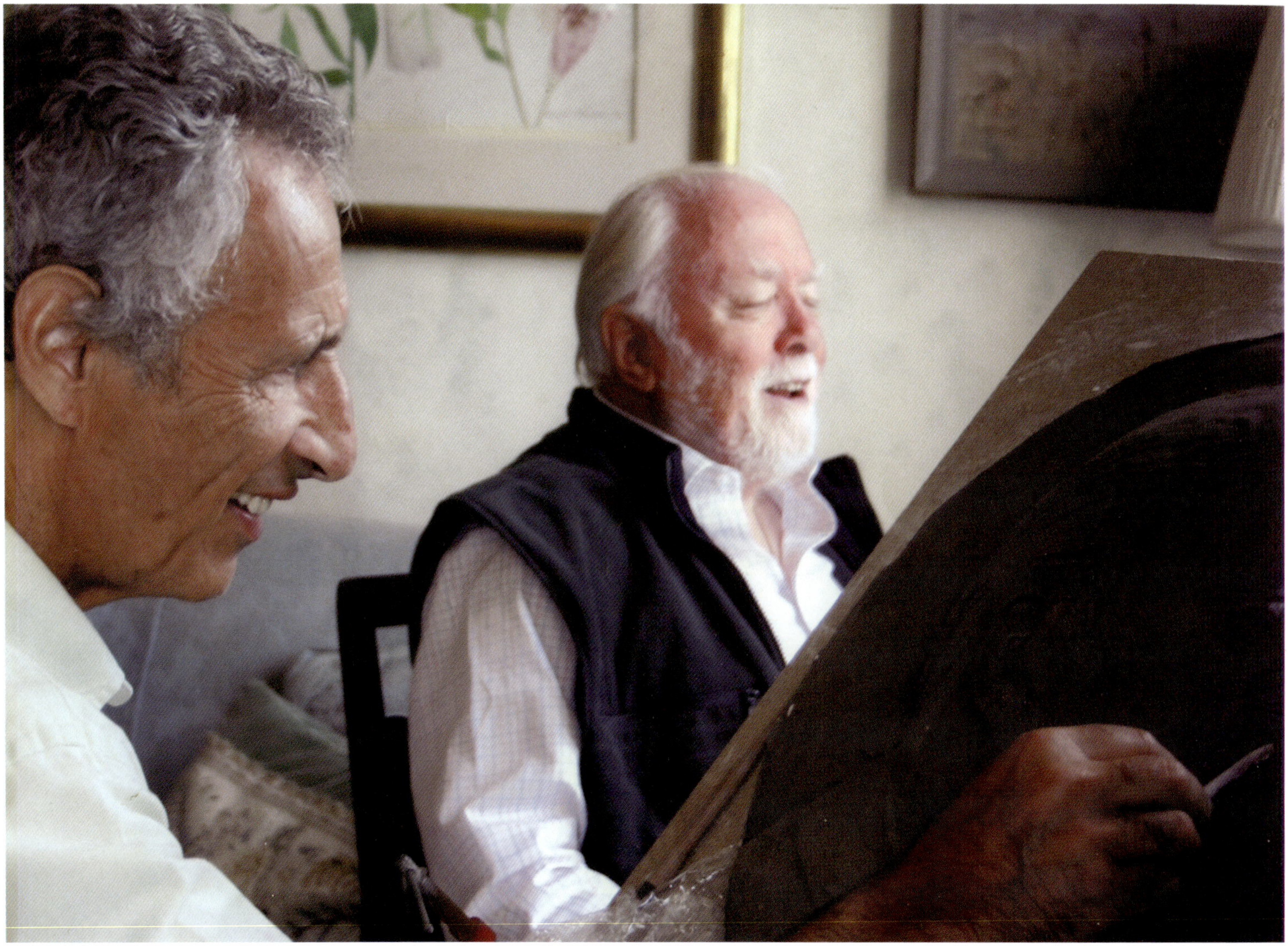

Raphael with Richard Attenborough

Chapter 7

Commissions with Consequences

AT THE SAME time as he was running Tower Mint, Raphael continued to undertake private commissions. As he declared, 'I have never refused a commission'. While still a student at Camberwell he had put an advertisement in the Times: 'Young sculptor seeks portrait commissions'. This produced good results, among them a portrait of the eminent biblical scholar Dr Hugh J. Schonfield, modelled by Raphael in Schonfield's house in Hyde Park Square. Further commissions included portraits of the hairdresser Vidal Sassoon, the photographers David Bailey and Patrick Lichfield, the footballer Bobby Moore, the broadcaster Michael Parkinson, and the actors Joan Collins and Richard Attenborough. All were sculpted either in their homes or at their place of work. Where possible Raphael preferred to model his subjects in their own homes, while chatting to relax both his sitter and himself. 'The portraits that have worked best have been when I was so engaged that I didn't know I was working.' He was also commissioned to make a bronze bust of Sir Thomas Beecham for the Carnegie Hall in New York. Beecham was the first Englishman to take the Royal Philharmonic Orchestra to America, where the bust was to be installed. Raphael attended the unveiling at a ceremony in Carnegie Hall, carrying with him a signed letter from the Queen Mother. For a church in New Malden he carried out a Madonna and Child in bronze. Another Madonna and Child for Brentwood Cathedral was sculpted in cement, a material he enjoyed. 'I like cement because it can be more sympathetic to the environment. The sculpture is made in clay, a waste-mould is made and filled with cement, then the mould is chipped out to leave the cement sculpture.'

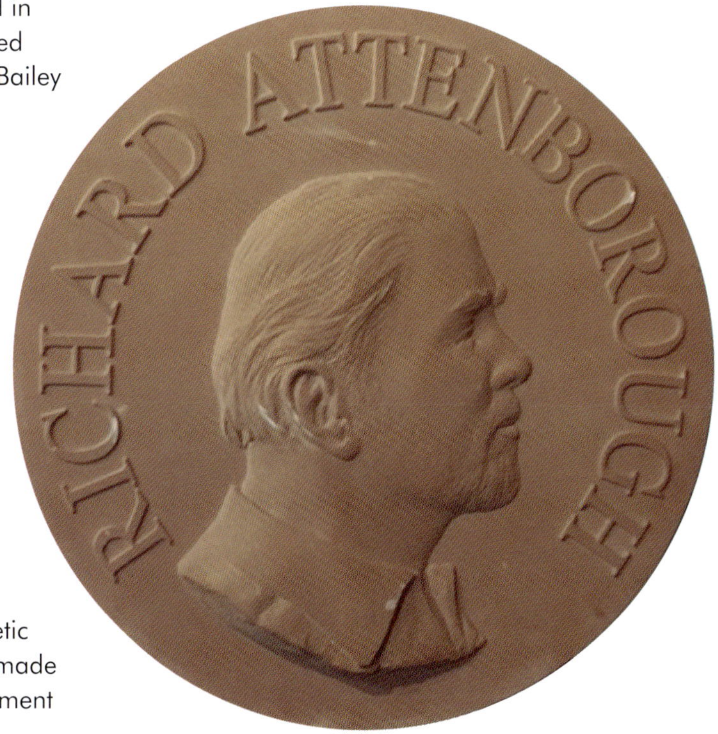

Bas relief of Richard Attenborough for Garrick Club

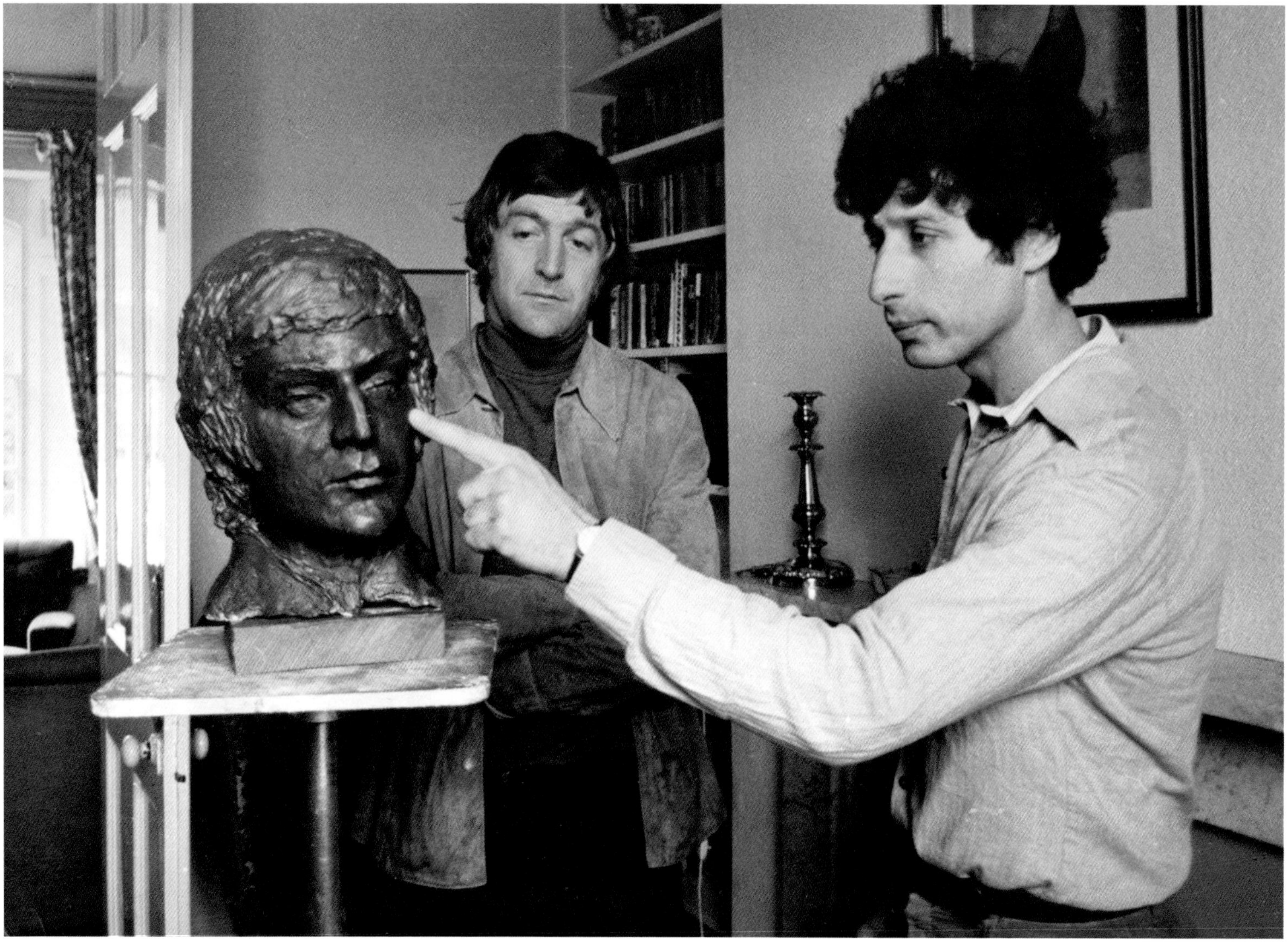

Raphael with Michael Parkinson, 1970

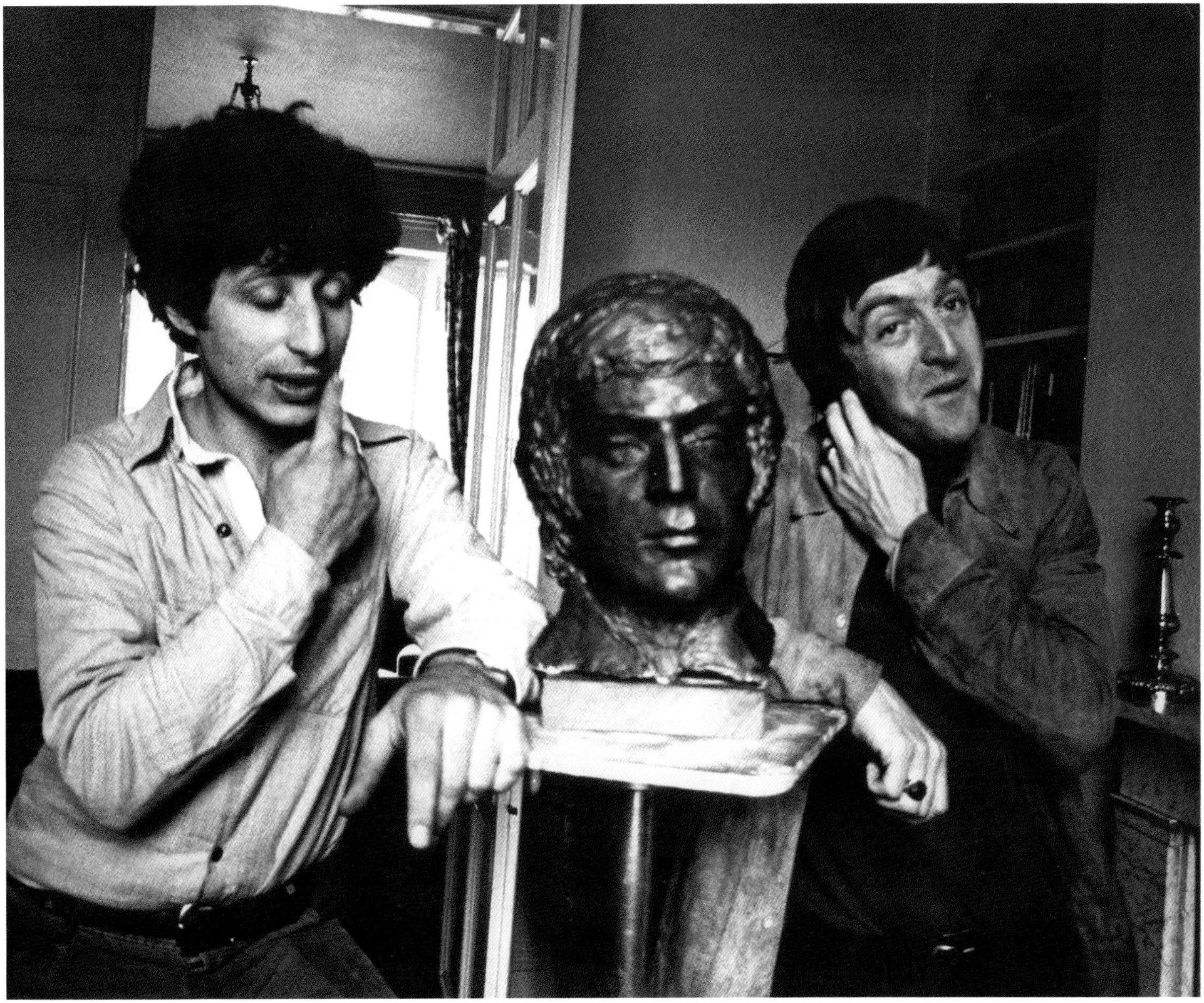

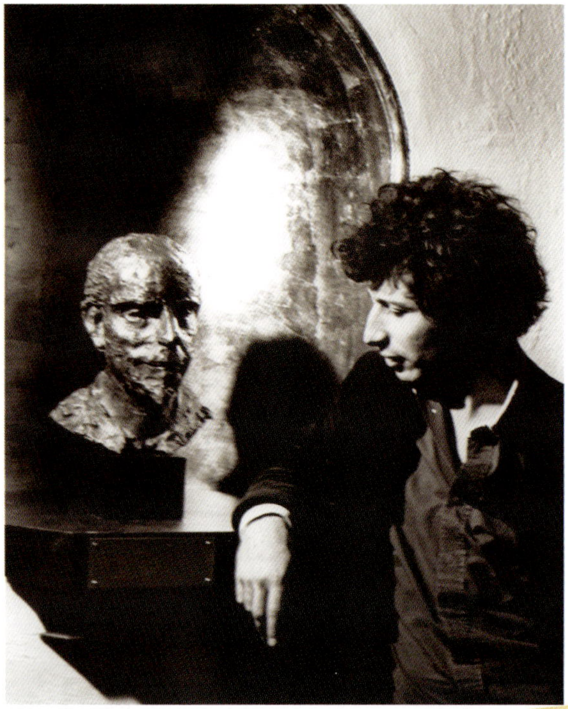

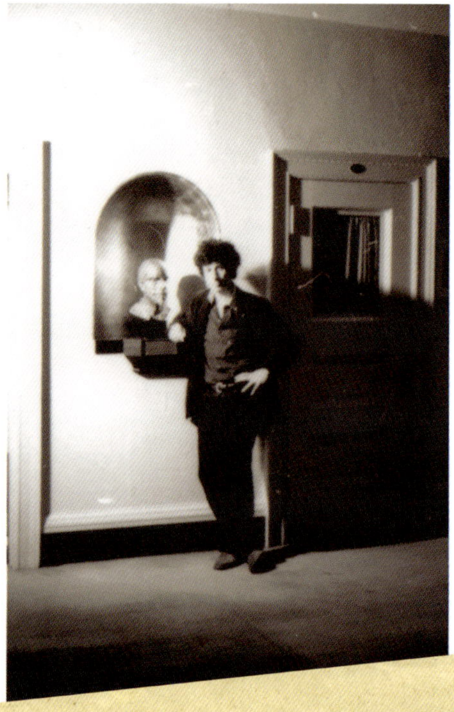

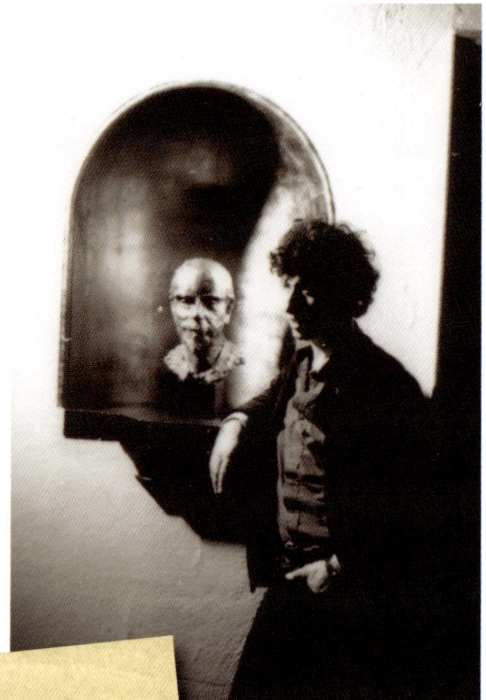

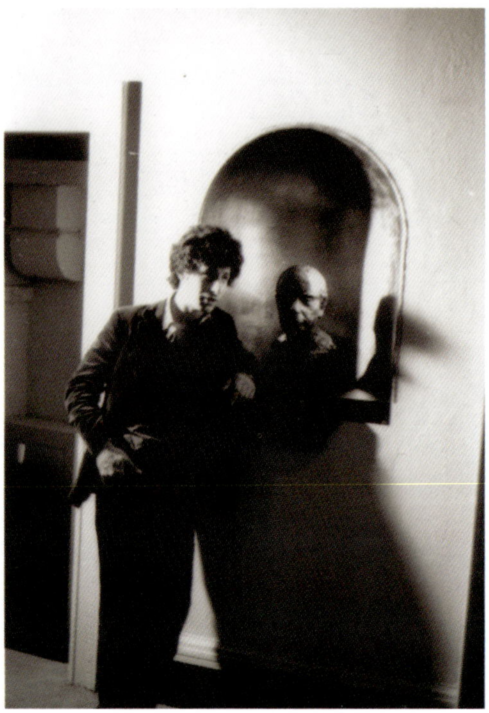

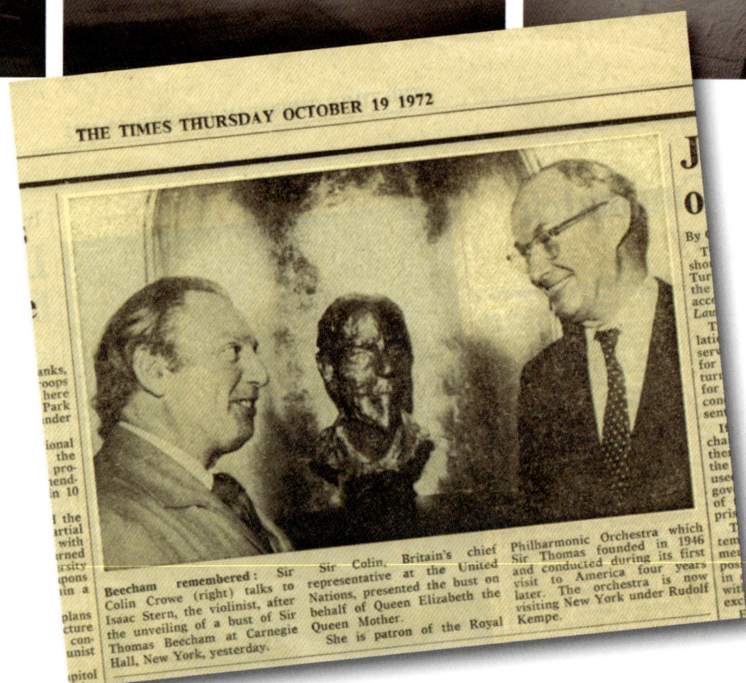

THE TIMES THURSDAY OCTOBER 19 1972

Beecham remembered: Sir Colin Crowe (right) talks to Isaac Stern, the violinist, after the unveiling of a bust of Sir Thomas Beecham at Carnegie Hall, New York, yesterday.

Sir Colin, Britain's chief representative at the United Nations, presented the bust on behalf of Queen Elizabeth the Queen Mother.

She is patron of the Royal Philharmonic Orchestra which Sir Thomas founded in 1946 and conducted during its first visit to America four years later. The orchestra is now visiting New York under Rudolf Kempe.

Sir Thomas Beecham at Carnegie Hall

In 1982 a momentous opportunity came his way. Raphael was invited, with seventeen other artists, to enter a national competition staged by the Royal Mint Advisory Committee on the Design of Coins, Medals, Seals and Decorations. The committee, established in 1922 with its current President HRH Prince Philip the Duke of Edinburgh, was looking for a new image of the Queen to replace Arnold Machin's outdated portrait that had been used on all UK currency since 1968. From among thirty-eight submissions it was Raphael's designs that were chosen – one for coins in general circulation and one for commemorative issues. These designs were current, from 1985 until 1997, on the coinage of other Commonwealth countries, including Australia, Gibraltar and Hong Kong, and are still in use today. His local newspaper, The Richmond and Twickenham Times, picked up the story. 'Artist Raphael Maklouf, who lives in Richmond, has won himself the commission of a lifetime. From January we will see his work every time we fish the change from our pockets, for he has re-designed the Queen's head which appears on every one of them.' [1]

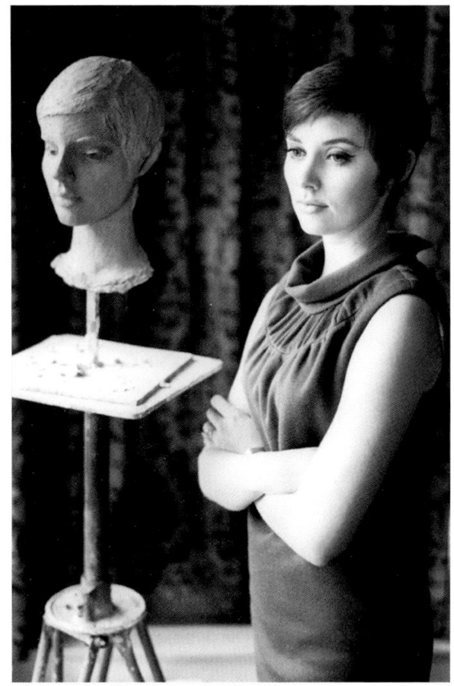

Beverly Sassoon

All the invited artists had been given a photograph of the Queen by Lord Snowdon from which to work. Raphael began designing his image from the photograph, but was dissatisfied with it. Although his designs had already been singled out, he requested, and was granted, a sitting with the Queen at Buckingham Palace. The *Daily Telegraph* quoted him as saying 'I told the Queen at a recent Garden Party that I did not think the photographs were very good. The Queen laughed and said "I will tell Lord Snowdon that". [2] With two sittings at Buckingham Palace Raphael was able to model the Queen in the round, and he used his portrait to improve his designs. As he testified, 'the Queen was incredibly warm and friendly... and I have tried to show that in my portrait... You don't need wrinkles to show age. Even a child could see that the skin and the jawline are those of an older person.' [3] All the daily newspapers reported the story of Raphael's portrait. Under a large photograph of him with his bronze the *Daily Mail* quoted him as saying 'The Queen gave me two sittings. I went into the yellow drawing room at Buckingham Palace with a footman carrying my bag of clay... The Queen was a wonderful sitter. She was relaxed and that communicated itself to me. But she was terribly busy... Obviously I am very proud. It's the height of a sculptor's ambition to create something that will last. When someone asks me what sort of work I do, I will be able to pull a handful of change from my pocket and show them.'[4]

In response to the criticism that the Queen's portrait did not look as old as her years, Raphael stressed that he was portraying a symbol, not simply a person. The Queen certainly approved, and a letter came from Buckingham Palace thanking Raphael for the gift of his bronze bust. In the *Daily Star* Andrew Morton wrote 'The Queen gets a new more mature look on Britain's coins next year. She is said to be delighted with the change, the first in 20 years. Yesterday sculptor Raphael Maklouf, who designed the effigy, said "It shows a happy, more mature Queen..." and added "It reveals her inner

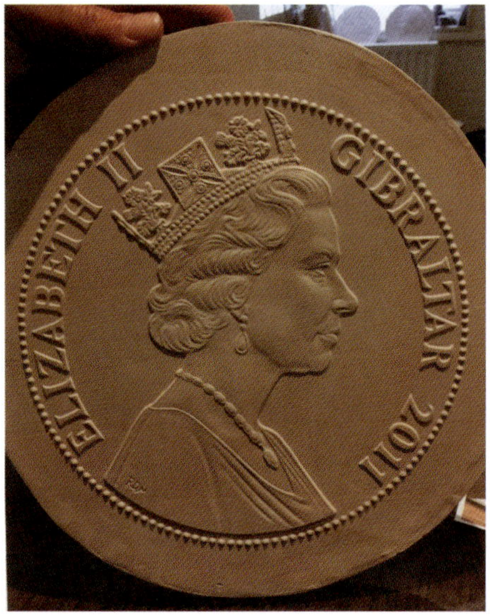

Plaster for Gibraltar coins

character and humanity. I don't think it is a severe look but she does seem to have more authority. Remember, I was designing a symbol, not a photograph..."' [5]

The *New York Times* ran a lengthy article about the whole project, entitled A New Coinage Portrait. 'At the outset of the contest, the mint had given each entrant the same photograph of the Queen: a side view taken by Lord Snowdon. Mr Maklouf studied other photos and took every opportunity to see her in person. For the most part, this involved catching glimpses of the Queen as she attended or drove to various state events. But on one occasion, Mr Maklouf received an invitation to a royal garden party at Buckingham Palace. That afternoon, he returned to his studio and sculptured a rough bust in clay. From that he produced and submitted models for four coin reliefs. "Some things come easily, others don't" the artist later remarked. "That day it just happened. It just gelled." Following his selection to sculpture the new effigy, Mr Maklouf requested and received a sitting by the Queen.' [6]

For the design of the coinage there was a specific brief, in which both history and protocol were involved. As the Royal Mint's bulletin pointed out, 'Collectors will notice at once that the Queen continues to be shown facing right. King George VI faced to the left and in accordance with a tradition which can be traced back to the seventeenth century whereby successive monarchs face in alternate directions on the coinage The Queen faces to the right. Some have claimed to see the origins of this tradition in the desire of Charles II to turn his back on Oliver Cromwell. But if any practical or political reason ever existed it has long been forgotten.' [7] Raphael's effigy for the circulating coins showed the Queen wearing the Royal Diadem used for the State Opening of Parliament together with a necklace and earrings, her head 'couped' (cut off at the neck), with his own initials, RDM, in tiny letters at the base of the neck. These letters are just visible through a magnifying glass. Raphael felt it important to add the D for David so that the RM might not be misconstrued as representing the Royal Mint. For the large commemorative coins parts of the Queen's shoulders were included in his design. The *Daily Express* noted that Raphael's effigy was only the third on British coinage since the Queen was crowned in 1953, and that she was said to be 'delighted' with the result. 'In the first year of minting no less than 788 million new-style coins will be pressed and issued by the Royal Mint. Their combined face value will be at least £220 million'. [8]

Raphael was present when the new coins were formally approved at Goldsmith's Hall at the conclusion of the Trian of the Pyx. The Trial of the Pyx, a ceremony dating back to the twelfth century, is the procedure in the UK for ensuring that newly minted coins conform to required standards. Over the centuries the ceremony has remained essentially the same: a trial presided over by a judge with an expert jury of assayers from the Worshipful Company of Goldsmiths. The Pyx is the boxwood chest in which coins are placed for presentation to the jury.

Opposite: Raphael working on the Queen's head

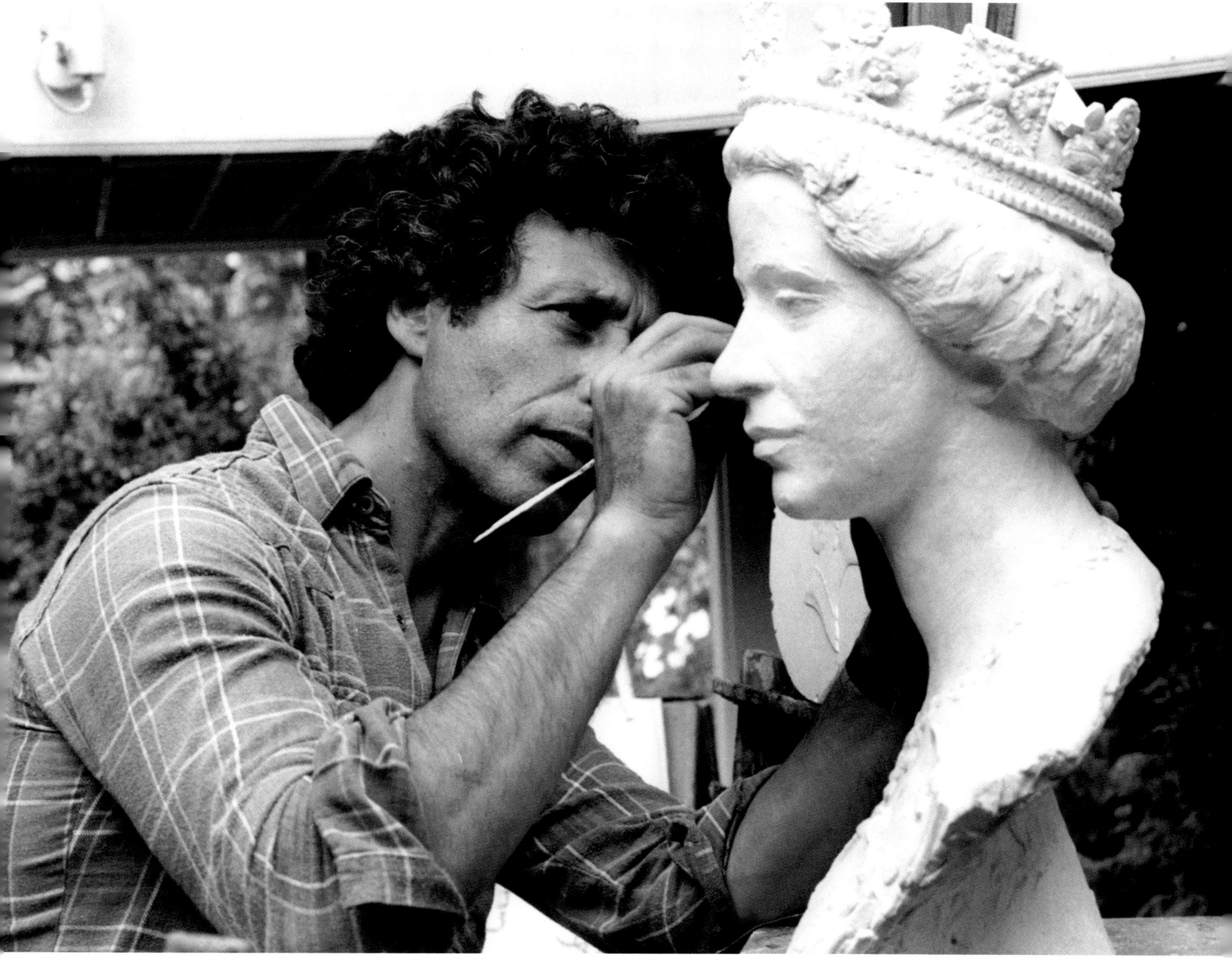

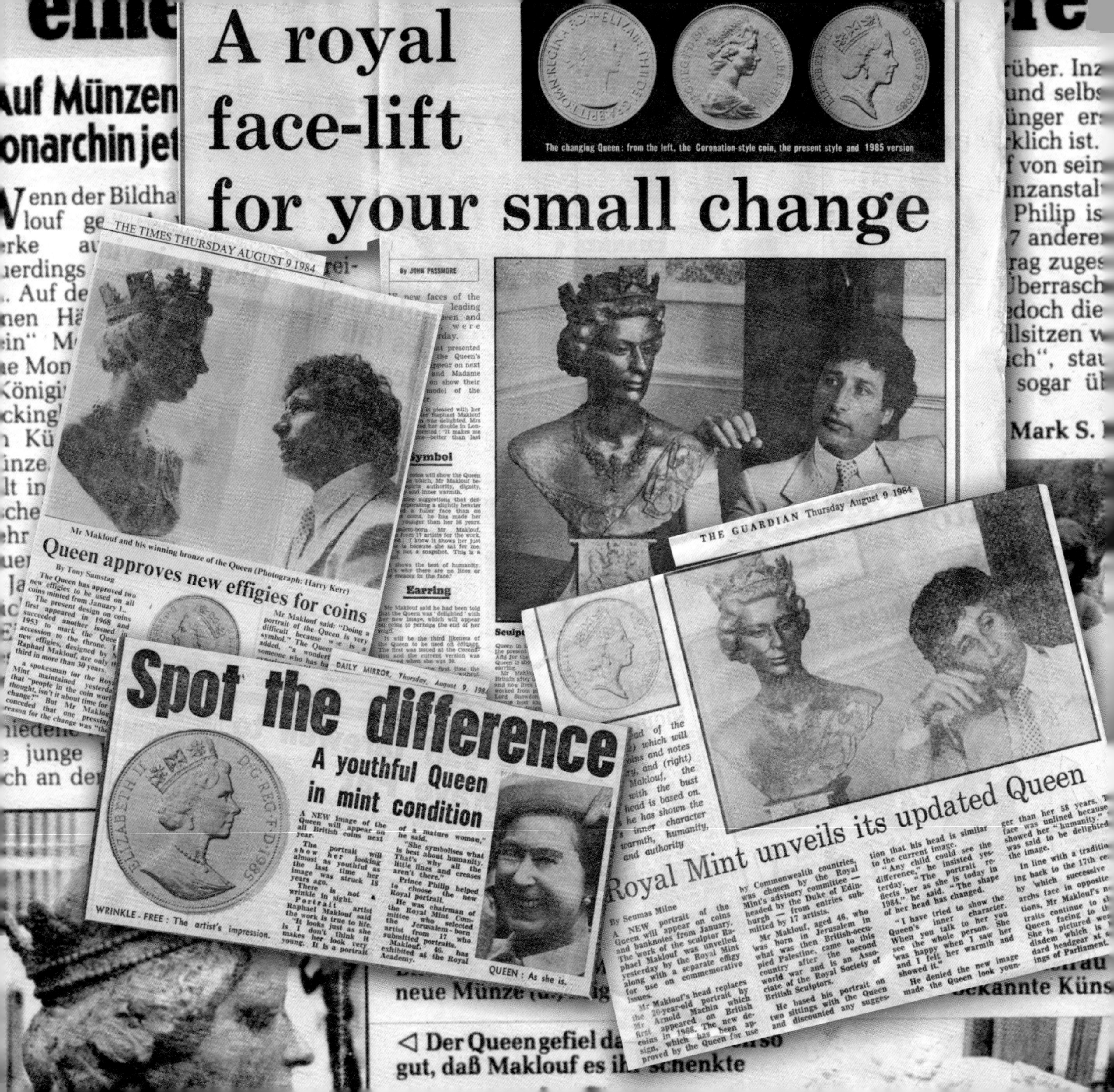
A royal face-lift for your small change

The changing Queen: from the left, the Coronation-style coin, the present style and 1985 version

By JOHN PASSMORE

Symbol

Earring

Mr Maklouf said he had been told that the Queen was 'delighted' with her new image, which will appear on coins to perhaps the end of her reign.

It will be the third likeness of the Queen to be used on coinage. The first was issued at the Coronation and the current version was issued when she was 38.

THE TIMES THURSDAY AUGUST 9 1984

Mr Maklouf and his winning bronze of the Queen (Photograph: Harry Kerr)

Queen approves new effigies for coins

By Tony Samstag

The Queen has approved two new effigies to be used on all coins minted from January 1.

The present design on coins first appeared in 1968 and succeeded another issued in 1953 to mark the Queen's accession to the throne. The new effigies, designed by Mr Raphael Maklouf, are only the third in more than 30 years.

A spokesman for the Royal Mint maintained yesterday that "people in the coin world thought, isn't it about time for a change?" But Mr Maklouf conceded that one pressing reason for the change was "the

Mr Maklouf said: "Doing a portrait of the Queen is very difficult because she is a symbol." The Queen ... added, "a wonderful ... someone who has ...

DAILY MIRROR, Thursday, August 9, 1984

Spot the difference

A youthful Queen in mint condition

A NEW image of the Queen will appear on all British coins next year.

The portrait will show her looking almost as youthful as the last time her image was struck 15 years ago.

There is not a wrinkle in sight.

Portrait artist Raphael Maklouf said the work is true to life.

"It looks just as she is. I don't think it makes her look very young. It is a portrait of a mature woman," he said.

"She symbolises what is best about humanity. That's why all the little lines and creases aren't there."

Prince Philip helped to choose the new Royal portrait.

He was chairman of the Royal Mint Committee which selected the Jerusalem-born artist from 17 who submitted portraits.

Maklouf, 46, has exhibited at the Royal Academy.

WRINKLE-FREE: The artist's impression.

QUEEN: As she is.

THE GUARDIAN Thursday August 9 1984

...ead of the ...) which will ...oins and notes ...y, and (right) Maklouf, the ... with the bust ... head is based on. ...s he has shown the ...'s inner character warmth, humanity, and authority

Royal Mint unveils its updated Queen

By Seumas Milne

A NEW portrait of the Queen will appear on coins and banknotes from January. The work of the sculptor Raphael Maklouf was unveiled yesterday by the Royal Mint along with a separate effigy for use on commemorative issues.

Mr Maklouf's head replaces the 20-year-old portrait by Mr Arnold Machin which first appeared on British coins in 1968. The new design, which has been approved by the Queen for use by Commonwealth countries, was chosen by the Royal Mint's advisory committee — headed by the Duke of Edinburgh — from entries submitted by 17 artists.

Mr Maklouf, aged 46, who was born in Jerusalem in what was then British-occupied Palestine, came to this country after the second world war and is an Associate of the Royal Society of British Sculptors.

He based his portrait on two sittings with the Queen and discounted any suggestion that his head is similar to the current image.

"Any child could see the difference," he insisted yesterday. "The portrait reflects her as she is today in 1984," he said. "The shape of her head has changed.

"I have tried to show the Queen's inner character. When you talk to her you see the whole person. She was happy when I saw her and I felt her warmth and showed it."

He denied the new image made the Queen look younger than her 58 years. The face was unlined because ... showed her "humanity." ... was said to be delighted ... the image.

In line with a tradition ... ing back to the 17th ce... by which successive ... archs face in opposite ... tions, Mr Maklouf's n... traits continue to ... Queen facing to the ... She is pictured we... diadem which is ... dard headgear at ... ings of Parliament.

Auf Münzen ... Monarchin jet...

Wenn der Bildha... louf ...

neue Münze ...

◁ Der Queen gefiel da... so gut, daß Maklouf es ihr schenkte

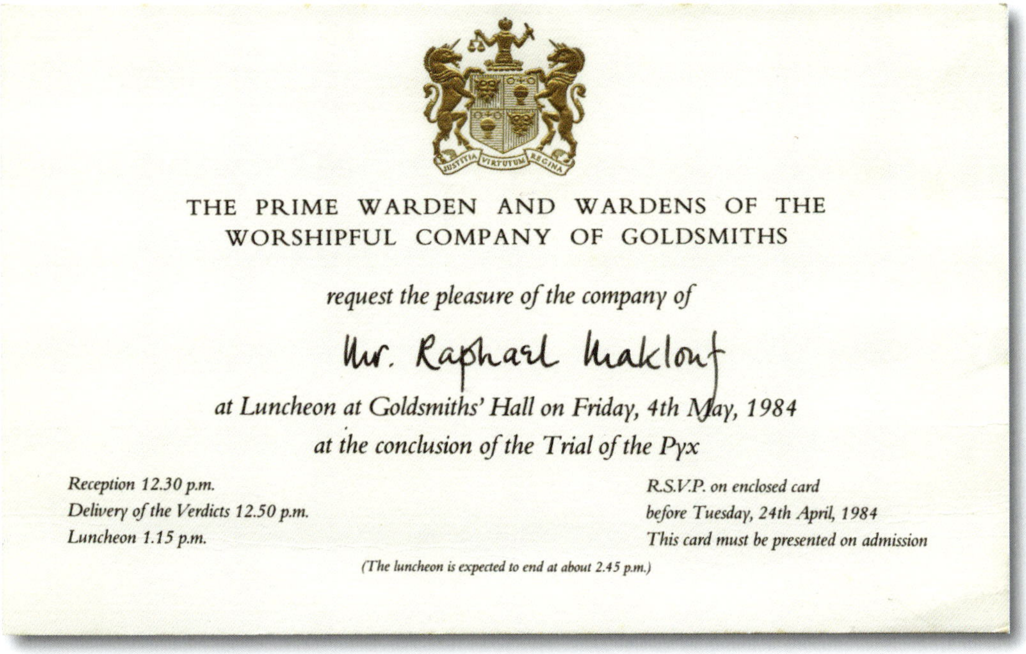

THE PRIME WARDEN AND WARDENS OF THE
WORSHIPFUL COMPANY OF GOLDSMITHS

request the pleasure of the company of

Mr. Raphael Maklouf

at Luncheon at Goldsmiths' Hall on Friday, 4th May, 1984
at the conclusion of the Trial of the Pyx

Reception 12.30 p.m.
Delivery of the Verdicts 12.50 p.m.
Luncheon 1.15 p.m.

R.S.V.P. on enclosed card
before Tuesday, 24th April, 1984
This card must be presented on admission

(The luncheon is expected to end at about 2.45 p.m.)

Invitation to the trial of the Pyx

Raphael's timing was, once again, immaculate. There was an extraordinary symbiosis between his sculptural and his minting activities, the artist chosen to sculpt the Queen's effigy for coinage also being involved in the minting of coins. His public reputation was much enhanced. The following limerick arrived on a postcard from Marillyn's cousin in France:

> Said the Queen – It is sad truth to tell
> On my coins I am not looking well
> I will send for Maklouf
> He'll improve on the truth
> And from now he'll be Saint Raphael. [9]

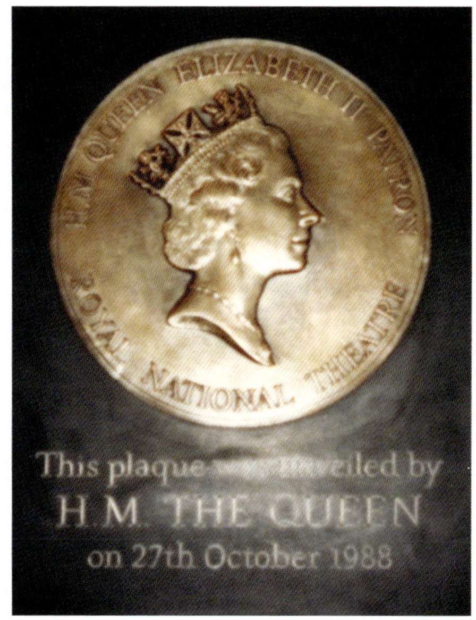

Plaque in the lobby of the National Theatre

Raphael's effigy of the Queen's head continued to circulate widely. In 1984 it was used to commemorate the official opening of the Thames Flood Barrier at Woolwich, opened by the Queen. In 1989 his royal portrait was used on the bi-metal £2 coin. The *Independent* newspaper ran a large notice: 'The Royal Mint proudly announces A Commemorative Coin of the Realm – the £2 Bill of Rights Coin. The Reverse designed by Mr John Lobban... The Obverse... features the portrait of Her Majesty Queen Elizabeth II by Mr Raphael Maklouf...' [10]

There followed a steady flow of commissions for portrait busts. After his sittings with the Queen, he modelled the Duke of Edinburgh. He was also invited to 10 Downing Street to

Plaster of Margaret Thatcher and letter from Margaret Thatcher

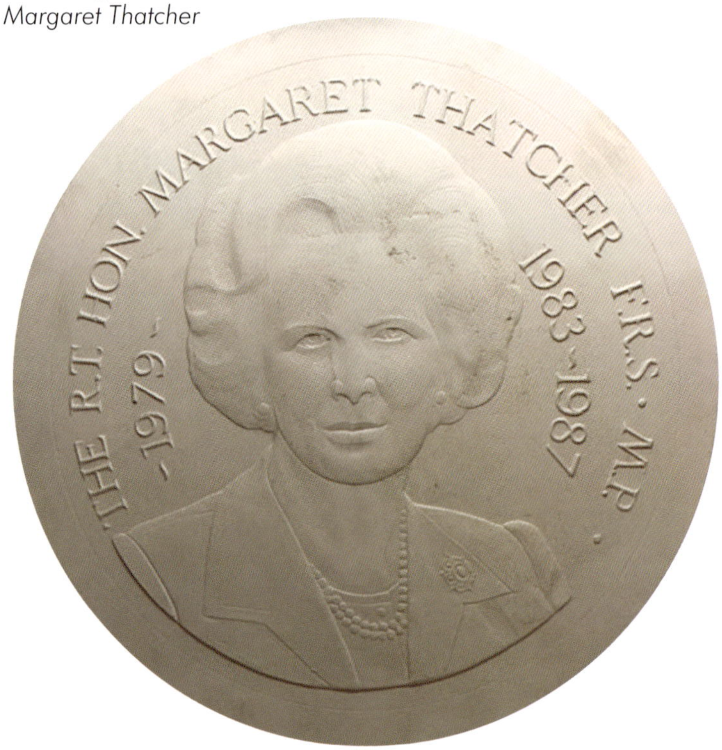

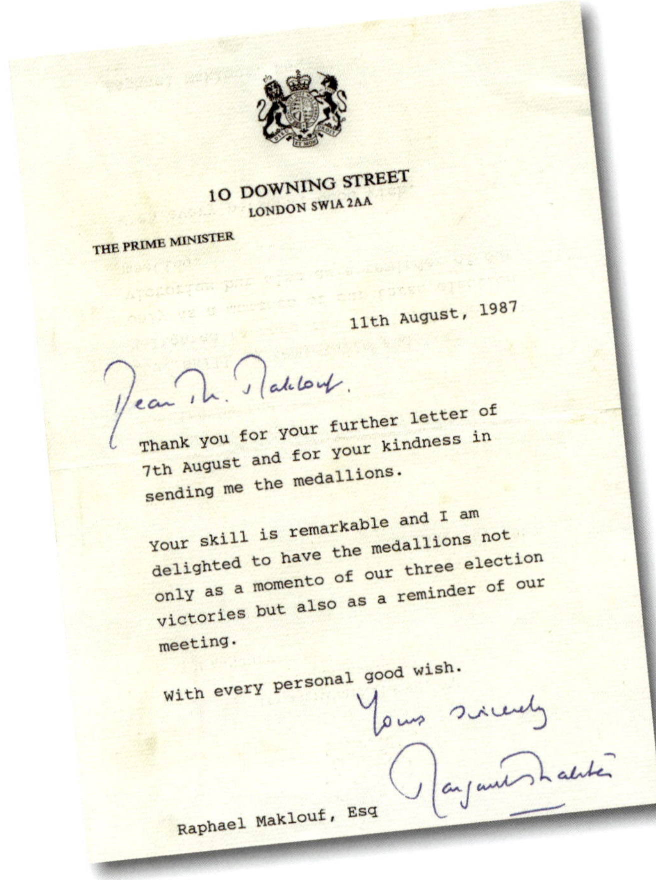

10 DOWNING STREET
LONDON SW1A 2AA

THE PRIME MINISTER

11th August, 1987

Dear Mr. Maklouf.

Thank you for your further letter of 7th August and for your kindness in sending me the medallions.

Your skill is remarkable and I am delighted to have the medallions not only as a momento of our three election victories but also as a reminder of our meeting.

With every personal good wish.

Yours sincerely

Margaret Thatcher

Raphael Maklouf, Esq

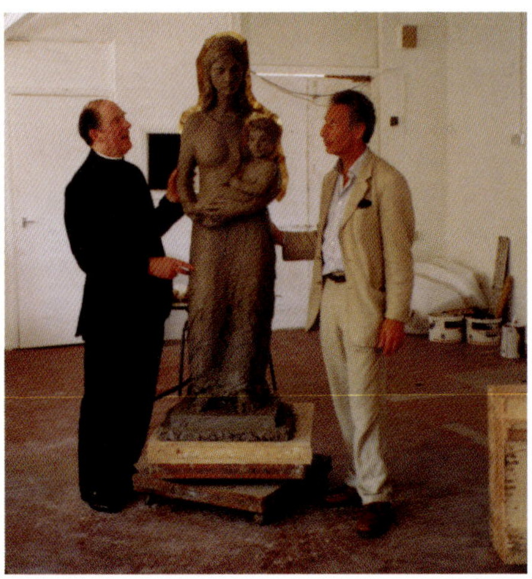

The Bishop of Brentwood with clay model of Madonna and Child

model the Prime Minister, Margaret Thatcher. As he recalled, 'Mrs Thatcher was nervous about being sculpted. She showed me a plate with her portrait on it, presented to her by Mao Tse Tung, and asked me if I thought it had any value.' Raphael's portrait was depicted on a medal to celebrate Mrs Thatcher's third election as Prime Minister. The gift of the medal to her elicited a warm response.

'10 Downing Street, 11 August 1987
Dear Mr Maklouf,
Thank you for your further letter of 7th August, and for your kindness in sending me the medallions.
Your skill is remarkable and I am delighted to have the medallions not only as a memento of our three election victories but also as a reminder of our meeting.
With every personal good wish,
Yours sincerely,
Margaret Thatcher.' [11]

In 1991 Raphael received a sculpture commission in which he was able to express his very personal style of 'Painting-Sculpture'. The Bishop of Brentwood, who had seen his portrait bust of the Queen, wanted bas-relief roundels representing the fifteen Stations of the Cross to encircle the interior of his cathedral. Brentwood Cathedral, England's newest cathedral, largely rebuilt by Quinlan Terry in the form of a basilica and attached to the shell of a small Gothic Revival church of 1861, was the first cathedral built in Britain in the classical style since St Paul's Cathedral. The Bishop wanted the fifteen roundels representing the Stations of the Cross in the following order: Jesus condemned to death; Jesus receives the Cross; Jesus falls the first time; Jesus is met by his mother; Simon of Cyrene is forced to help Jesus with the Cross; Veronica wipes the face of Jesus; Jesus falls the second time; Jesus speaks to the women of Jerusalem; Jesus falls for the third time; Jesus is stripped of his garments; Jesus is nailed to the Cross; Jesus dies on the Cross; Jesus is taken down from the Cross; Jesus is laid in the sepulchre; Jesus is risen in Glory.

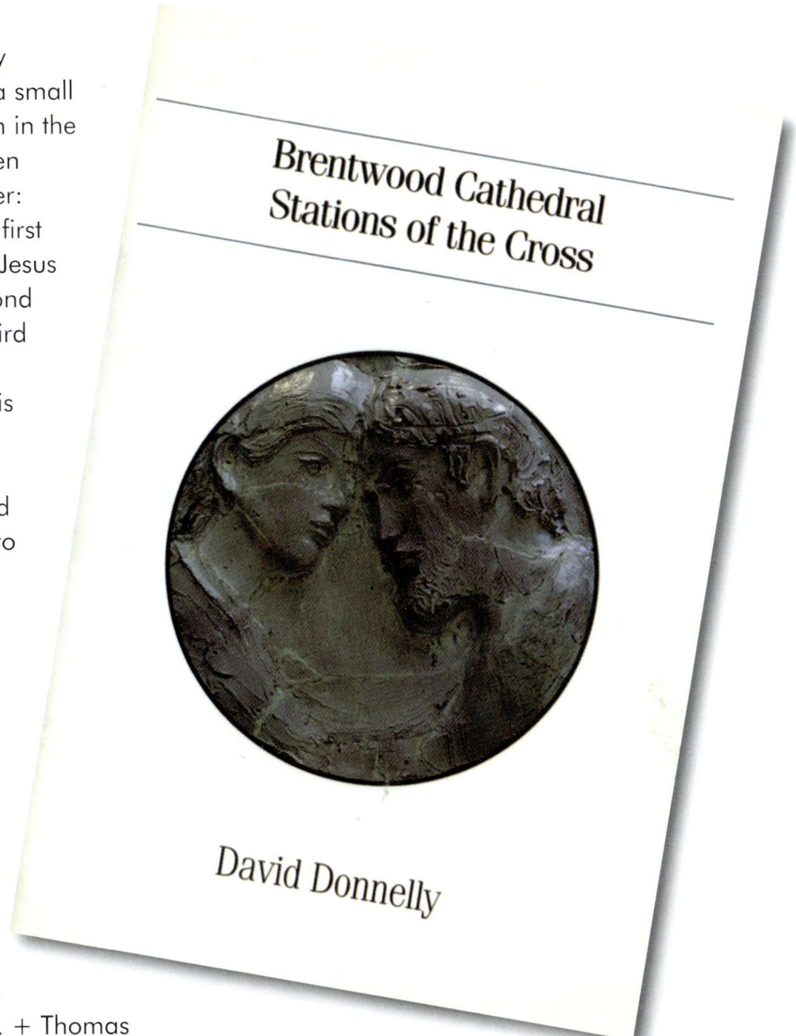

Brentwood Cathedral booklet

As Raphael recounted, 'someone had left a pot of money to rebuild the cathedral., and the Bishop wanted fifteen Stations of the Cross to go around it. I said I thought there were only twelve. "No, no" said the Bishop, originally there were fifteen. They were all to be heads, placed very high up. I sketched some heads and juggled them around. Luckily at that time I had bought a working pottery near Exeter with two huge walk-in kilns, so I was able to fire those big heads in them. The last one blew up in the kiln and I had to put it together again. It turned out to be the best one. When I told the Bishop he said "that's quite alright – it's the work of God", because, as it happened, it represented the Ascension.' [12] Brentwood Cathedral's booklet states 'The Stations, set in the roundels of the Cathedral, are in white glazed terracotta... Like many great artists, Raphael Maklouf has left each Station slightly "unfinished". As he says, one cannot begin to tell the whole story, but can merely suggest and leave the rest to our imagination. + Thomas McMahon, Bishop of Brentwood.' [13] A gold-plated medallion of the Bishop, and twenty sterling silver commemorative coins, were struck by Tower Mint for the cathedral.

Another intriguing commission was to make a small sculpture of the Queen's corgis. This was written up in the Sunday Express in an article entitled *How much is that Dorgi?* 'Now, for the first time, the Queen has allowed three of her pets to be immortalised by the renowned sculptor Raphael Maklouf. The exclusive, handmade limited edition models, in hallmarked sterling silver, are to be sold on behalf of the Animal Health Trust, of which

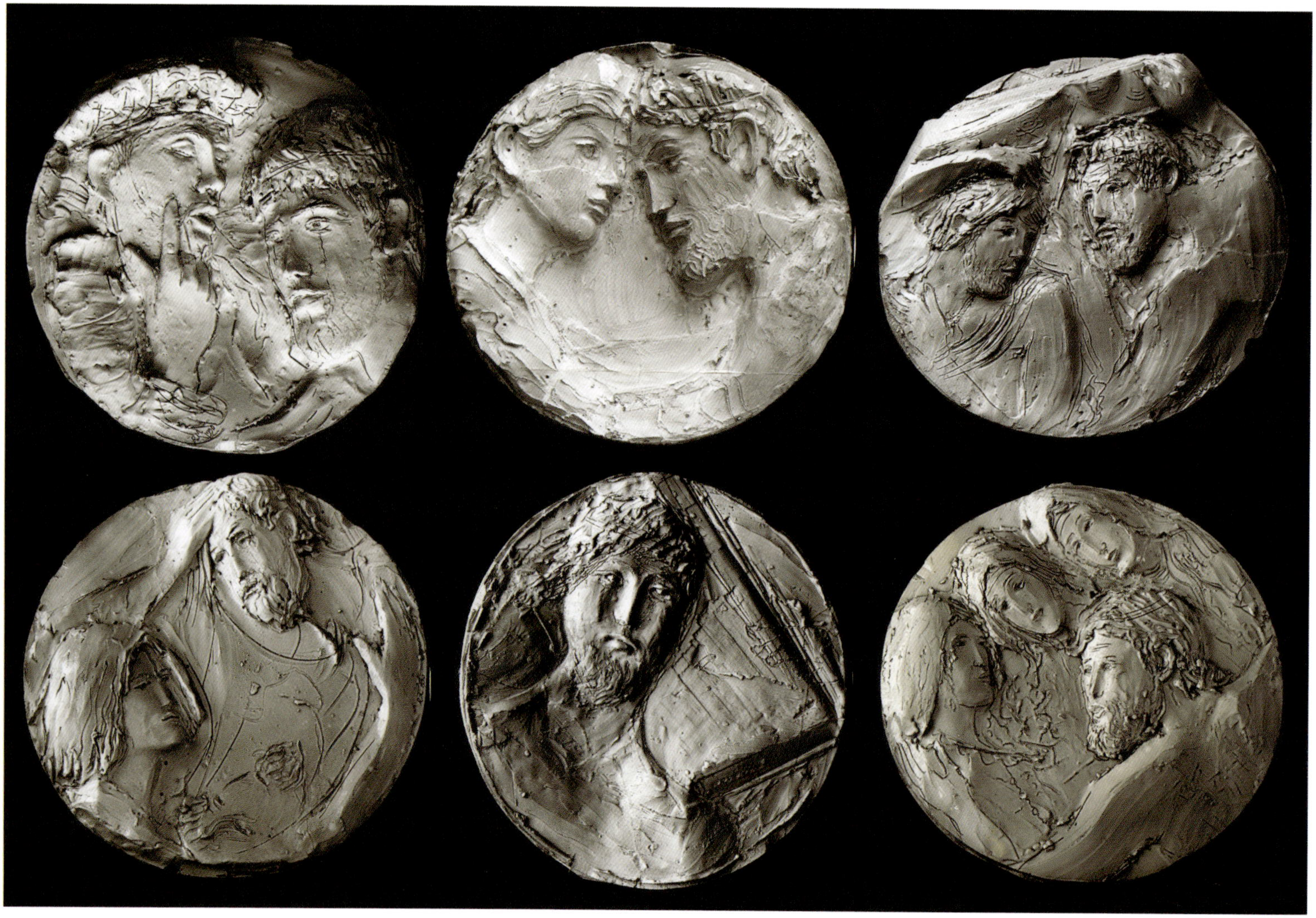

Bas relief Stations of the Cross in Brentwood Cathedral

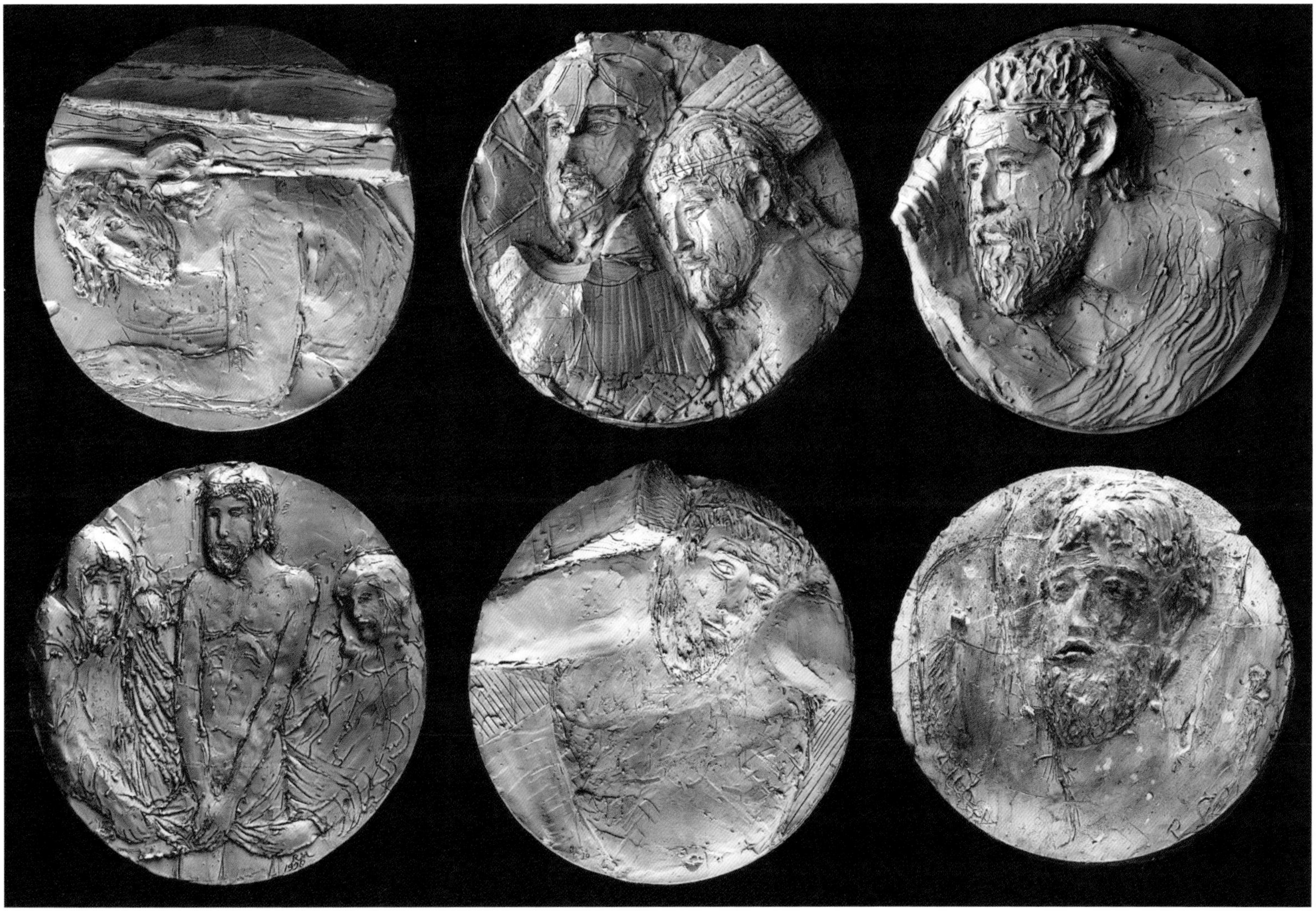

Bas relief Stations of the Cross in Brentwood Cathedral

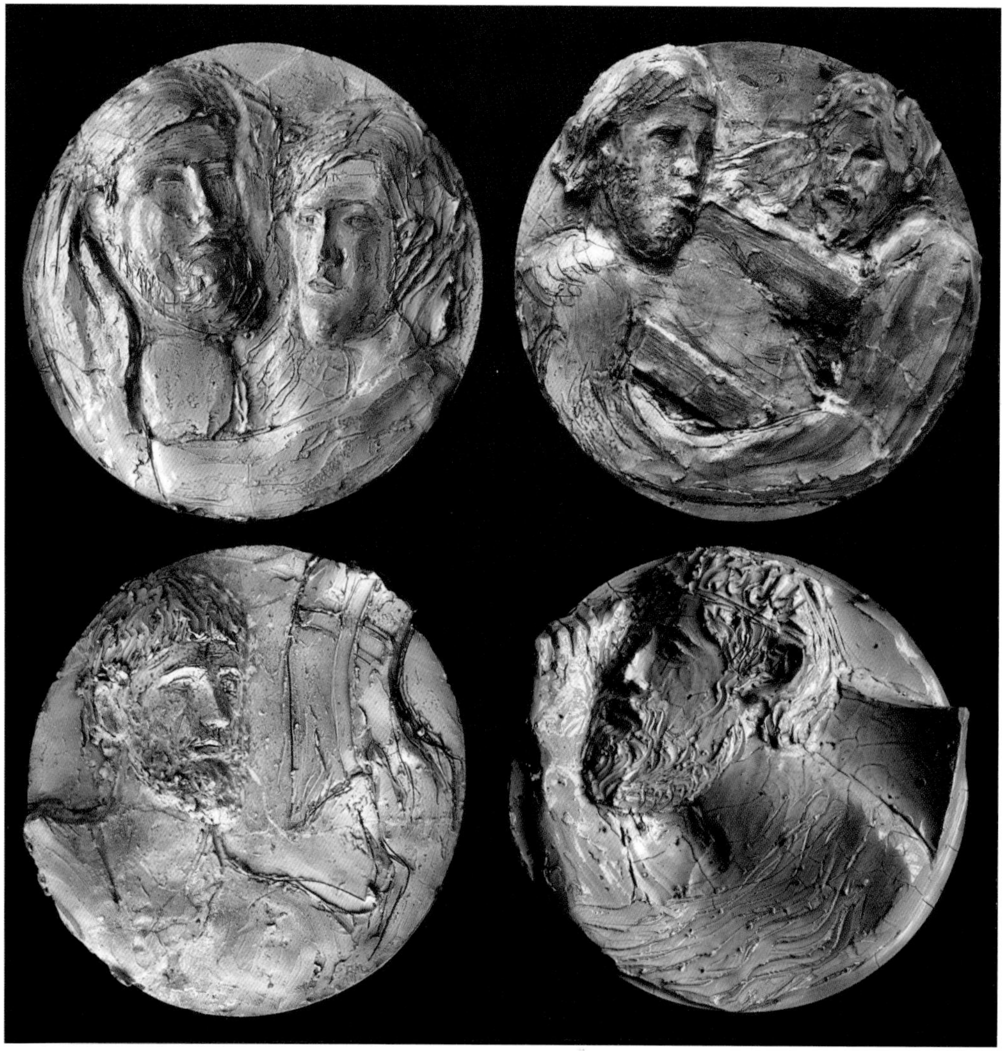

Bas relief Stations of the Cross in Brentwood Cathedral

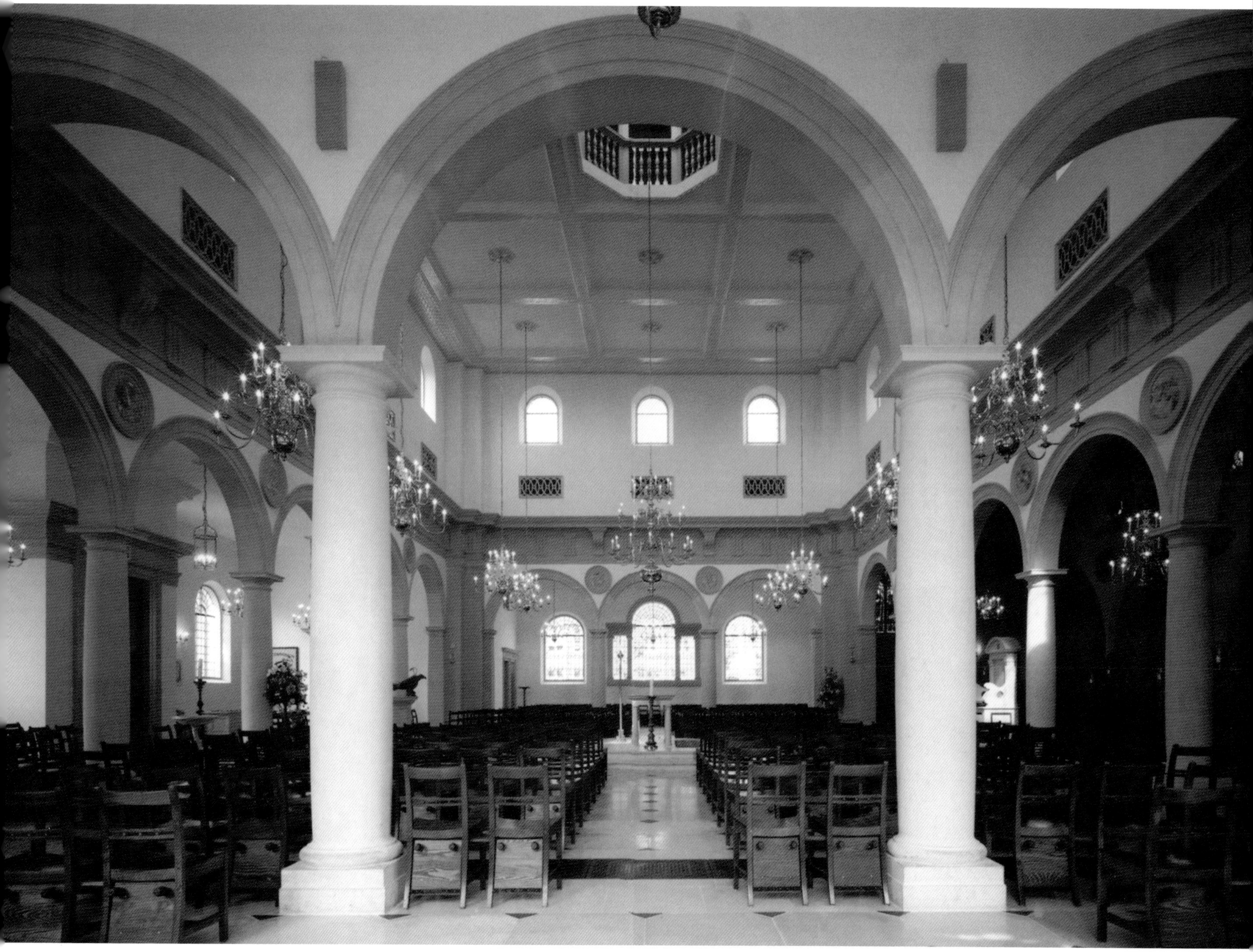

Interior of Brentwood Cathedral, terracotta roundels by Raphael Maklouf

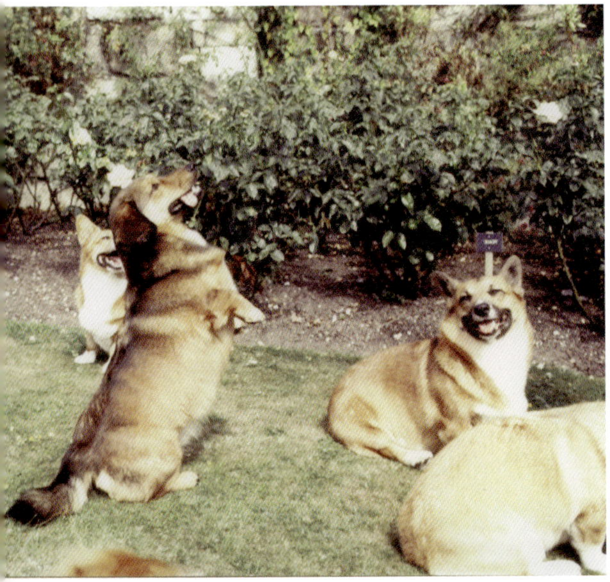

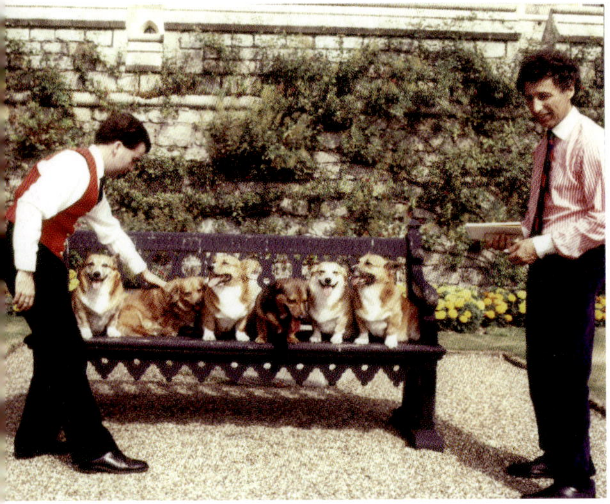

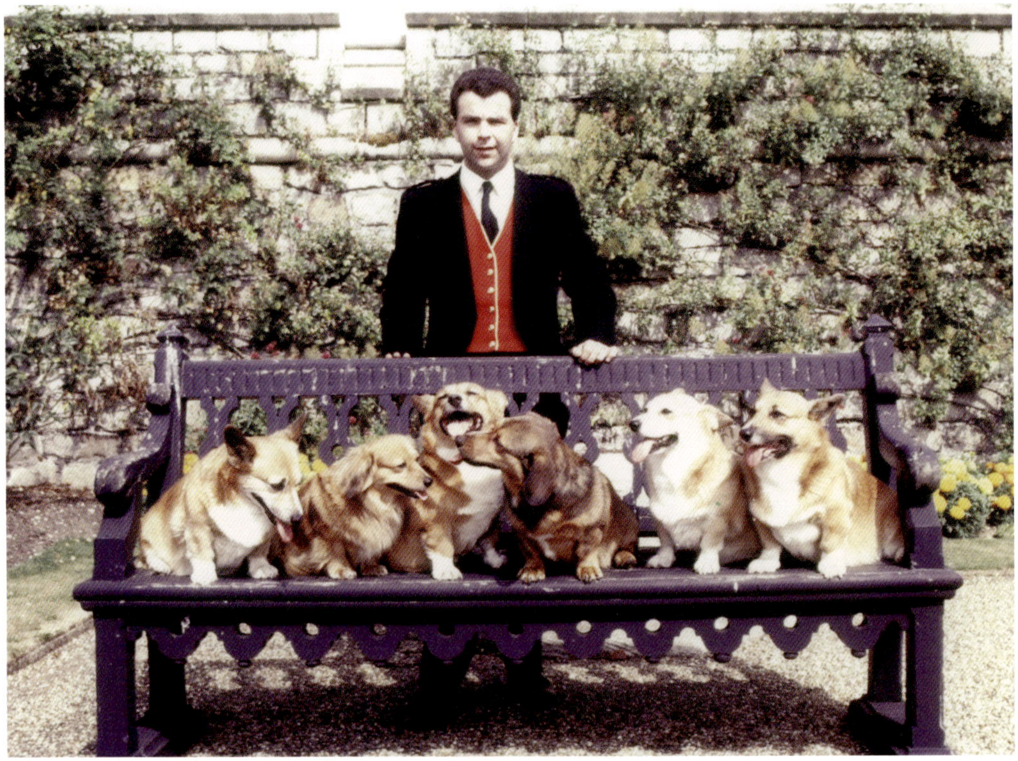

The Queen's corgis and dorgis at Windsor. Photographed by Christina Gascoigne

the Queen is patron... "I hadn't portrayed dogs before and I'd been told that corgis could be quite aggressive, but they were incredibly friendly. I went to Windsor Castle and spent the best part of a day with a sketchbook, while photographer Christina Gascoigne took black and white photographs. I remember it was a very hot day, and we were outside, when suddenly the corgis all shot off, yapping like mad. They had seen the Queen on horseback riding in the distance and they went tearing off after her. They are obviously terribly fond of her, and she of them.' [14]

Raphael's growing reputation meant that he became involved with several charities including the Army Benevolent Fund. This brought invitations to colourful and entertaining military occasions. Raphael had also been elected a Fellow of the Royal Society for the Encouragement of Arts, Manufactures and Commerce (RSA), the British organisation committed to enriching society through ideas and actions and finding innovative practical solutions to current social challenges. He was invited to be on a selection committee for good design in coins and medals. Founded in 1754, the RSA was granted its Royal Charter in 1847, and the right to use the term *royal* in its name by King Edward VII in 1908. Notable members past and present have included Charles Dickens,

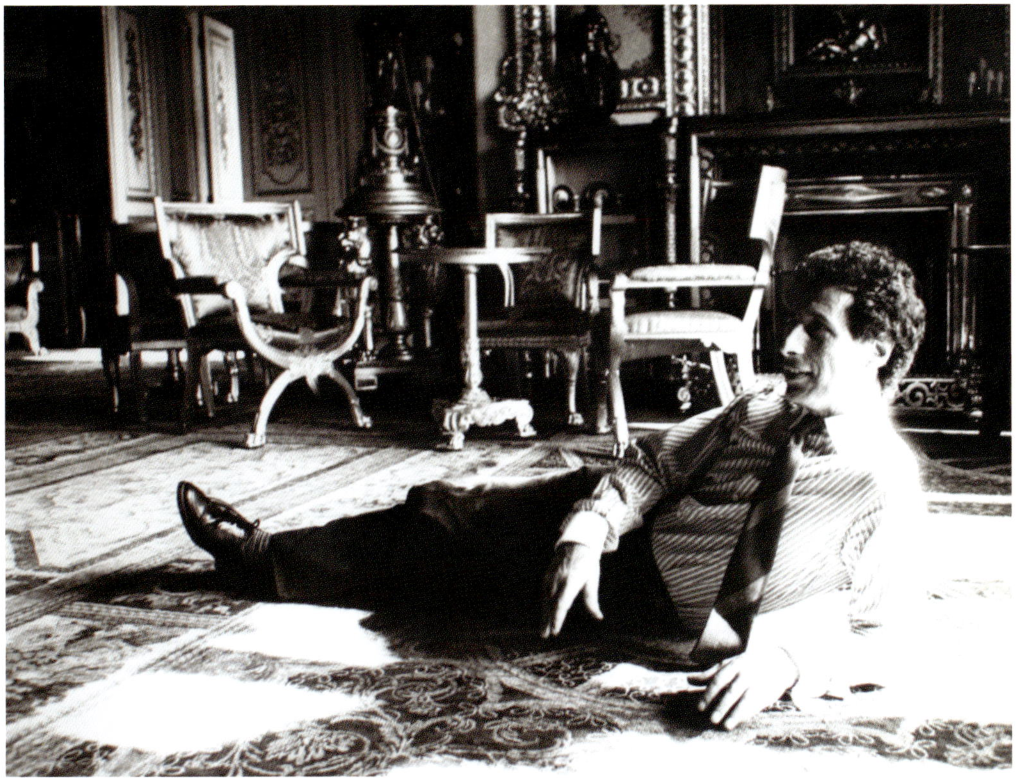

Raphael at Windsor Castle

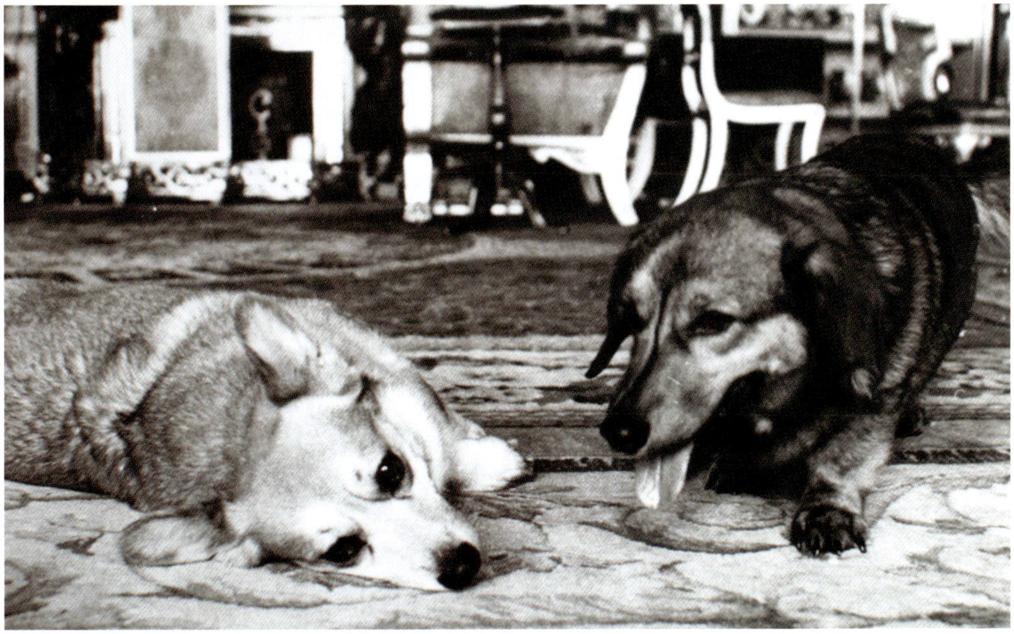

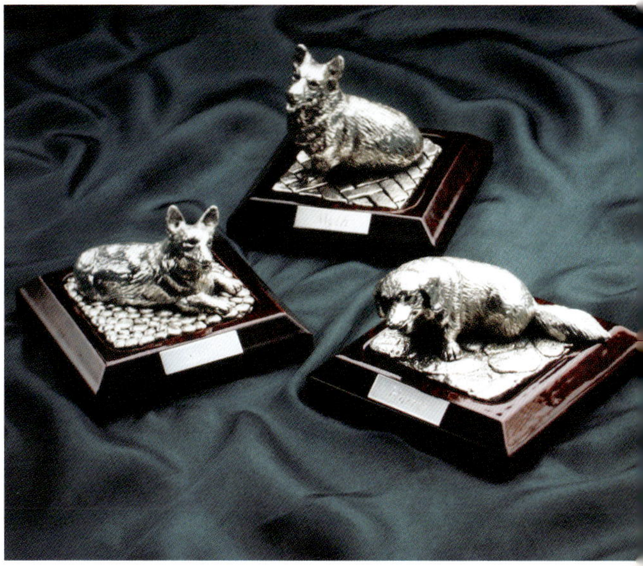

The Queen's corgis and dorgis commissioned by the Animal Health Trust

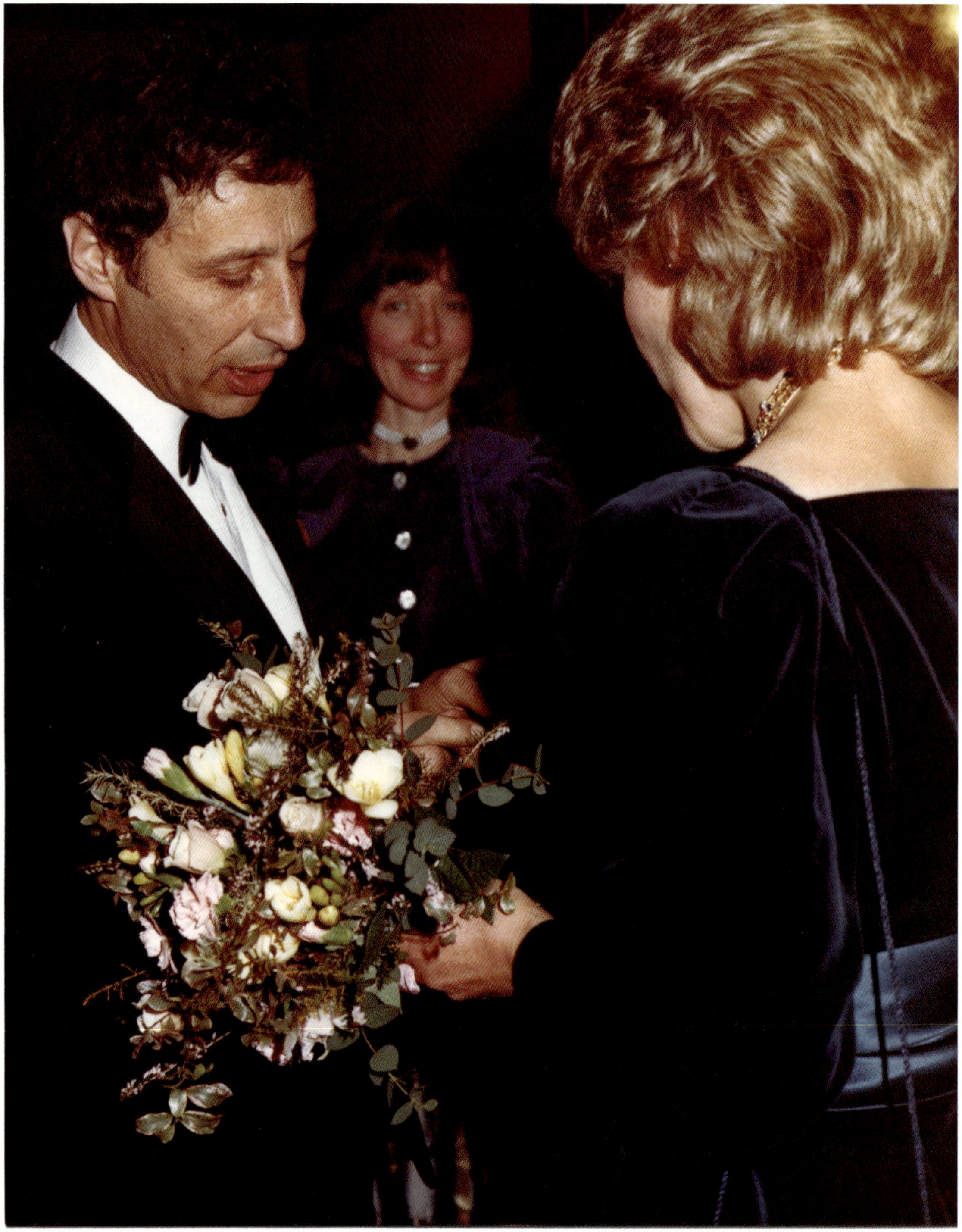

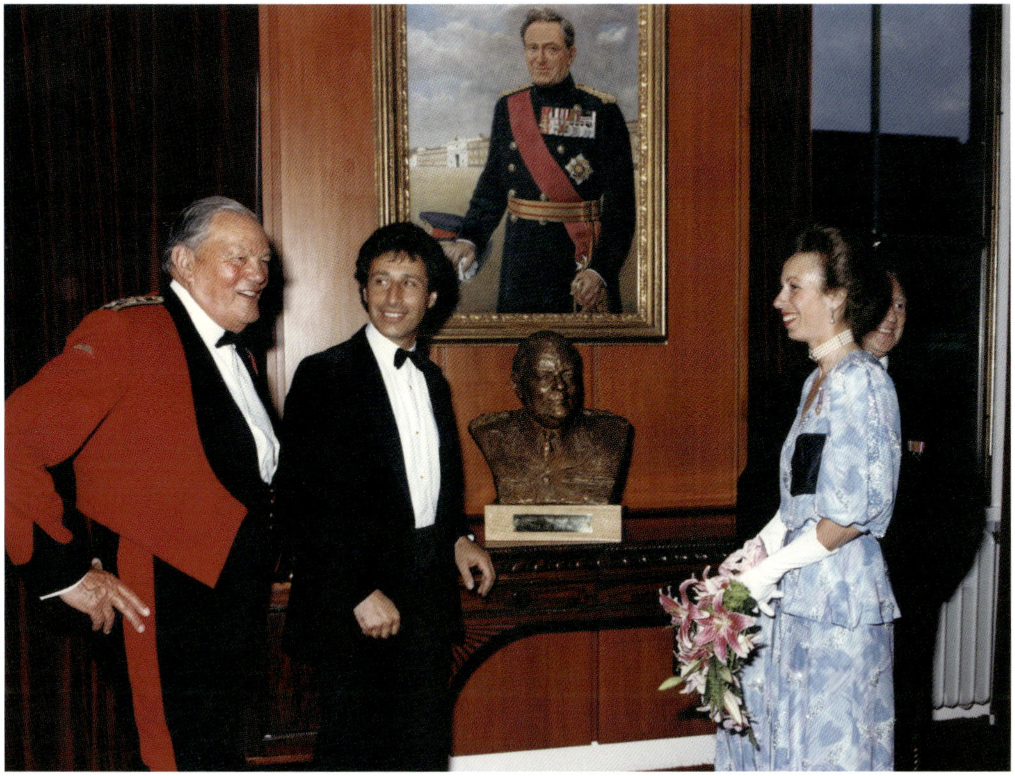

Unveiling of portrait bust of General Sir John Mogg by the Princess Royal

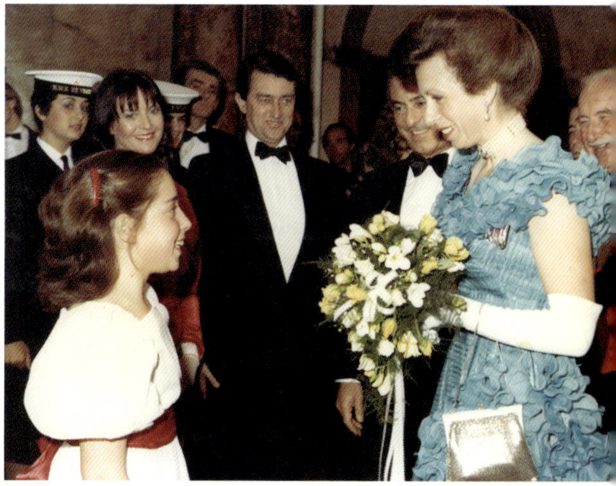

Events at the Army Benevolent Fund. Laetitia presenting a posy to Princess Anne

Adam Smith, Benjamin Franklin, Karl Marx, William Hogarth, Stephen Hawking and Tim Berners-Lee. It has about eighty fellows worldwide, and the Princess Royal has recently replaced the Duke of Edinburgh as its President.

In 1984 Another exclusive body, the Royal British Society of Sculptors, elected Raphael to its membership as a Fellow. The RBS, which received its royal patronage in 1911, has a selected membership of around six hundred professional sculptors. It was founded in 1904 to promote excellence in the art and practice of sculpture. Raphael was also made an Honorary Fellow of the University of the Arts, London, Europe's largest university, a federation of six art colleges: Camberwell, Central St Martins, Chelsea, the London College of Communication, the London College of Fashion, and Wimbledon College of Art. In his speech at the conferment ceremony held in the Banqueting House at Whitehall, Raphael referred particularly to those artists who struggle alone and need help to succeed. He contrasted the convivial glitter of the occasion with the lonely occupation of artists starting out on their life's work. He pointed out that only a few succeed while many fall by the wayside, and stressed the importance of remembering those others who had not succeeded.

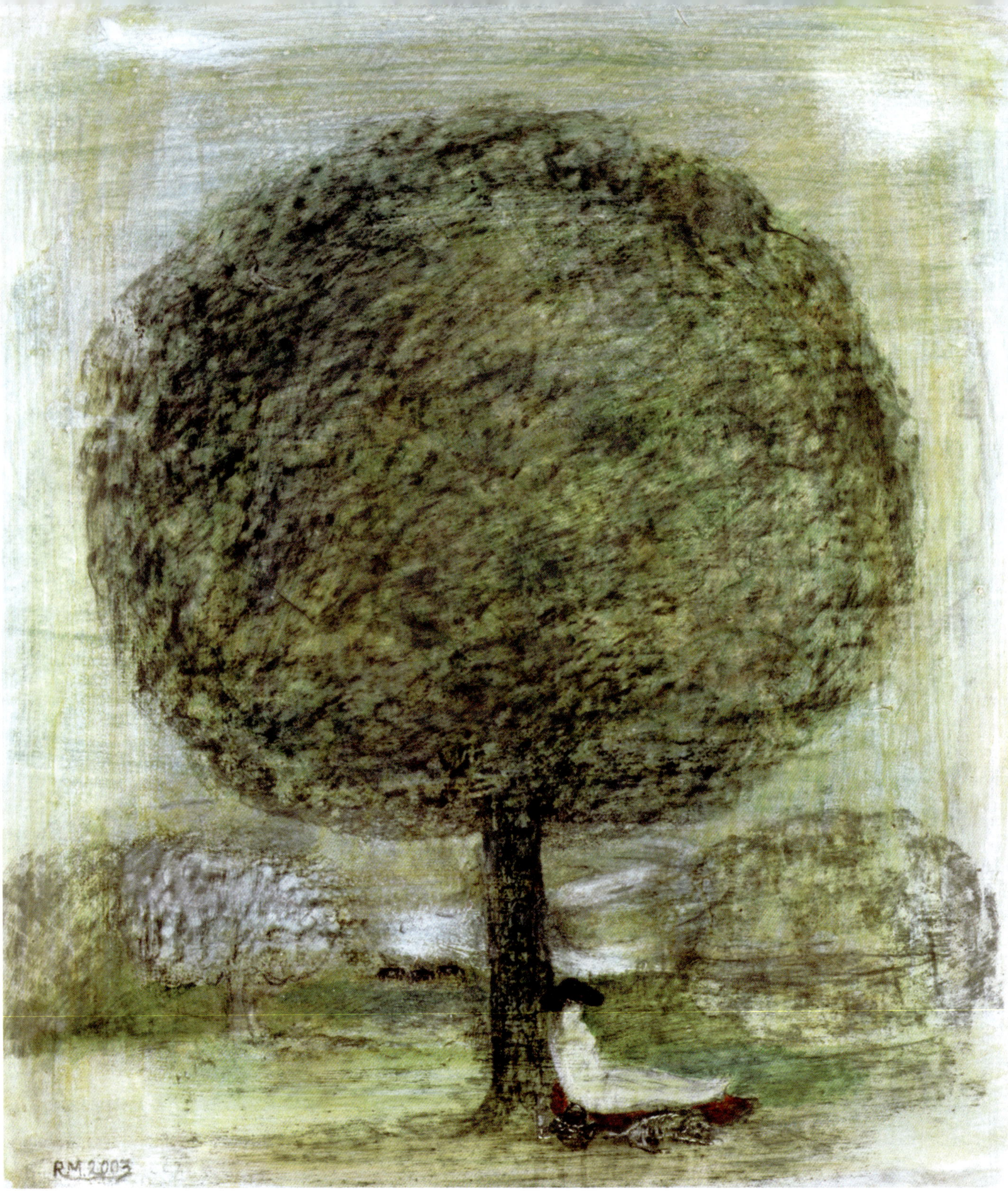
RM 2003

Chapter 8
Leaves of the Tree

WHILE RUNNING THE Mint, Raphael had less time to pursue his own work. Although he occasionally designed effigies of heads, for the most part he employed freelance artists to sculpt his medals and coins. Instead of making sculpture, in his spare time he painted. The main subject of his paintings throughout the years has been the Tree of Life. The tree has always been an important symbol for him, as is the Mimosa tree in the courtyard of the Mint. As well as representing life and growth, the tree in the Garden of Eden tells the story of humanity. The story of human love is picked up in Raphael's paintings of a gondolier in love with a girl. Set in Venice, a girl, reclining in the pose of a Giorgione Venus, waits for her gondolier lover. These are dream images, imaginative musings on life and love. Raphael's handling of paint is delicate and free, the marks exploratory, the tones built up with glazes. Raphael is a tonal painter, not a colourist, and it may be that his childhood eye problems, which forced him to keep his eyes shaded, damaged the colour receptors of his retinas. Tonal values can best be judged with half-closed eyes, while colour is received on the retina with eyes wide open. Raphael's paintings have a monochrome connection with his sculpture, particularly with the 'painterly' sculpted heads in the Stations of the Cross at Brentwood Cathedral. As he asserts, 'Painting is my muse'.

Although Raphael's paintings come from his imagination, his imagery is nevertheless derived from things seen or experienced in the outside world. He has remained a figurative artist, true to the spirit of Vogel's teaching. Like Vogel, he believes that Art should have the touch of the artist's hand, that unique touch being as important as the concept in the mind. He bemoans the loss of hand skills, the loss of imagery based on the visible world, and the way that intellectualising seems to have abolished intuition. The reduction of art to little more than a curator's label telling the viewer what to think, leaves him totally bemused. His beliefs and disbeliefs are echoed in one of his treasured books, Tom Wolfe's *The Painted Word,* written in the 1970s when the wave of Abstraction was rolling over America. Wolfe's engaging and provocative tirade satirises the gradual reduction of Art to a sort of visual Nothingness.

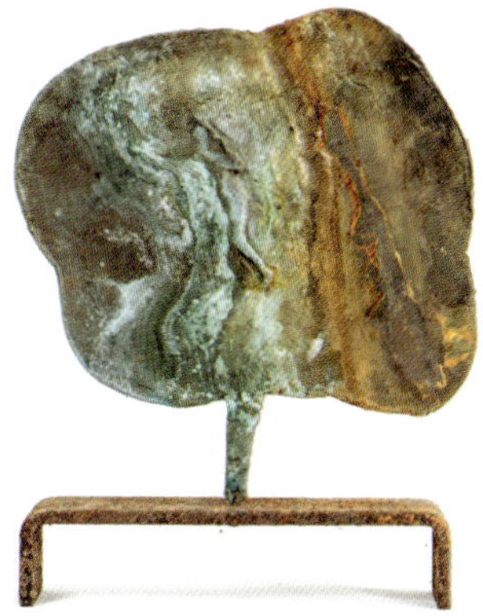

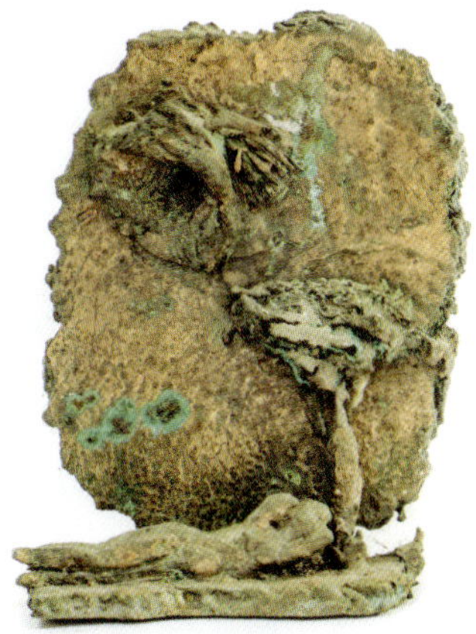

Small bronzes, The Garden of Eden
Photos by Kirsten Scully

Opposite: Tree series 2003
Photo by Paul Webster

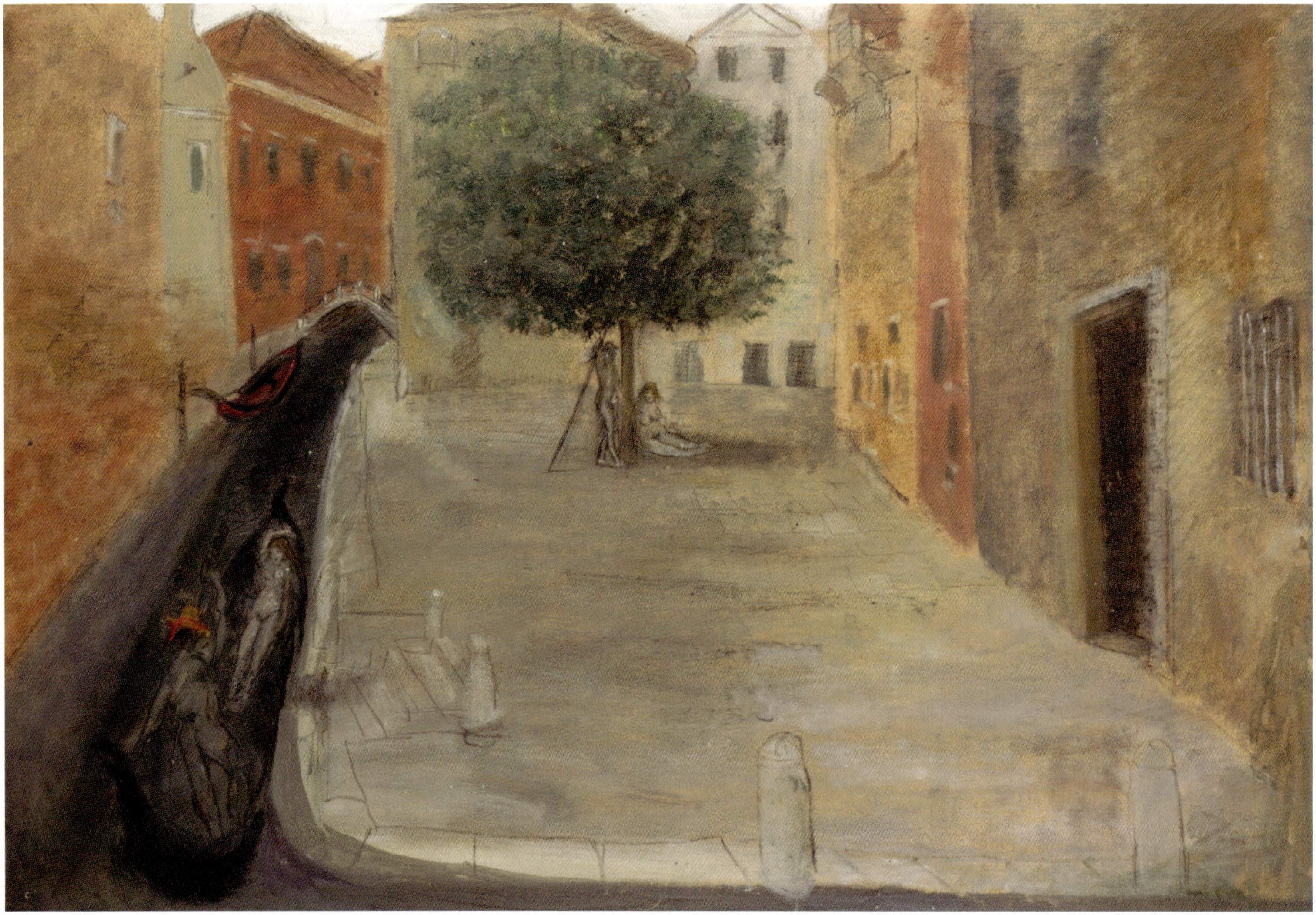

Venice Gondolier series
Photo by Paul Webster

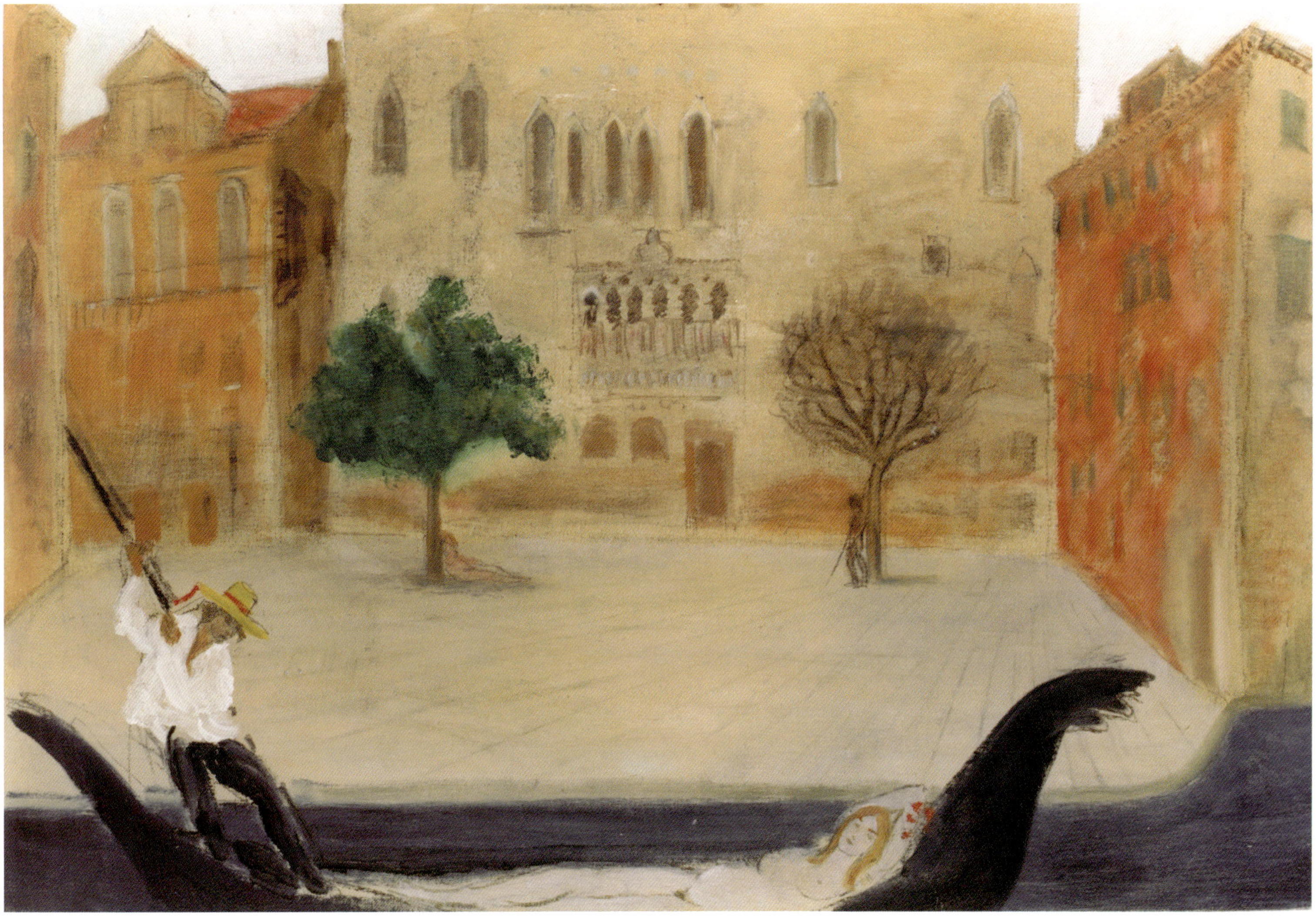

Venice Gondolier series
Photo by Paul Webster

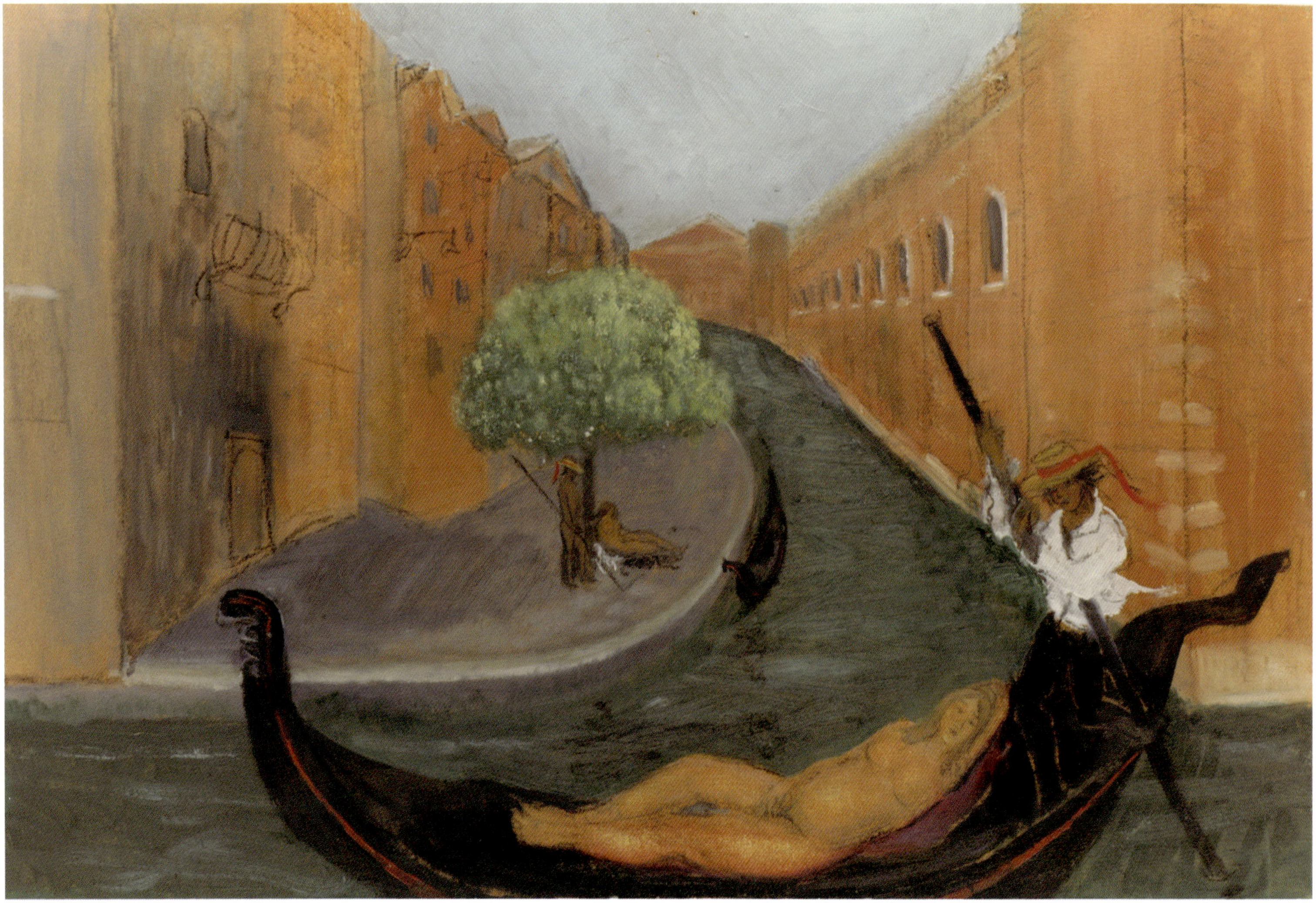

Venice Gondolier series
Photo by Paul Webster

Venice Gondolier series
Photo by Paul Webster

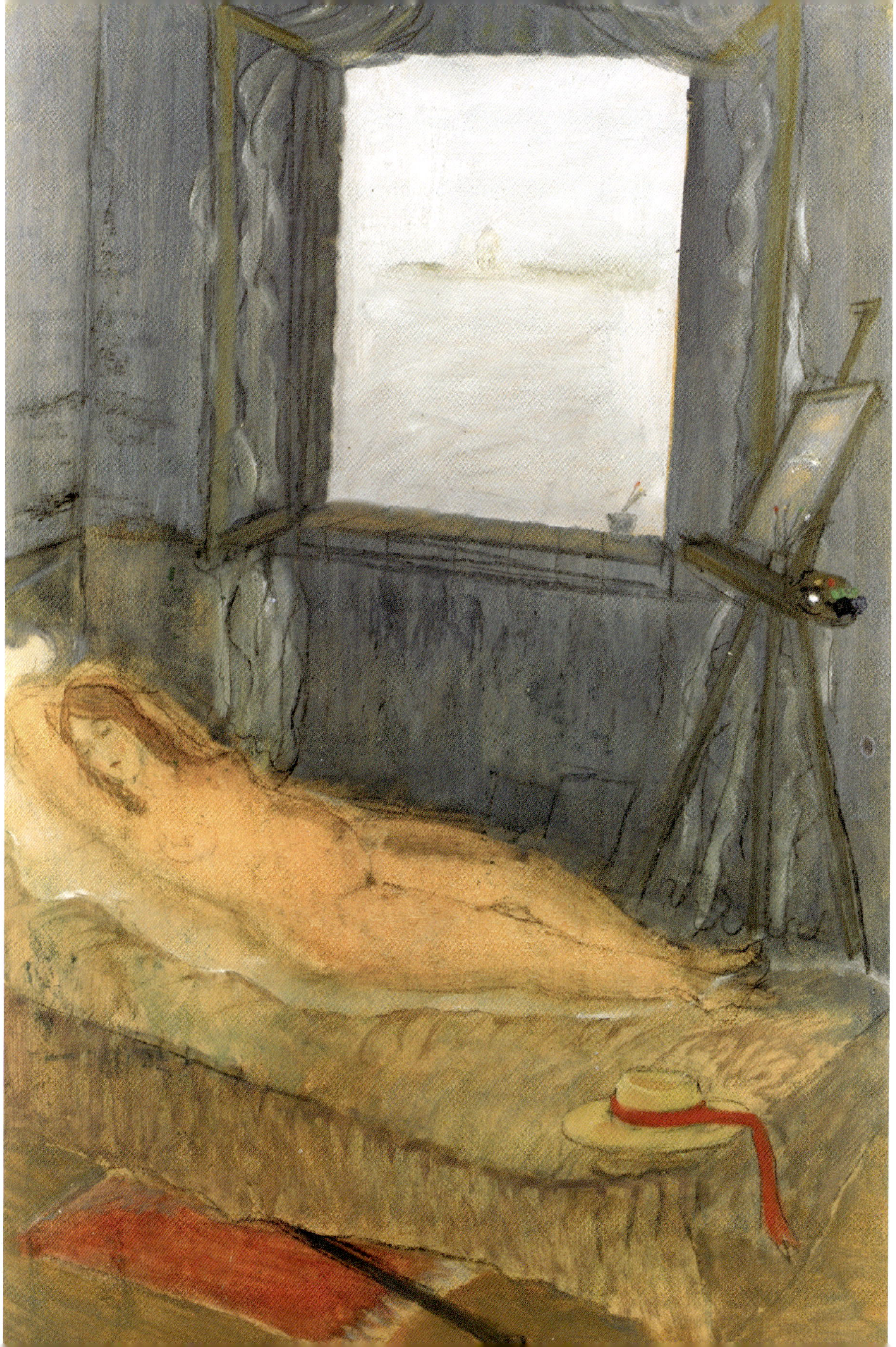

'How far we have come! How religiously we've cut away the fat! In the beginning we got rid of nineteenth-century story-book realism. Then we got rid of representational objects. Then we got rid of the third dimension altogether and got really flat... Then we got rid of airiness, brushstrokes, most of the paint, and the last viruses of drawing and complicated designs.... And how about the painting frame?.... what about this nice sweet bourgeois idea of hanging up pictures in the first place... We've gotten rid of illusion, representational objects, the third dimension, pigment (or most of it), brushstrokes and now frames and canvas – but what about the wall itself?... What about the very idea of the gallery or museum. ..Wasn't there something impossibly retrograde about the whole thing?... Back to business... the monomaniacal task of *reduction*. What about the idea of a permanent work of art at all, or even a visible one?   Out of that objection came Conceptual Art...'
'And there, at last, it was! No more realism, no more representational objects, no more lines, colours, forms and contours, no more pigment, no more brushstrokes, no more evocations, no more frames, walls, galleries, museums, no more gnawing at the tortured face of the god Flatness, no more audience required, just a 'receiver' that may or may not be a person or may or may not be there at all, no more ego projected, just "the artist" in the third person who may be anyone or no one at all, for nothing is demanded of him, nothing at all, for that got lost in the subjunctive mode – and in that absolutely dispassionate abdication, of insouciant withering away, Art made its final flight... and came out the other side as Art Theory! Art Theory, pure and simple, words on a page, literature undefiled by vision, flat flatter, flattest, a vision invisible...' [1]

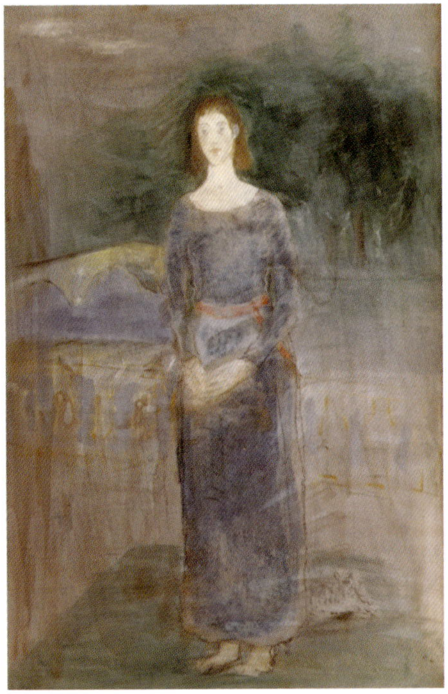
Marillyn

In this morass of intellectual anarchy, Raphael saw that art students were floundering. He deplored the direction in which art schools were heading and decided to try and do something about it. With philanthropic intent he went to his old alma mater, Camberwell, and proposed the idea of a competition to sculpt a portrait head. 'It was my initiative from Tower Mint to hold the portrait head competition, for this reason: I was going to the degree shows every year and seeing mostly installations, nothing much made by hand, or things already made and just put together. I was concerned about how the students when they leave are going to continue working and make a career for themselves because (a) they won't have access to the huge studios of the art schools and (b) portrait heads don't take up so much room. I found that there is a market out there - many people want portraits of their children, or garden sculpture – and it's relatively inexpensive if you don't use bronze. I still think it's unfair not to teach them a craft as a way of surviving when they leave the art colleges. I decided the way to encourage them was to give this prize. When I told the Dean my idea, she was enthusiastic. She said "Good idea, go and see the sculpture tutors." When I went to the senior sculpture teacher I asked if he had any head armatures and he looked blank. I said "you do have some clay, don't you?" He said "we used to, but we don't have much call for it". When I asked if the students wanted to carve rather than model, he told me they would have to find their own materials. The sculpture tutors didn't want their students diverted, so they

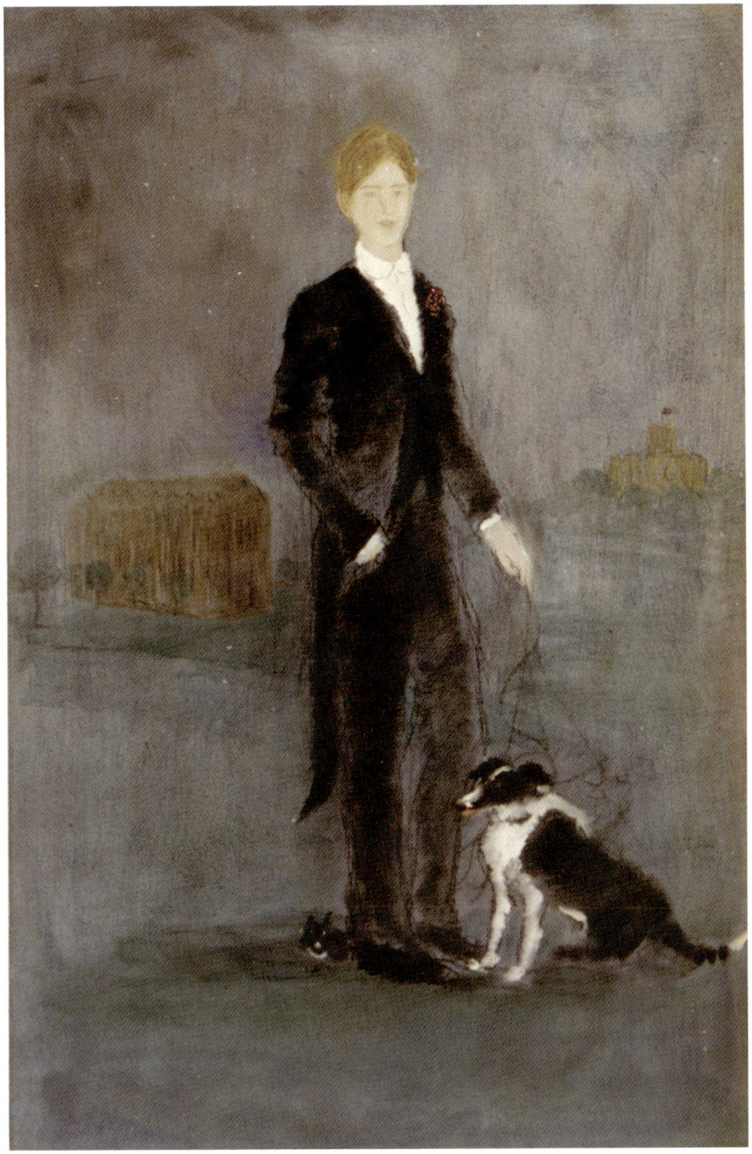

Edmund and Oscar

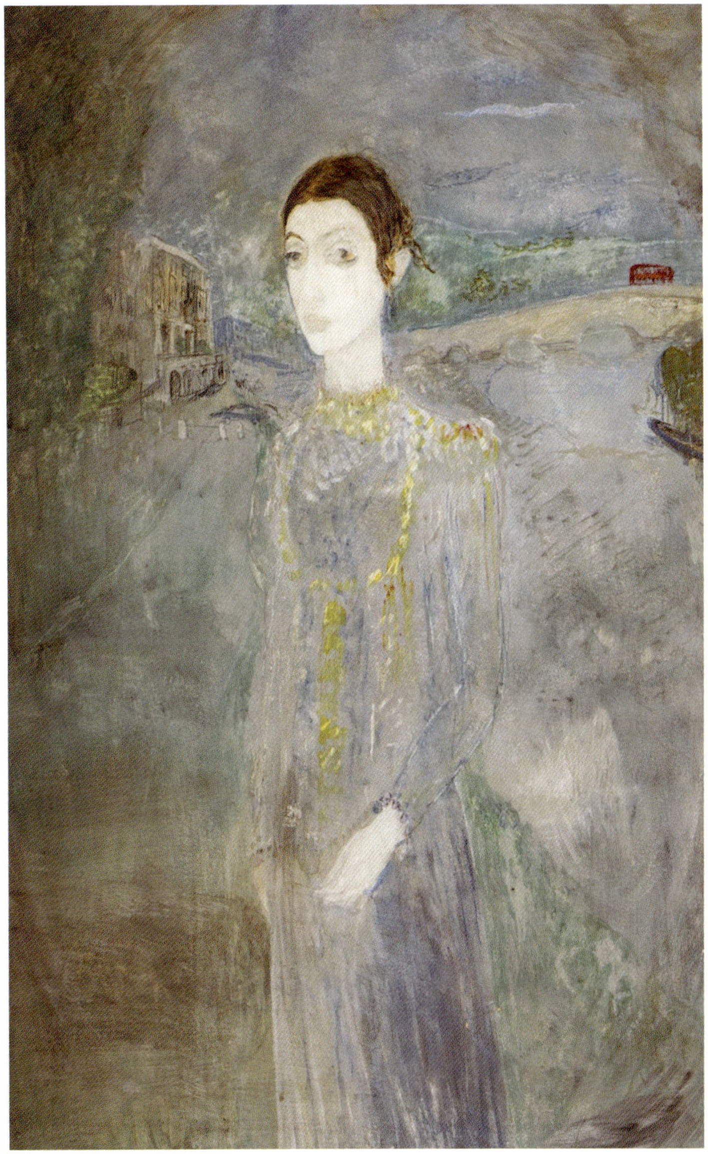

Marillyn

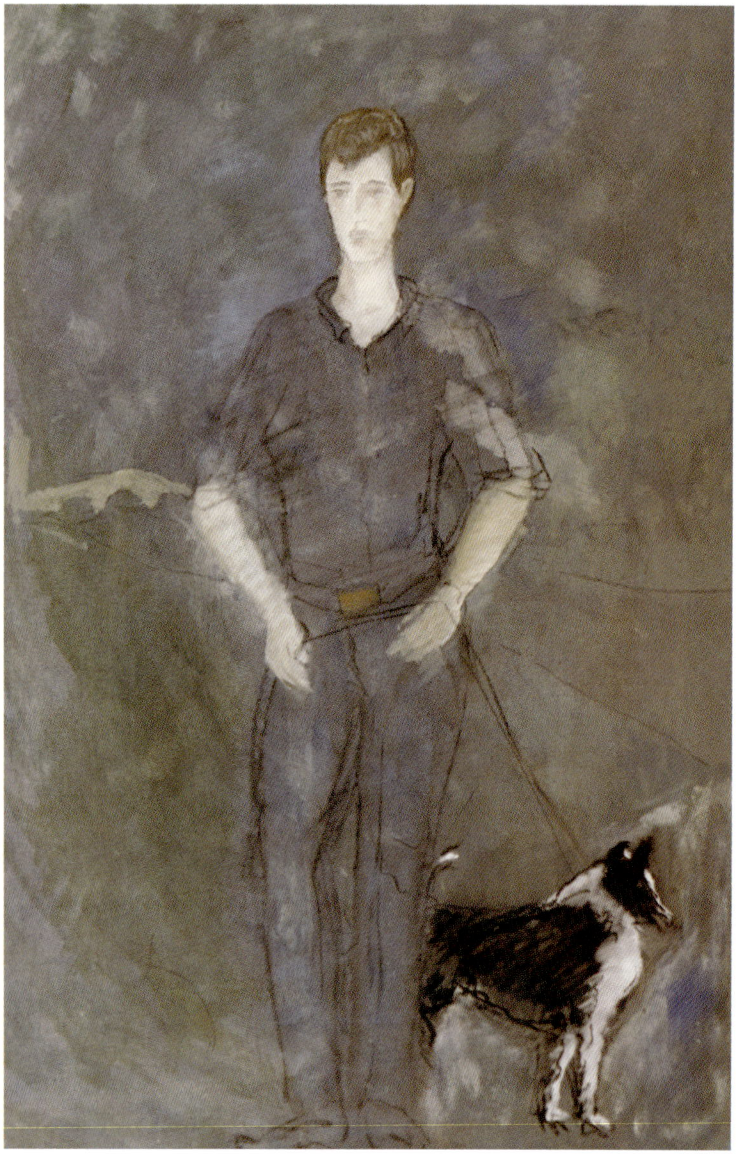

David and Oscar

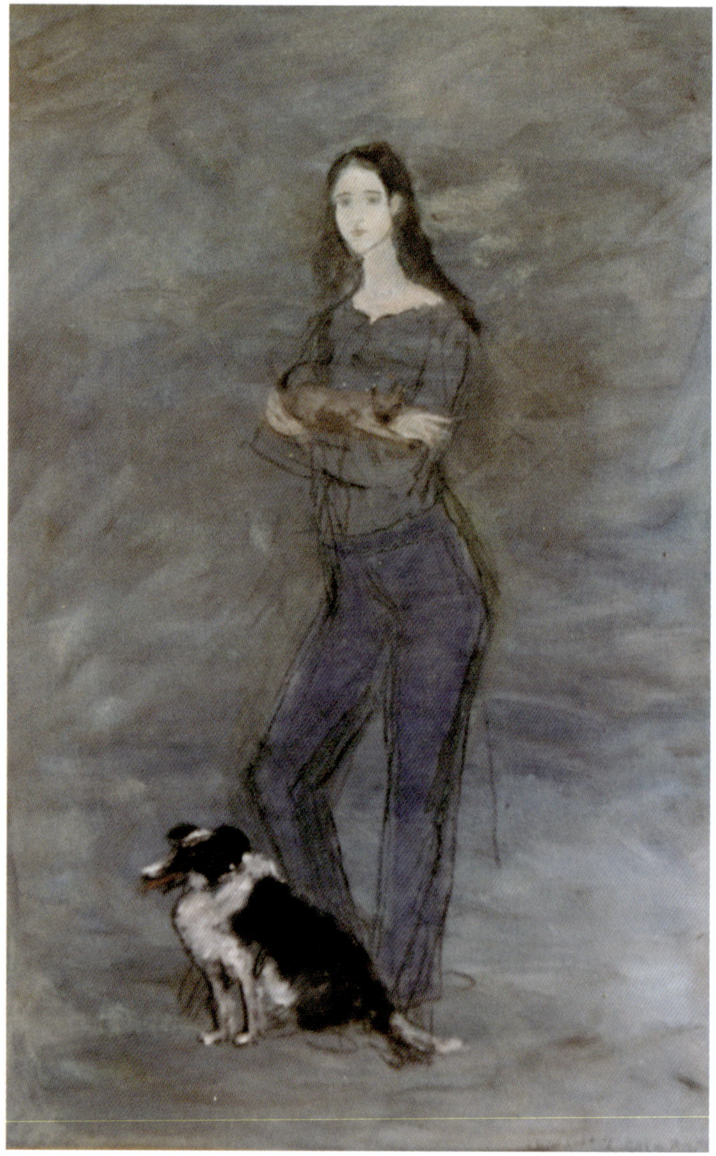

Laetitia and Oscar

allowed only the first years to take part in my project. There were eight of them. My idea was to show them how to draw the outline of a lifesize portrait, how to make casts, how to mix plaster. In two weeks you can't do much, but we did do some casting.' [2]

Raphael offered the substantial prize of £2000 for the best portrait head created from the model. A friend who lived locally agreed to sit for the whole two weeks. Raphael wanted the students to use their eyes and hands, to concentrate, to look really hard, to discover the characteristics of that particular head, find the shape of the skull underneath, and then model it. Above all they should make an accurate portrait, not merely an approximation. He encouraged them: 'You've got to look. It's hard work, it doesn't come easy, but you'll get more out of it.'

Raphael's project, recorded by Martina Habulin in a film entitled *The Sculpture Class with Raphael Maklouf* , gives a vivid picture of his practical approach to teaching. As he pointed out, 'students now are not learning a craft, although they are learning to use their imagination. But you can't teach imagination. You can, though, teach a craft that enables you to use your imagination and express yourself. My opinion is that constant practice means you don't have to concentrate on the technical aspect, you can concentrate on the creative side.' The film shows him first visiting the studios where his eight students were at work on their own projects. One girl student was making an assemblage out of popcorn packets. As Raphael said, 'if you didn't call this Sculpture, I would have no problem. I'd call this Creative Therapy – finding out what's inside you'. Another girl was making a Performance piece with three white-clad people on a plinth being abusive to passers-by. The point of the piece was in the audience reaction. As he reiterated, 'nowadays in order to be noticed you have to be outlandish. That's not creative. Art has now become curatorial. Artists now are the curators who find things and put them together. It's sad because there is something so basic about getting a bit of clay and seeing something in it and making something. My brief in the competition was for the students to create a portrait of the sitter that looked like the sitter, to exercise the craft and make it look like the model. I wanted them to concentrate on the technical side. The great artists work outside themselves – they don't even know they are working. They don't have to try and be different or individual – they are already themselves.' [3]

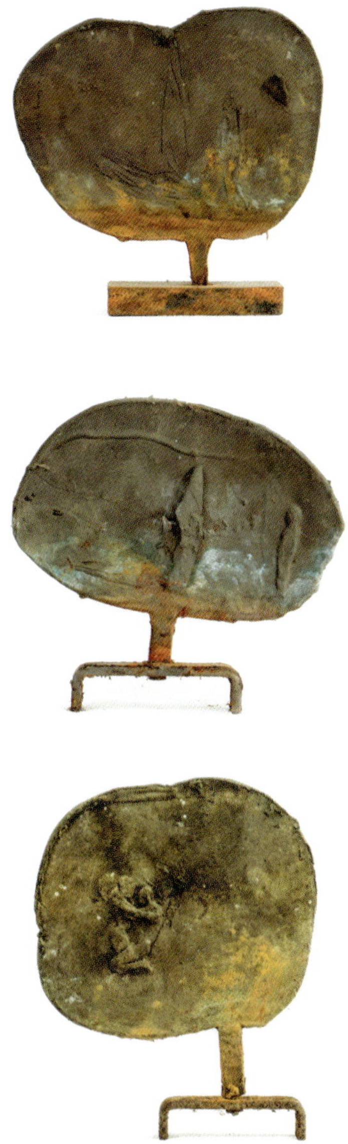

Small bronzes of Garden of Eden
Photos by Kirsten Scully

Raphael's teaching methods were based on the years of experience built up from his student days when Vogel had given him a teaching job at Camberwell. 'Although I was very young I had the mantle of being a teacher and took on that persona.' He offered his group of students straightforward constructive advice, encouraging them to draw before they started to model, because it would help them to think in the round. They were asked to look for simple shapes, to visualise the model in terms of squares, circles and triangles. 'We are all made of these very simple shapes.' He advised getting the sitter to talk in order to keep her animated, and said that on no account should the students work

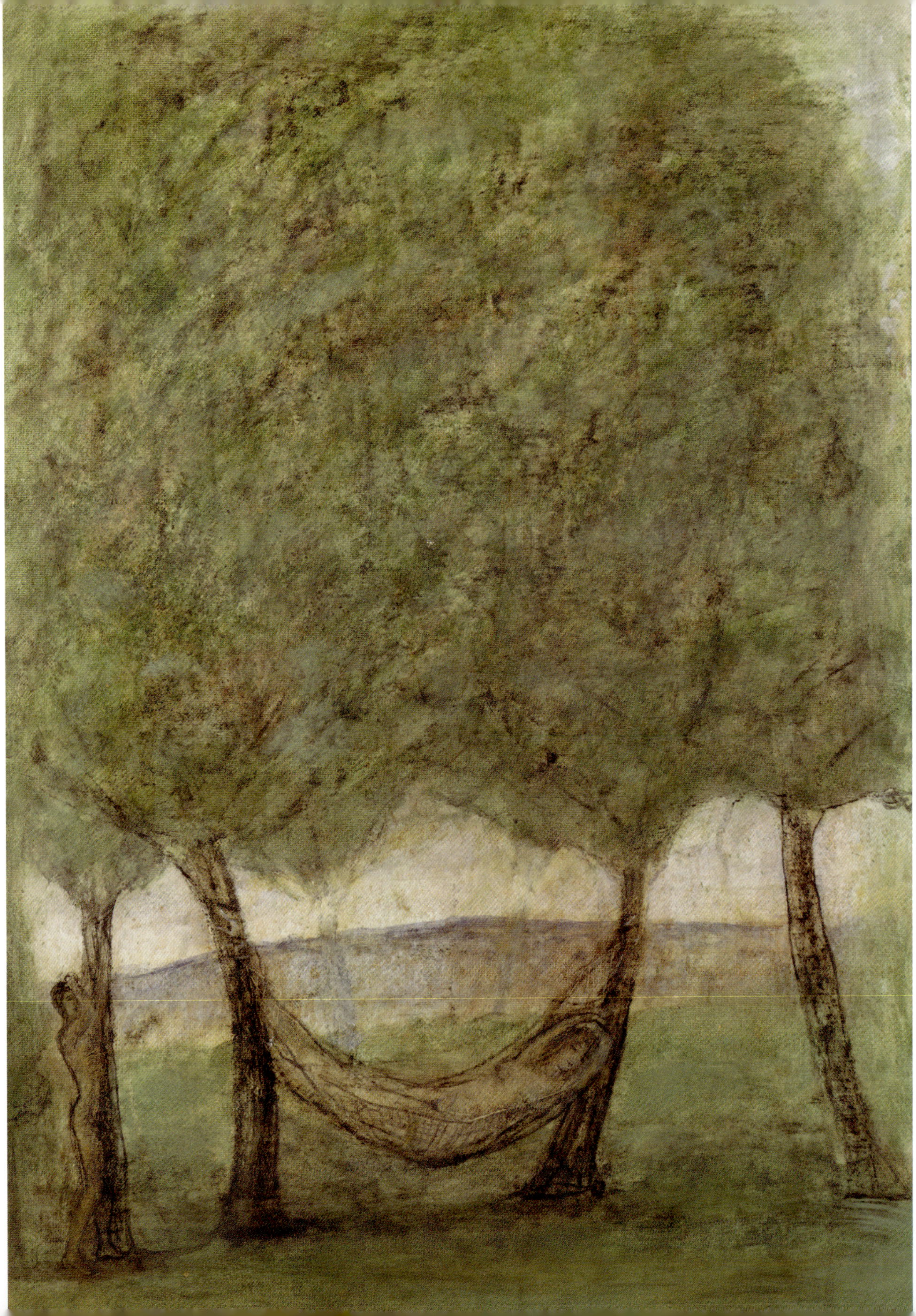

Tree series
Photo by Paul Webster

in silence. When the prizegiving came, two of the better students shared the prize, but Raphael was disappointed by the results. 'Every one of those heads ended up as a self-portrait. One always makes oneself in a sculpture – you put yourself in there without wanting to. It's natural. The difficulty is not to make too much of yourself. '

From Camberwell days onwards Raphael had enjoyed teaching and was always ready to pass on his knowledge. He was happy for his son Edmund to bring two Eton school-friends who wanted work experience to come to the Mint. The working conditions at the Mint were primitive, certainly not an environment that required suits and ties. Raphael was amused to see his two young pupils appear for their first day's work very smartly dressed, obviously not expecting manual work.

Raphael's sculpture intrigued his children, as Laetitia recalled. 'I would beg my father to do a death mask of me. For some reason I was obsessed with having one. It took a long time, and there's a certain amount of trust involved, because you have to breathe through two straws stuck up your nostrils and you can only communicate by tapping the hand of the person doing it. I remember getting very hot under the plaster and panicking a bit. My father held my hand and told me it would be over soon. When we made the mould and produced the actual death mask out of plaster, the amazing thing was that, although it was a true representation of my face, it looked nothing like me, whereas the sculptures my father made looked exactly like me.' [4]

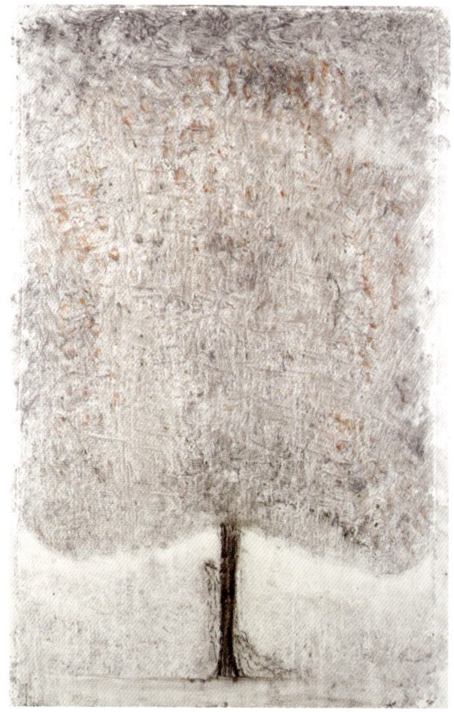
Tree series
Photo by Paul Webster

An important addition to the Tower Mint portrait project had been the filming of it. The medium of film has always attracted Raphael. As his son David attested, 'he's very interested in films and watches a lot of movies. He once got himself a role in a film. He's also interested in environmental issues, and made a film, *The Kanasee,* about the effect of Europeans on Native Americans, writing most of the script himself.' In 2010 Raphael featured in an art film series made by BBC in seven episodes, *How to get a Head in Sculpture*. This was advertised as 'a journey through the most enduring subject for world sculpture, the human head'. Taking part were Raphael and six other artists: Martin Jennings, Marc Quinn, David Mach, Tom Price, Anthony Caro and Maggie Hambling. The actor David Thewlis had his head sculpted by three different sculptors, while Dr Rowan Williams, then Archbishop of Canterbury, the painter Maggi Hambling, and the art critic Rachel Johnson discussed Art's principal long-standing preoccupation – our own selves. All acknowledged the unique power of the imaged head to focus emotion and to impress. Martin Jennings pointed out that the Emperor's head, shown on coinage as a symbol of power and value, was an early form of advertising. Anthony Caro maintained that getting a likeness was a less important part of the sculptor's task, because the subject becomes 'a mixture of what it's of, and the sculptor who is making it'. For Caro the making of a sculpture was an intense form of appreciation – '*Love* is what sculpture is about'. The film shows Raphael working directly from the model, deciding to 'idealise'

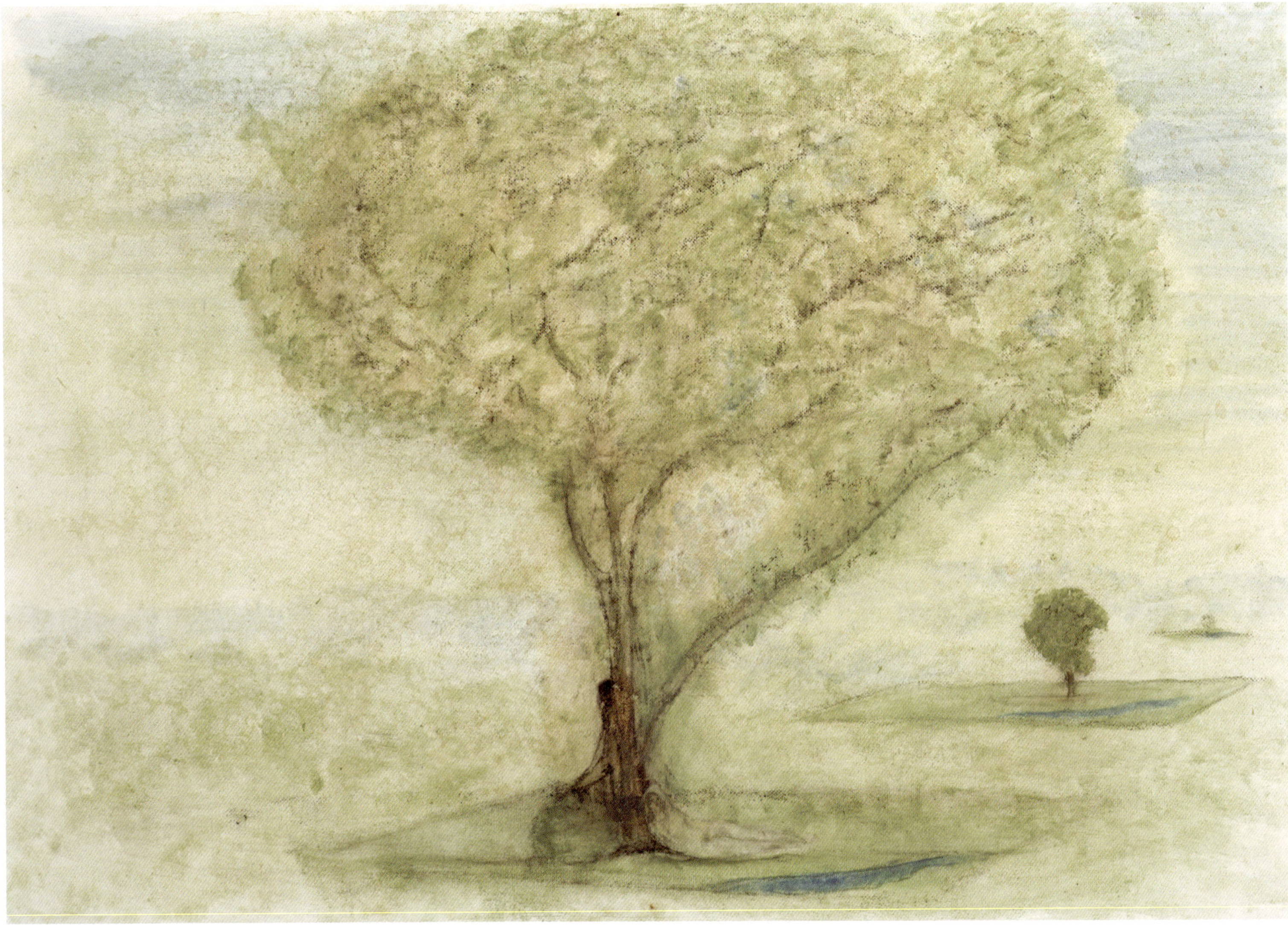

Tree series
Photo by Paul Webster

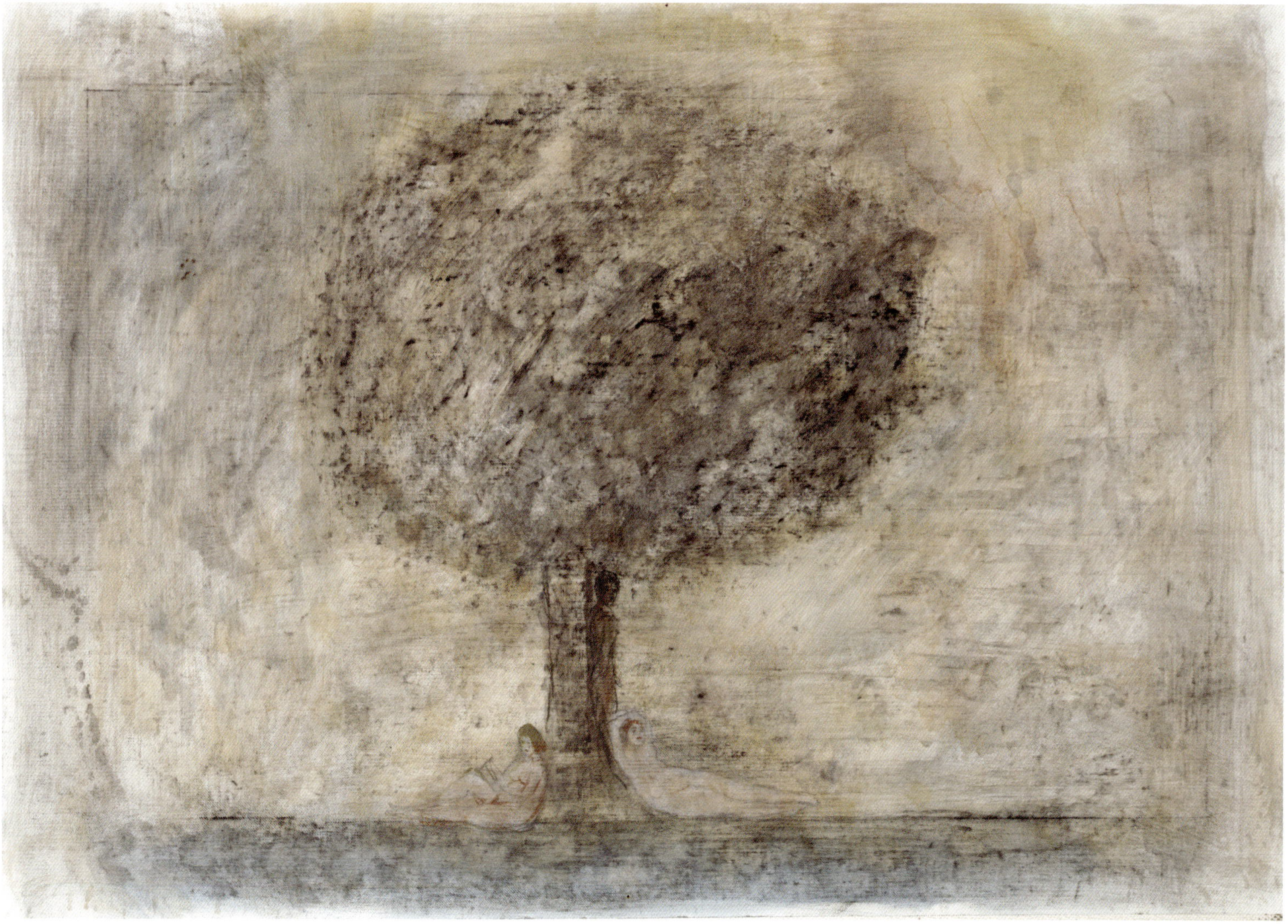

Tree series
Photo by Paul Webster

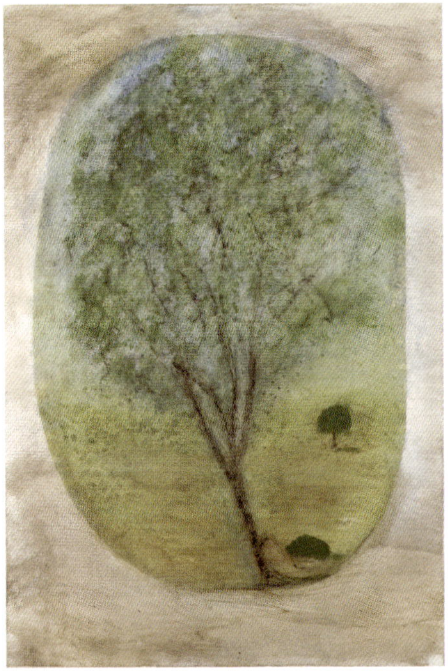

Tree series
Photo by Paul Webster

David Thewlis slightly and turn him into a 'ruler'. As a portraitist Raphael was well used to being observed at work, and the film shows him working fast, instinctively, and completely unselfconsciously. [5]

Raphael has always deplored the current imperative to be original at all costs. 'None of us are original – we all take on the past. If you live in the western world you see things differently from the eastern world. You are influenced by your surroundings. You can't help being of your age, being influenced, and there's nothing wrong with it. I do think there has been a hypocritical shift by many artists. They have asked "How can I be different?". The shark, the unmade bed, the pile of bricks – once you do that you become a celebrity and it doesn't matter what you do after that. It has very little to do with art. Picasso only had to sign his name – a simple thing, a signature. Once a celebrity all you have to do is sign your name. And the museums and galleries, these "cathedrals of art" where people go to worship, make things look different, holy.' [6]

Summing up his own work, Raphael maintains 'I have never tried to be original. We are all original. One just does what one does. I've tried to marry the idea of commercial with art – a portrait not necessarily made to express yourself, but made to commission. Apart from my painting, I work mostly from life. What interests me is how different people are. When they sit for you they invariably talk about themselves. I can give so many instances of people talking spontaneously about their lives while I'm working, and their faces reflect what they are thinking about. I've always found the portraits that have worked best are those when I didn't realise I was working. I think that happens to musicians and others. Watching Djokovic playing tennis, you know it's instinctive. If you have to think, it doesn't work. You go into a sort of inner memory. A pianist is a typical example. Because you know where the notes are you can concentrate on what you are saying. It's the same with sculpture – that's when you get the high. I have rarely suffered from sculptor's block. Sometimes when you haven't particularly liked a person you start to hear about their life and suddenly the whole thing changes. People have moods. You try and catch the mood.' [6]

Raphael's Tree of Life has many leaves on its many branches, and is as multi-faceted as its creator. From the most obscure beginnings Raphael has built a unique life, always living in the present, making the most of the opportunities that have arisen, and maintaining his serenity through all difficulties. As Horace wrote (in Dryden's translation):
Happy the man, and he alone,
He, who can call today his own;
He who, secure within, can say,
Tomorrow, do thy worst, for I have lived today.

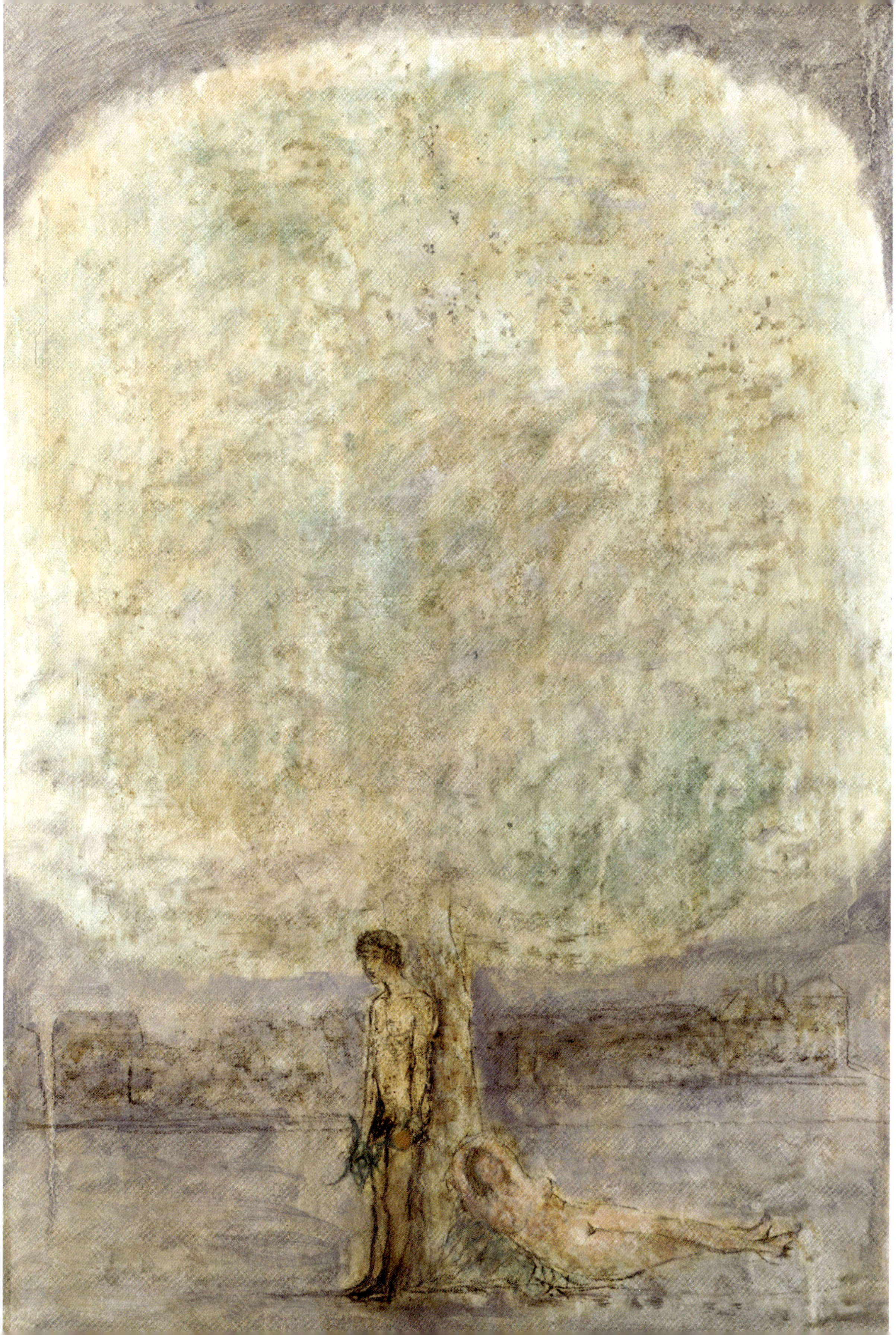

Tree series
Photo by Paul Webster

Endnotes

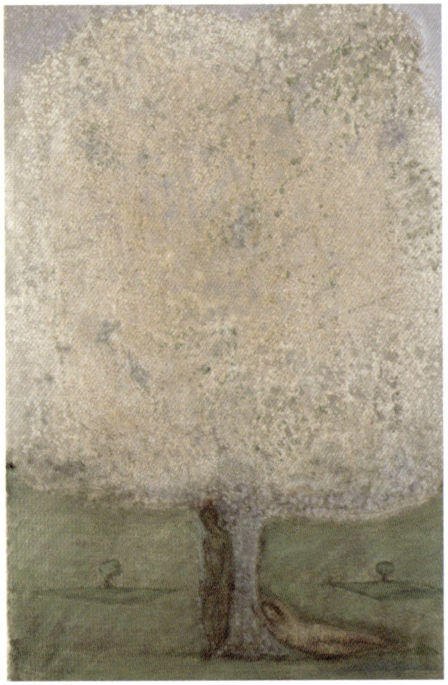

Tree series
Photo by Paul Webster

Chapter 2 Prospects in Palestine

1 Paper from the Cinquième Colloque International, Jerusalem, 9-12 April 1984

Chapter 3 British Beginnings

1 Raphael Maklouf, recorded interview with Jenny Pery, March 2015

2 Raphael Maklouf, ibid

3 Raphael Maklouf, ibid

4 Quentin Crisp, quoted by Geoff Hassell, *Camberwell School of Arts and Crafts,* Antique Collectors Club, 1995

5 Raphael Maklouf, recorded interview with Jenny Pery, March 2015

Chapter 4 The Archangel's Apprenticeship

1 Raphael Maklouf, recorded interview with Jenny Pery, March 2015

2 Raphael Maklouf, ibid

3 E.H.Gombrich, Foreword to catalogue, *Karel Vogel Retrospective Exhibition*, South London Art Gallery, 30 November – 29 December 1962

4 Michael Snowden, recorded interview with Jenny Pery, August 2016

5 Michael Snowden, ibid

6 Teresa Sladen, recorded interview with Jenny Pery, January 2016

7 Raphael Maklouf, recorded interview with Jenny Pery, July 2015

8 Raphael Maklouf, ibid

9 Michael Snowden, recorded interview with Jenny Pery, August 2016

10 *Evening Standard*, 27 June 1961

11 Raphael Maklouf, recorded interview with Jenny Pery, July 2015

12 Raphael Maklouf, ibid

Chapter 5 The Pursuit of Love
1 Marillyn Maklouf, written 2017 after interview with Jenny Pery, March 2015
2 David Hepher, *Grain of Concrete – Utopia and Entropy,* Flowers Gallery New York, 2016
3 Marillyn Maklouf, written 2017 after interview with Jenny Pery, March 2015
4 Gwilym Lewis DFC, *Wings over the Somme 1916-1918,* first published Longdown Press Ltd, Bristol, 1976; Bridge Books, Wrexham, Clwyd, 1994
5 Gwilym Lewis DFC, ibid
6 Gwilym Lewis DFC, ibid
7 Marillyn Lewis, recorded interview with Jenny Pery, March 2015
8 Raphael Maklouf, recorded interview with Jenny Pery, March 2015
9 Raphael Maklouf, ibid
10 The *Daily Telegraph*, April 1968
11 Raphael Maklouf, recorded interview with Jenny Pery, March 2015
12 David Maklouf Lewis, recorded interview with Jenny Pery, February 2016
13 David Maklouf Lewis, ibid
14 David Maklouf Lewis, Email to Jenny Pery, 8 February 2016
15 Laetitia Maklouf, Email to Jenny Pery, February 2017
16 Gwilym Lewis, letter to Raphael Maklouf, 28 December 1983, Maklouf Archive

Chapter 6 Tower Mint
1 Raphael Maklouf, recorded interview with Jenny Pery, July 2015
2 Raphael Maklouf, ibid
3 Raphael Maklouf, ibid
4 Raphael Maklouf, recorded interview with Jenny Pery, July 2016
5 Jane Poole, interview with Jenny Pery, July 2016
6 Jane Poole, ibid

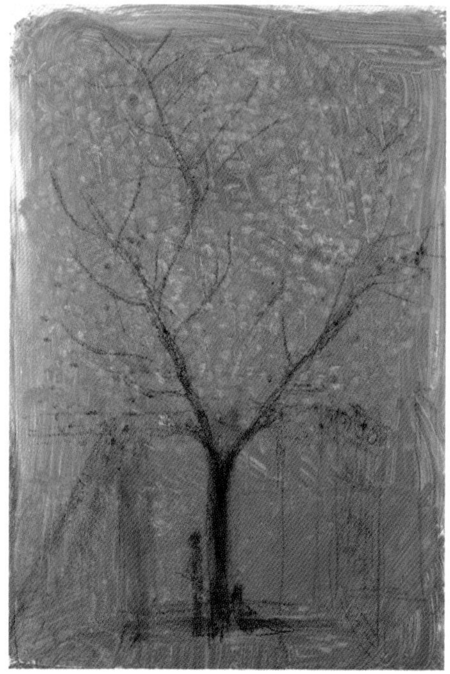

Tree series
Photo by Paul Webster

Chapter 7 Commissions with Consequences
1 The *Richmond and Twickenham Times*, 1984
2 The *Daily Telegraph*, 1984
3 Raphael Maklouf, recorded interview with Jenny Pery, March 2015
4 The *Daily Mail*, 9 August 1984
5 The *Daily Star*, 9 August 1984
6 The *New York Times*, 19 August 1984
7 *The Royal Mint Coin Club Bulletin* Issue No 13 1984

8 The *Daily Express*, 10 August 1984
9 Postcard from Collioure, France 1984, Makolouf Archive
10 The *Independent*, 1989
11 Margaret Thatcher, letter to Raphael Maklouf, 11 August 1987, Maklouf Archive
12 Raphael Maklouf, recorded interview with Jenny Pery, July 2016
13 Stations of the Cross, Brentwood Cathedral Booklet, 1994
14 The *Sunday Express*, 12 July 1992

Chapter 8 Leaves of the Tree
1 Tom Wolfe, *The Painted Word,* Picador New York, 1975
2 Raphael Maklouf, recorded interview with Jenny Pery, July 2016
3 The Sculpture Class with Raphael Maklouf, film by Martina Hambulin, 2015
4 Laetitia Maklouf, Email to Jenny Pery, February 2017
5 How to get a Head in Sculpture, BBC Film, 2015
6 Raphael Maklouf, recorded interview with Jenny Pery, December 2015
7 Raphael Maklouf, ibid

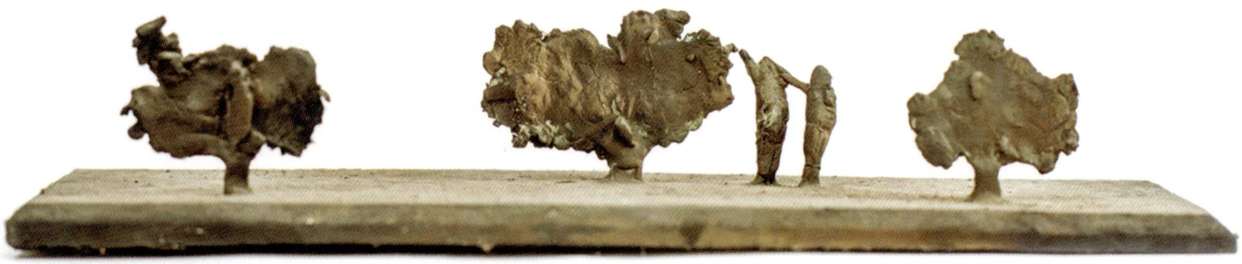

Small bronze, The Garden of Eden
Photo by Kirsten Scully

Acknowledgements

My thanks go first of all to Raphael and Marillyn Maklouf for their kindness and hospitality, and for making the creation of this book such fun. I am also indebted to their son David Maklouf Lewis and Raphael's sister Ruth Carter for invaluable insights into a unique character. Further thanks go to Jane Poole at Tower Mint, and fellow students Teresa Sladen and Michael Snowden, for giving up their time to reminisce with me. I am also grateful to Halsgrove's Simon Butler and Sharon O'Inn, with whom I have worked so happily.

Jenny Pery